KINGS and VIKINGS

Scandinavia and Europe
AD 700–1100

P. H. Sawyer

Methuen
London and New York

To
Bibi

First published in 1982 by
Methuen & Co. Ltd
11 New Fetter Lane, London EC4P 4EE

Published in the USA by
Methuen & Co.
in association with Methuen, Inc.
733 Third Avenue, New York, NY 10017

British Library Cataloguing in Publication Data
Sawyer, P. H.
Kings and Vikings: Scandinavia and Europe
AD 700–1100
1. Vikings   2. Europe – Civilization – History
I. Title
940   CB353

ISBN 0-416-74180-0
ISBN 0-416-74190-0 Pbk

Library of Congress Cataloging in Publication Data
Sawyer, P. H.
Kings and Vikings.

Bibliography: p.
Includes index.
1. Vikings.   2. Scandinavia – Civilization.
3. Christianity – Scandinavia.   4. Europe – History –
476-1492.   I. Title.
DL65.S254   1982   940'.04395   82-12539
)-0
SBN: 0 416 74190 8 *(pbk.)*

Photoset by Rowland Phototypesetting Ltd
Bury St Edmunds, Suffolk
Printed in Great Britain at
the University Press, Cambridge

Contents

List of plates

List of figures

Preface

Many books on the Vikings have been published recently and some apology or explanation ought perhaps to be offered for adding to their number. This book is, in effect, a sequel to my *Age of the Vikings*, first published in 1962. That title was somewhat misleading for it was not a general study of the Vikings but rather an attempt to question some of the assumptions made about them. It was, however, my ambition to write a general survey and this seems a good time to attempt such a work of synthesis. In the past twenty years there have been many important advances in Viking studies, as the recent exhibitions in London, Copenhagen and elsewhere have made clear. In the next twenty years there will certainly be many new developments that will make this account of the Age of the Vikings obsolete. It is, indeed, my hope that this book will stimulate discussions that will contribute to its own obsolescence.

This book could not have been written without the help generously given by many people and institutions. Among the latter I thank the University of Leeds and the British Academy for grants towards travel costs. Particular thanks are due to members of staff in the university libraries of Leeds and Gothenburg. I am also indebted to many people and institutions for the gift of publications that would otherwise have been very difficult to obtain, and for help in obtaining the illustrations used here.

Many friends and colleagues have spent time, often a great deal, showing me excavation sites and the material from them, answering questions and discussing problems; in particular, in the British Isles, Peter Addyman, Ian Crawford, David Gaunt, Richard Hall, Rory McTurk, Christopher Morris, Donnchadh Ó Corráin and Breandán Ó Ríordáin; in Germany, Kurt Schietzel and Ingrid Ulbricht; in the Netherlands, Jan Besteman, J. A. Trimpe Burger, W. A. van Es and H. H. van Regteren Altena; in Normandy, Lucien Musset; in Iceland, Kristján Eldjárn and Thór Magnússon; in Denmark, Mogens Bencard,

Preface

Ole Crumlin-Pedersen, Steen Hvass, Olaf Olsen, Thorkild Ramskou, Else Roesdahl and Ingrid Stoumann; in Norway, Per Sveaas Andersen, Charlotte Blindheim, Aslak Liestøl, Irmelin Martens and Thorleif Sjøvold; in Sweden, Kristina and Björn Ambrosiani, Anders Carlsson, Dan Carlsson, Inga Hägg, Åke Hyenstrand, Jan Peder Lamm, Agneta and Per Lundström, Erik Nylén, Bengt Schönbäck and Börje Westlund. I have also been helped on numismatic matters by Kirsten Bendixen, Michael Dolley, Bengt Hovén, Peter Ilisch, Bernd Kluge, Brita Malmer, Michael Metcalf, Thomas Noonan and Tuuka Talvio. Roberta Frank, Walter Goffart, Gillian Fellows Jensen, Simon Keynes, Niels Lund, Janet Nelson, Ian Wood and Patrick Wormald all read the whole book in draft and the final version owes much to their advice and criticism. To all I should like to express my thanks.

P. H. Sawyer

Note on references

In order to avoid overloading this book with references, general literature on most major topics and sites is indicated in the bibliographical note (pp. 147–54) rather than in the text. For many points of detail references are only given to the relevant articles in *KHL*, most of which have good bibliographies. References are given for the Norwegian and Swedish runic inscriptions that are mentioned, but not for the Danish. The latter may be located easily in Moltke 1976 or in *Danmarks Runeindskrifter*, ed. L. Jacobsen and E. Moltke, 2 vols, København (1941–42).

Abbreviations

AA	*Acta Archaeologica.* Copenhagen.
AB	*Annales Bertiniani,* ed. Grat, Vielliard and Clémencet 1964, cited in the translation by Janet Nelson, see p. 150.
Adam of Bremen	*Gesta Hammaburgensis Ecclesiae Pontificum,*ed. Trillmich and Buchner 1961, cited in the translation by Tschan 1961 (reference by book and chapter).
ANOH	*Aarbøger for nordisk Oldkyndighed og Historie.*
ARF	*Annales Regni Francorum,* cited in the translation by Scholz 1970.
ASC	*Anglo-Saxon Chronicle,* cited in the translation in *EHD* 1.
BAR	British Archaeological Reports.
CNS 1	*Corpus Nummorum Saeculorum ix–xi qui in Suecia reperti sunt,* ed. B. Malmer *et al.,* 1 *Gotland,* 2 parts published, Stockholm 1975–7 (hoards referred to by part and number).
DB	Domesday Book.
EHD	D. Whitelock, *English Historical Documents c. 500–1042* two editions, London 1955, 1979 (texts referred to by number).
EI	*Encyclopedia of Islam,* second ed. vols I–IV, Leiden and London 1960–78.
Gä	*Gästriklands Runinskrifter,* ed. Sven B. F. Jansson = *Sveriges Runinskrifter* xv, Stockholm 1981 In progress.
KHL	*Kulturhistorisk Lexicon for nordisk middelalder,* 22 vols, København and elsewhere 1956–78.
MLUHM	*Meddelanden från Lunds Universitets Historiska Museum.*

Abbreviations

NAR   *Norwegian Archaeological Review.*

NIYR   *Norges innskrifter med de yngre runer*, ed. M. Olsen, 5 vols, Oslo 1941–50.

SBVS   *Saga-Book of the Viking Society.*

Sö   *Södermanlands Runinskrifter*, ed. E. Brate and E. Wessén = *Sveriges Runinskrifter* III, Stockholm 1924–36.

U   *Upplands Runinskrifter*, ed. E Wessén and Sven B. F. Jansson = *Sveriges Runinskrifter* vi–ix, Stockholm, 1940–58.

VA   *Vita Anskarii*, ed. Trillmich and Buchner 1961, cited in the translation by Ian Moxon, see p. 150 (referred to by chapter).

Set justice aside then, and what are kingdoms but fair thievish purchases? For what are thieves' purchases but little kingdoms, for in thefts the hands of the underlings are directed by the commander, the confederacy of them is sworn together, and the pillage is shared by the law amongst them? And if those ragamuffins grow up to be able enough to keep forts, build habitations, possess cities, and conquer adjoining nations, then their government is no more called thievish, but graced with the eminent name of a kingdom, given and gotten, not because they have left their practices, but because now they may use them without danger of law. Elegant and excellent was that pirate's answer to the great Macedonian Alexander, who had taken him: the king asking him how he durst molest the seas so, he replied with a free spirit: 'how darest thou molest the whole world? But because I do it with a little ship only, I am called a thief; thou, doing it with a great navy, art called an emperor.

St Augustine, *City of God*, iv.4

1

The Age of the Vikings: an introductory outline

For three centuries, beginning shortly before the year 800, north-west Europe was exposed to attacks by Scandinavians, who had discovered that great wealth could be gathered by plundering or threatening the rich communities of the British Isles and Frankia. These raiders were called by many names – pagans or gentiles, as well as Northmen or Danes – but one of the words used by the English, and probably by the Scandinavians themselves, Viking, has become generally accepted as the appropriate term, not only for the raiders but also for the world from which they came. These centuries were, for Scandinavia as well as the parts of Europe they threatened, the Age of the Vikings.

The first Vikings probably returned home with their spoils, but in the course of the ninth century, as the attacks became more ambitious, many leaders were content to stay in the west as conquerors of English kingdoms, or in strongholds around the Irish coast, while others were granted land, more or less reluctantly, by Frankish rulers. These conquests and fiefs offered good opportunities for members of the Viking bands to settle permanently and those who did were quickly assimilated, learning the languages and accepting the religion of their neighbours. Some, however, preferred to take their chance in the virtually empty Atlantic islands of Iceland and the Faroes. Iceland, in particular, offered spacious opportunities to the first settlers. They began to arrive in about 870 and there was then a steady stream of immigrants, from Scandinavia as well as from the British Isles, until by about 930 the best land had been taken. This eventually led some Icelanders to move on to Greenland where, by the end of the twelfth century, some 300 farms had been established. In the eleventh century, some Greenlanders or Icelanders had reached the coast of North America: one of their settlements has been found at L'Anse aux Meadows in Newfoundland (Ingstad, 1970; Schönbäck, 1974; 1976). There were probably others, but there is no evidence of any permanent Scandinavian settlement in America. Icelanders later believed, probably correctly, that the opposition of the indigenous population – Eskimos or Indians – was too strong.

While some Scandinavians were raiding, conquering and colonizing in the west, others were doing much the same in the lands east of the Baltic, attracted by the Islamic silver that was then reaching Russia.* Towards the end of the eighth century, a little before the first Viking raids in the west, Muslim merchants began visiting Russia to buy the produce of its forests and the Arctic north and, as a result, large numbers of Islamic silver coins, called dirhams, were taken there and by the middle of the ninth century Scandinavians, known as *Rus*, were taking part in this trade. They established bases in several parts of Russia, collecting furs and slaves as tribute from the local populations to sell in markets on the Volga and elsewhere (see p. 122). As in the west, these Scandinavian emigrants were soon assimilated into native cultures; the princes of Kiev were indeed much like the dukes of Normandy.

Scandinavians were undoubtedly responsible for many great changes during the Viking Age. By colonizing the Atlantic islands they extended Europe, while elsewhere they played a significant part in reshaping political structures. As raiders they were disruptive, even destructive, but as conquerors and colonists they made a more positive contribution, not least by stimulating commerce and encouraging the growth of towns.

These centuries also saw many changes in Scandinavia, partly as a result of the closer contacts that then existed with Christian Europe. After their conquest of Frisia and Saxony, completed shortly before 800, the Franks attempted, by diplomacy, evangelism and threats of force, to gain some influence over their new neighbours, the Danes. Their efforts contributed to the transformation of Scandinavian society which had, however, long been subject to external influences, thanks to the demand in Frankia and Britain for the furs, amber and walrus ivory that Scandinavians were well placed to supply (see p. 66). There had already been a lively demand for northern goods in Roman times and the trade continued, on a reduced scale, after the collapse of the Roman Empire in the west. In the seventh and eighth centuries the traffic was largely in the hands of Frisians who were ideally placed between the

---

* Russia as a recognized country did not then exist. The term will, however, be used here for convenience to refer to the European areas of present-day USSR including provinces that, strictly speaking, never formed part of Russia.

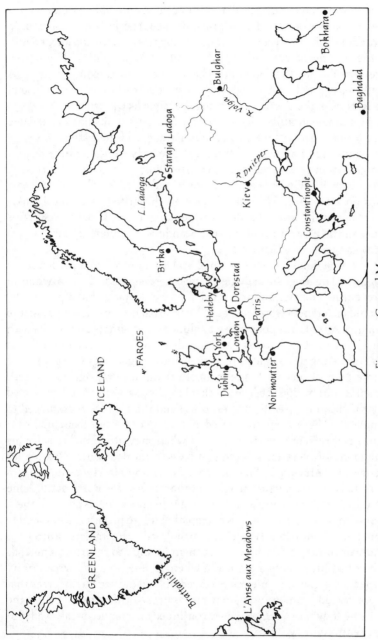

Figure 1 General Map

two worlds, and were familiar with both. As a result, Scandinavians became aware of new ideas whose influence is perhaps most obvious in Scandinavian art. Technological developments were, however, even more significant, particularly in the craft of ship-building. It was from western Europe that Scandinavians learned how to equip their boats with masts, and by the eighth century they had mastered the use of sails, thus making long sea ventures possible (see p. 76).

Scandinavian kings did not at first take part in distant raids. They had other sources of wealth, including trade, and their kingdoms were too unstable to allow long absences. The only ninth-century Danish kings known to have led raids on western Europe chose targets close to their frontier: Godfred attacked Frisia, and Horik's only reported raid was on Hamburg. The Viking raids on the British Isles and Frankia were rather the work of exiles – former kings or failed claimants. It was only in the eleventh century that Scandinavian rulers themselves led attacks against the British Isles.

The first raids were on a small scale, and directed against coastal targets. The English and the Franks were successful for a while in preventing any significant extension of these attacks, but after 830 the Frankish defences were weakened by internal political disputes and the Vikings seized the opportunity to plunder more important towns with such success that there was an immediate increase in the number and size of raiding fleets, and a great extension of their range (see p. 81). For more than twenty years the main effort was directed against western Frankia, but by 866 the heart of that kingdom was effectively protected by fortifications (see Figure 14, p. 87) and the Vikings then turned to England. There they conquered two kingdoms and dismembered a third before being beaten by Alfred when they attempted to seize his kingdom of Wessex. Alfred's success coincided with a period of renewed confusion in Frankia, and the Viking effort was once again directed there, in particular against the areas east and north of the Seine that had earlier been relatively resistant to attack. In response to these renewed raids fortifications were rapidly built to protect the vulnerable towns and churches (Figure 15, p. 90), and the raiders suffered a number of major defeats causing them, in 892, to return to England. They had little success there and when, in 896, this last 'great army' broke up, some of its members stayed in England settling in areas that were already under Scandinavian control; others returned to the continent, where Viking activity continued on a reduced scale well into the tenth century.

By then the opportunities for Vikings in western Europe were becoming very limited. Fortifications had reduced the chance of quick results and, in 911, Rouen and the lower Seine were granted to a Viking leader to protect Paris and its region. Alfred had shown that there was little hope of extending Scandinavian conquests in England and the best land in Iceland had already been claimed. Only Ireland and, for a while, the areas of England that had already been taken over by Scandinavians, offered much hope for any unsettled Vikings who remained in the west. Few young Viking warriors would, however, have wanted to do so, for there were then unprecedented opportunities to win great wealth in the lands east of the Baltic.

In the ninth century only small quantities of Islamic silver had reached eastern Scandinavia, but in the early tenth century the situation changed dramatically thanks to the very large increase in the quantity of silver reaching Russia. For about fifty years after 910 Swedes and Gotlanders were extraordinarily successful in tapping this wealth, although how they did so is uncertain. It has been claimed that it was a trading balance, but it is more likely to have been plundered or taken as tribute by force (see p. 125). The treasure that reached Scandinavia in the first half of the tenth century accelerated the changes that were already taking place. Markets that had originally supplied western merchants now increasingly served local demands. Merchants travelled great distances to bring goods to the wealthy people of, for example, Mälardalen or Gotland, and craftsmen gathered at seasonal markets throughout the Baltic region to make the tools, weapons, jewellery, clothing and combs that the people both wanted, and could afford (see p. 129).

In the 1960s the flow of Islamic silver to Scandinavia dried up almost completely, and the stability of the region was undermined by fierce competition for the available resources. There are hints of this in the texts that begin to shed light on the Baltic and Scandinavia at the end of the tenth century: it was at this time that the most important markets, at Hedeby and Birka, were fortified. There was also a renewal of Viking attacks on western Europe, where the main target was England, by then a rich kingdom with a government that was sufficiently well organized to be able to collect large sums of money, if necessary by taxation, to buy off the invaders (see p. 45). From 991 a succession of Scandinavian leaders attacked England and, in the end, a Danish king, Sven, conquered it. He died soon after his triumph but his son Knut followed his example. As king, Knut was able to use

England's wealth to support his ambitions in Scandinavia, but his Anglo-Danish Empire was short-lived; the machinery of government was inadequate to sustain it.

The old English dynasty regained power in 1042, and later attempts by Scandinavians to tap England's wealth had little success, thanks to greatly improved defences. The Norwegian king, Harald Hardrada, was killed at Stamford Bridge in 1066, and the great invasion planned by a Danish king (another Knut) in 1085 was abandoned. England was thereafter undisturbed by such threats. There were further attempts by one Scandinavian king to extend his power in the British Isles: the Norwegian king Magnus made two expeditions, but was killed on the second and his death, in 1102 in Ulster, truly marks the end of the Viking Age.

The Scandinavia from which Knut, Harald and Magnus came was very different from the homeland of the first Viking raiders (see p. 145). There were fewer kings and they had greater power. The machinery of government was more elaborate, and royal coinages were minted throughout Scandinavia. Towns and markets flourished in most areas, and many were under the control of royal agents. However, the greatest change was the conversion to Christianity. This began, effectively, in the tenth century, and by the early eleventh century the dominant classes in society in all but the most remote areas had accepted the new religion. Conversion did not, however, mean the end of the Viking Age, for the last attacks on the British Isles were led by Christian kings.

The Age of the Vikings began when Scandinavians first attacked western Europe and it ended when those attacks ceased. Once the west was closed to them, Scandinavians were forced to look for new ways to win fame and fortune, and many did so as crusaders. Some, such as the Norwegian king, Sigurd, in Jerusalem, while others followed the more 'Viking' tradition by crusading against the still pagan Slavs, Balts and Finns (Christiansen, 1980a).

Our knowledge of the Vikings, and of the world from which they came, largely depends on Christian sources, first written by the Vikings' victims but later, after their conversion, by Scandinavians themselves. These sometimes elaborate and often entertaining attempts by later generations to explain their Viking past have played a large part in forming modern ideas about that period. They were, however, written for patrons and audiences of the twelfth century or later, and whatever their value as evidence for the pagan past, they

6

more obviously illuminate their own time. It therefore seems desirable to begin with some account of the circumstances in which they were written, for which we have a relative abundance of evidence, and to consider how these circumstances affected attitudes to the past, before embarking on the task of interpreting the more elusive evidence from the Viking Age itself.

2

The twelfth century

The medieval kingdoms of Denmark, Norway and Sweden were at very different stages of development in the early twelfth century. Denmark was the smallest, although its boundaries extended far beyond those of the modern country; its southern boundary was the River Eider and it included the provinces of Skåne, Halland and Blekinge in what is now southern Sweden. This territory had been one kingdom for at least a century, but that did not mean that it was politically stable, and for over twenty-five years after 1131 it was disrupted by disputes between rival members of the royal family. These eventually led, in 1157, to the partition of the country between three cousins, but by the end of that year two had been killed and the survivor, Valdemar, was recognized as king throughout the whole of Denmark. He retained the throne and was succeeded in turn by his two sons, Knut (1182–1202) and Valdemar II (d. 1241). They all had to contend with aristocratic opposition and local separatism, but this was to some extent countered by the initial success of their expansionist policy in the southern Baltic at the expense of both Germans and Slavs. In 1215 Valdemar II even conquered Estonia, and established a Danish base at Reval, but this vastly enlarged territory did not long remain under Danish control; by 1227 Valdemar's authority was once again limited to the area over which his father had ruled seventy years earlier.

In 1100 Norway similarly acknowledged one king, but his authority did not extend far inland. The distances involved were nevertheless vast, and in many areas the king had to be content to acknowledge the right of local chieftains to rule as they thought fit. Twelfth-century Norway is perhaps better considered as an overlordship, and as in Denmark, there were violent struggles between rival contenders for the throne. These became acute after the death of the crusading king Sigurd in 1130, and lasted for some fifty years, until Sverri successfully fought his way to general acceptance. These rivals claimed to be members of the royal family, some with more reason than others.

The early development of the Swedish kingdom is very obscure. Accounts written in the thirteenth century and later treat eleventh-century Sweden as a single kingdom in which the Svear of Mälardalen were united with the Götar in acknowledging the Uppsala king. But this is certainly an over-simplification. The Götar were themselves divided into the Västgötar and the Östgötar by Vättern, and as late as 1081 Pope Gregory VII addressed a letter to two kings of the 'Visigoths', by which he probably meant the Götar (Wessén, 1960, p. 6n). In the early twelfth century the Västgötar and the Svear chose different kings – the former elected Magnus, son of the Danish king, Niels, while the Svear chose Ragnvald, who was later killed by the Västgötar when he claimed authority over them. For more than a century after that there was competition, often violent, between the rival dynasties for control of Svealand, but the details are not known because of the inadequacy of our sources. We may, however, be confident that in Sweden, as in Norway, royal authority was severely circumscribed by the power of local chieftains and leading freemen.

By the beginning of the twelfth century Christianity had long been more or less accepted throughout Scandinavia. By about 1120 seven bishoprics had been established in Denmark, at Schleswig, Ribe, Århus, Viborg, Børglum, Roskilde and Lund; Norway had three, at Oslo, Bergen and Nidaros; while there were five in Sweden, Skara, Linköping, Strängnäs, Sigtuna and Västerås (Gallén, 1958). The foundation of a bishopric depended on royal support, and the contrast between the episcopal organization of Denmark and Norway at that time underlines the differences in the development of royal authority in the two countries. In Sweden, at least some of the bishoprics had been created for different kingdoms: Skara for the Västgötar, Linköping for the Östgötar and Sigtuna for the Svear. Kings were indeed the most enthusiastic supporters of Christianity, for the new religion had much to offer them. It was a royal religion and its literature, notably the Old Testament, described a world very much like their own in which the success of kings as they led their armies in search of glory and gain depended on their obedience to the will of God. It is hardly surprising that some Scandinavian kings, like other barbarian rulers before them, were willing to accept that the God of the Christians was more powerful than other gods, and this lesson was reinforced by their awareness of the achievements, wealth and magnificence of their great contemporaries in Germany and England.

The conversion brought to the service of kings a literate priesthood some of whom had had the opportunity of obtaining a relatively good education. It would certainly be wrong to suggest that the Church introduced literacy into Scandinavia – runic writing had been used for a wide variety of purposes: inscriptions, messages and letters, as well as magic charms, long before the arrival of the first missionaries (Liestøl, 1971). But the Church was responsible for encouraging a more extensive use of writing, and the production of a written literature in which history bulked large. One early consequence of Christianity in Scandinavia, as elsewhere in barbarian Europe, was the attempt to interpret the past of the newly-converted people, and to place them in a wider historical context, that is, to define their place in Christian history. That need was most urgently felt by Icelanders who, as colonists in a new land, were particularly eager to understand their links with their homeland. Scandinavian historical traditions were in fact written down in Iceland even earlier than in Scandinavia. The first surviving work is *Íslendingabók* (the Book of the Icelanders) written by Ari Thorgilsson between 1125 and 1132. Ari may also have had some part in the compilation of *Landnámabók*, a detailed account of the colonization of Iceland, the first version of which was probably written at that time, and he also reports that in the winter of 1117 some of the laws were written down.

Icelanders began to compose sagas in the twelfth century, first about Norwegian kings and Icelandic bishops, later about the families who were believed to have played a prominent part in the history of the country. These sagas, and other Icelandic writings, have probably done more to shape modern ideas about the Viking Age than anything else, and those ideas have consequently been deeply influenced by the circumstances of twelfth- and thirteenth-century Iceland, the world in which Ari and the saga writers lived. The earliest work to survive, *Íslendingabók*, is very short and begins with an account of the discovery of Iceland, its settlement, and various important stages in the organization of the new community, the bringing of the law from Norway, the division of the country into Quarters, and the establishment of assemblies for both local districts and for the whole country – the annual Althing. Ari also briefly describes the settlement of Greenland. However, most space is devoted to the conversion and to the achievements of the first two bishops, Ísleif and his son Gizur, whose episcopates covered the period 1056–1118. Throughout the work, one of Ari's most obvious aims was to set these events in the chronology of the universal Church, measured in *Anno Domini*. A less obvious but

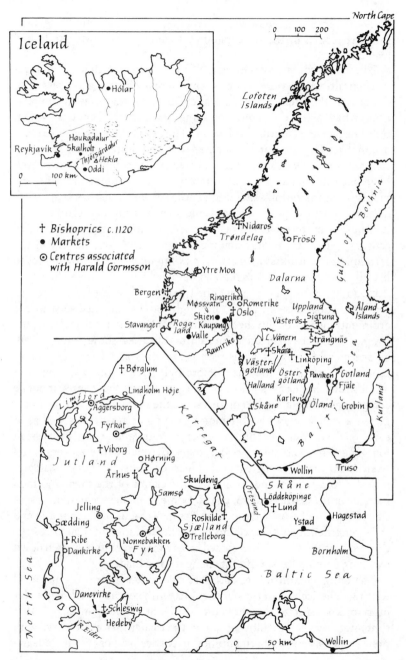

Figure 2 Scandinavia

no less important purpose was to emphasize, and perhaps exaggerate, the part played in the conversion of Iceland by his own family and friends.

Landnámabók survives in several late versions which have obviously been altered in various ways, but there seems no good reason to doubt that they reflect the general character of the original compilation, which gave the names of some 400 settlers, amongst whom thirty-nine were identified as leaders. The descendants of some of these original settlers are noted, together with the Scandinavian ancestors claimed for a few of them. The motive for its compilation may well have been in part antiquarian interest, which would account for the inclusion of many folk-tales and anecdotes, but it also served a more directly practical purpose: as a register of property claims. It is therefore a more reliable guide to the situation in the early twelfth century, when it was first compiled, than to the early history of the settlement (Benediktsson, 1976). *Landnámabók* makes no attempt to list all the original settlements, some of which have been shown by excavation to have been abandoned before the end of the eleventh century (Thórarinsson, 1976), although some abandoned settlements are mentioned, probably because their land was still valuable. In the course of the twelfth and thirteenth centuries some estates were enlarged, while others were reduced in size, and later versions of *Landnámabók* were modified accordingly (Rafnsson, 1974, pp. 166 –81). Much emphasis is placed on the genealogies, but these cannot be accepted as reliable records of ancestry: the manipulation of genealogies is a well-known phenomenon in the modern world as well as in early medieval Europe (Dumville, 1977). In Ireland, where the passion for genealogy was even greater than in Iceland, the eleventh and twelfth centuries saw a great deal of learned adjustment of genealogies in order to reinforce and 'authorize' the claims of the men who then had power (Ó Corráin, 1978, p. 34). Some Icelanders, chieftains especially, may well have welcomed the enhancement of their status and the strengthening of their claims by the modification of their ancestry: the two centuries which had passed before they were first written down was long enough for significant changes to be made.

Changing circumstances also affected other forms of historical writing. The Icelandic sagas of the thirteenth century tend to give far more prominence to the ancestors of the most powerful men at that time, notably the Sturlungs, than do the earlier historical works with their emphasis on southern families, in particular those from Oddi and

Haukadalur who played such an important part in the conversion and the early history of the Icelandic Church. Stories were told, or at least written down, about Snorri *goði* and Egil Skallagrímsson in the thirteenth century, not in the twelfth (Meulengracht Sørensen, 1977, pp. 82–3).

A particularly clear example of the rewriting of history to reflect changing circumstances is provided by the two sagas about the settlement and conversion of Greenland (Magnusson and Pálsson, 1965). According to the earlier of these, the *Saga of the Greenlanders*, the leader of the settlement, Erik the Red, died before Christianity reached Greenland. *Erik's Saga*, written later, describes the conversion of Erik's son Leif in Norway and his arrival in Greenland, where his father was reluctant to accept the new faith. Erik's wife, Thjódhild, however, did so with such enthusiasm that she not only refused to sleep with him until he followed her example, which 'annoyed him greatly', but also built a church some distance away from their farm. When, in 1961, the remains of a tiny church with a graveyard were discovered some 200 metres from the site identified as Erik's farm, it was accepted as dramatic confirmation of the accuracy of the saga, for most Greenland churches are much closer to farms than that (Krogh, 1965). More recently, the remains of another, apparently earlier, farm have been discovered very close to 'Thjódhild's church'. It appears that when *Erik's Saga* was written the original farm had been abandoned and a new one built, but that the chapel or its remains, survived 'some distance away' from the farm. The story in *Erik's Saga* offered a convenient explanation for this unusual circumstance (Magnusson, 1980, pp. 217–20).

Some historical adjustments were more significant. It was, for example, believed by some Icelanders that their ancestors had emigrated from Norway to escape the growing power of the Norwegian king, Harald Finehair. They were, however, well aware that some of the colonists did not come direct from Norway but from the British Isles, where they, or their fathers, had originally settled after leaving Norway. It was therefore necessary to explain how Harald could have been responsible for an emigration from the British Isles. The solution was found in an apocryphal extension of Harald's power to the British Isles, an achievement for which there is no independent evidence and which was probably modelled on that of a later Norwegian king, Magnus, who did indeed make two expeditions to the British Isles (Sawyer, 1976).

Kings and Vikings

Despite the apparently widespread belief in Iceland that the colonists had fled from the power of a Norwegian king, some Icelanders in the twelfth century were keenly interested in Harald and his descendants. Ari himself wrote an account of them that has not survived. The most remarkable monument to the Icelandic preoccupation with Norwegian kings is the collection of royal sagas, the *Heimskringla*, written in the first half of the thirteenth century by, or to the order of, Snorri Sturluson. There were several reasons for his interest. First, the early Icelandic writings were by church leaders, or were composed with their encouragement, and the Icelandic bishops tended to be supporters of royal power. In addition, for many Icelanders the best way to gain wealth and fame was to serve Norwegian kings, who naturally welcomed the service of men who spoke the same language, but came from a distant land and so were less likely to become involved in internal Norwegian disputes. One particular service which Icelanders performed was that of court poet (skald) whose task was to compose poems in praise of his lord. These poems were elaborate compositions, mostly in what was appropriately called *dróttkvætt* (the metre fit for the *drótt* – the king's retinue). Many of these verses were used by, and quoted in the 'historical' sagas written in the twelfth and thirteenth centuries, and that is how they have been preserved. This poetry was therefore a very important element in Icelandic culture and greatly influenced the Icelanders' ideas about their past, powerfully reinforcing their interest in kings, especially the kings of Norway.

Historical writing began later in Norway than in Iceland, but its themes and sources were largely the same (Holtsmark, 1961). The earliest efforts were lives of the royal saint Olaf, killed in 1030, and a Latin *Vita* of him had already been translated into Norse by the middle of the twelfth century. The earliest Norwegian attempts to give a general account of their history were the *Historia de antiquitate regum norwagiensium* by Theodricus, an anonymous *Historia Norvegiae*, and a vernacular work, *Ágrip af Nóregs konunga sögum* (Compendium of the Histories of the Kings of Norway), all written shortly before or after 1200. These drew heavily on the evidence of skaldic verse also used by Saxo Grammaticus, whose *Gesta Danorum*, completed in the early thirteenth century, is a most comprehensive attempt to interpret Danish history. There are naturally great differences between the interpretations offered by Saxo and by the Norwegian or Icelandic writers. The treatment of Olaf Tryggvason is a good illustration of this. For the Icelanders and Norwegians, Olaf, who was believed to have begun the systematic conversion of Norway, was a hero, and his Danish opponent, Sven Forkbeard, a villain. In Saxo the roles are reversed, and Olaf is presented as stupid, brutal and untrustworthy. It is instructive to compare their accounts of the events that led to Olaf's death in battle against Sven in 1000. Saxo makes the Norwegian the aggressor, seeking revenge for Sven's trickery in depriving him of 'two most splendid matches' – the widowed Swedish queen, Sigrid, and Sven's own daughter, Thyri (x.12). According to the Norwegian and Icelandic accounts, Olaf rejected Sigrid because she refused to become a Christian and he did marry Thyri (described as Sven's sister, not daughter). It was in attempting to recover lands that rightly belonged to Thyri that he was attacked by Sven and his allies.

Such differences are not surprising. Conflict between Danes and Norwegians had been a recurrent theme in their history and the consequent prejudices were deep-rooted. There are, however, some revealing differences in the attitudes of different Danish historians, in particular Saxo and his contemporary Sven Aggesen, whose *Brevis Historia* was completed before Saxo's work. A good example of their different treatment of the same material is provided by the story of Thyri, wife of the Danish king, Gorm. The only contemporary evidence for her is a runic inscription on a stone at Jelling, 'King Gorm made this memorial for his wife Thyri *tanmarkar bot*'. The interpretation of this inscription has been the subject of much dispute; it has even been suggested that the last phrase, whatever its meaning, referred not to Thyri but to Gorm. Neither Saxo nor Sven had any doubt that it referred to Thyri, but their attempts to make sense of it are very different (Strand, 1980, pp. 159–65). According to Sven, Denmark had, thanks to Gorm's weakness, been forced to pay tribute to the German emperor who was eager to have Thyri as his empress rather than the queen of a tributary land. When he proposed this, she explained that a vast sum would be needed to compensate Gorm for his loss. It was therefore agreed that for three years the Danish tribute should be paid to her so that she could accumulate the necessary amount. Meanwhile, she summoned the Danes to build the great wall called *Danevirke* to protect Jutland from Germany, and successfully duped the Germans into thinking that it was designed to protect Germany from Gorm's inevitable wrath. When, after three years, the emperor sent an army to fetch his bride, she declared: 'What the emperor demands and claims, I decline; what he desires, I shun . . . I will at once free the tributary Danes from the yoke of slavery and never more honour or submit to you.' And so, wrote Sven, Thyri redeemed a whole country.

Saxo's account is even more fantastic. Thyri, Gorm's wife, was daughter of an English king, Æthelred, and only agreed to marry on condition that she was given Denmark as her morning gift. Gorm and Thyri had two sons, Knut and Harald, who attacked England, so impressing their grandfather that he bequeathed England to them. Thyri did not complain at being disinherited; she considered it an honour rather than an insult. Gorm had sworn that he would kill any messenger who brought news of his elder son's death, so when Knut was killed in Ireland no one dared to tell him. Thyri therefore resorted to trickery. She dressed the old king in filthy clothes and gave him other signs of grief until he asked whether they indicated that Knut was dead. She answered that he himself had declared it and 'by her answer she made her husband a dead man, and herself a widow, regretting her misfortune'. Harald then succeeded his father, attempted to enlarge his possessions, but lost England. He was later forced to abandon an invasion of Sweden because the German emperor had seized the opportunity to invade Denmark 'which lacked royal leadership'. Harald drove the Germans back, but it was Thyri who started to build the *Danevirke*, 'a brave woman's imperfect plan, completed' Saxo explains, in his own days by Valdemar. She was, nevertheless, the protector of her land and freed Skåne from paying tribute to the Swedes.

In both accounts Thyri played a vital role in the defence of Denmark against the Germans, who were still a threat when Sven and Saxo were writing. Saxo enlarged her role by making her responsible for the liberation of Skåne, and in this and other ways belittled Harald's achievement. Both writers had the same overt purpose: to glorify the Danish kings Valdemar and Knut. Saxo was a most sophisticated and learned writer, well deserving the epithet *Grammaticus*, and he used various devices to qualify his praise and to hint at his disapproval of some aspects of royal policy. He was, in particular, opposed to an hereditary monarchy, and at various places in *Gesta Danorum*, including the opening section, emphasized the importance of the Danish tradition of electing their kings. The story of Thyri, as related by Saxo, contains several subtle hints of his disapproval of succession by inheritance rather than election. Harald inherited Denmark from his mother but proved to be a weak king and in the end, when he wished to erect a large monument to his mother's memory, the Danes drove him into exile. He was, it is true, succeeded by his son Sven, but only because the Danes *chose* Sven. The accounts of Thyri given by Sven and Saxo not only illustrate how contemporary preoccupations affected their interpretation of the past, they also show how freely both writers indulged in fantasy.

As sources for the history of times earlier than their own the *Brevis historia regum Dacie* and the *Gesta Danorum* are completely unreliable and untrustworthy. They both used various sources, and Saxo specifically acknowledges his debt to Icelandic poetry, but whatever they gleaned they adapted very freely to serve their own purposes. We may sometimes guess what lay behind their stories. Thyri's career seems to be elaborated from the description of her on the stone at Jelling that Gorm erected in her memory, but Saxo nevertheless makes Gorm die first. As the supposed builder of the *Danevirke* she may have been identified with Alfred's daughter Æthelflæd, who certainly did build fortifications, and at least one twelfth-century English historian, Henry of Huntingdon, believed that Æthelflæd's father was called Æthelred. Where their sources can be identified, it is sometimes possible to work out how they were used or misused, but when the sources are unknown we cannot check what Saxo or Sven did with them; their works therefore have very little, if any, value as evidence for the history of the Viking Age. For Norway, Denmark and the British Isles we are fortunate in having a variety of other sources that make it possible to check some of Saxo's fantasies, but for Sweden, particularly in the tenth and eleventh centuries, there is very little alternative evidence, and a remarkable number of assertions about Swedish history at that time are still based on his work.

One of the main sources used by both Sven and Saxo was Adam of Bremen's *Gesta Hammaburgensis ecclesiae pontificum* completed shortly before 1075. Adam was very interested in Scandinavia and devoted the whole of the fourth, and last, book of his work to a description of what he called 'the islands of the north'. This interest was natural. Hamburg claimed primacy throughout Scandinavia, an authority that derived ultimately from the missionary efforts of the first bishop, Anskar. Adam was aware of the claims of his Church and on such ecclesiastical matters he was well informed, if partisan. He also learned much at first hand from the Danish king, Sven Estrithson. Kings are not necessarily well informed about their distant ancestors but, thanks to Sven and to his own Hamburg sources, Adam's work is of the greatest value for the mid-eleventh century. For earlier periods, when he is often the only source, he is sometimes fanciful, as he is in commenting on the more distant regions of the north in his own day. His anti-Norwegian prejudices did not derive from Sven alone; the reluctance of the Norwegians to acknowledge Hamburg's claims must have been an important factor. His attitude to the Norwegians is clearly displayed in his account of Olaf Tryggvason. After acknowledging that Olaf 'was the first to bring Christianity to his fatherland' (ii.36), he offers some extraordinary comments on him:

> Some relate that Olaf had been a Christian, some that he had forsaken Christianity; all, however, affirm that he was skilled in divination, was an observer of the lots, and had placed all his hope in the prognostication of birds. Wherefore, also, he received a by-name, so that he was called Craccaben. In fact they say that he was also given to the practice of the magic art and supported as his household companions all the magicians with whom that land was overrun, and, deceived by their error, perished. (ii.40)

As Adam recognized, Olaf was converted in England, and English influence was consequently very marked in the Norwegian Church. This, together with the fact that Anskar's missions never affected Norway, seriously undermined Hamburg's claims there. English churchmen also had some influence in Denmark, thanks to the Danish conquest of England, with consequences that Adam deplored.

Historical writing was a late development in Sweden (Carlsson, 1961). The earliest lists of kings were compiled in the thirteenth century and go back no further than the beginning of the eleventh century to Olof Skötkonung, supposedly the first Christian king. The earliest attempt to write a more general historical account of any part of Sweden may well have been *Gutasagan*, which has been claimed as a thirteenth-century text, although the early years of the fourteenth century seem more likely (Sjöholm, 1977, pp. 94–110). This very short account of the history of Gotland displays a preoccupation with the rights of the Gotlanders as against the bishop of Linköping and the Swedish king. It was probably a response to the attempts made by King Magnus Birgersson at the end of the thirteenth century to increase the naval obligations of the islanders, or the payments made if the service was not performed. *Gutasagan's* account of the voluntary submission of the pagan Gotlanders to an un-named Swedish king, and the arrangements then made for the payment of tribute may well be what some Gotlanders believed, but it is not to be taken any more seriously

The twelfth century

as evidence for the early history of Gotland than *Gutasagan*'s account of the arrival of Tjälvar, the first man, and the birth of his three sons – a myth that served to emphasize the independence of Gotland, and explained its division into three parts. *Gutasagan* is, in fact, a good example of an attempt to justify or claim privileges by an appeal to a distant past.

A similar motive may be suspected for the collections of provincial laws that were compiled for several parts of Scandinavia in the late twelfth and thirteenth centuries. These have to be seen against the background of conflict between local aristocracies and kings, and they also served to reinforce the rights of free landowners against the many men who had no land of their own (pp. 40–2). They may possibly incorporate old rules or procedures, but it is no easy matter to identify which they are. An inscription at Hillersjö in Uppland (U, 29), which describes a very complicated chain of inheritance that agrees well with the provisions of the late thirteenth-century Uppland Law, makes it possible to trace those customs back at least to the eleventh century, but such independent evidence is rare. Some of the clauses are certainly no older than the late thirteenth century despite their 'archaic' form (Hemmer, 1969), and a similarly late date is suggested by the occurrence of words borrowed from Low German (Utterström, 1975; 1978). It has been argued that alliteration is a sign of oral transmission and indicates great antiquity, but alliteration and other 'archaic' features are also found in the sections concerning the Church, which cannot be older than the eleventh century. Alliteration, which is more frequent in later collections than in the earlier ones, appears to have been deliberately adopted to give an impression of antiquity (Ehrhardt, 1977). Similar laws, sometimes in very similar words and occurring in different compilations, are more likely to be due to direct copying than to their independent survival from a primitive Germanic legal system, and there are good reasons for suspecting that some of the men who compiled them had studied in Bologna and consciously drew on their knowledge of Lombard Law (Sjöholm, 1977, pp. 120–62).

These Scandinavian legal collections show that their compilers were very much like the later medieval commentators on the early Irish laws, who delighted in elaborating very complicated and artificial schemes, weaving 'a crazy pattern of rabbinical distinctions, schematic constructions, academic casuistry, and arithmetical calculations' (Binchy, 1943, pp. 224–6). This is best seen in the very complex provisions concerning freedmen (p. 40) and rights of kinsmen to compensation after a slaying (p. 44), both of which are remarkable displays of ingenuity that had little relation to reality.

Interest in the Scandinavian past was not confined, in the eleventh and twelfth centuries, to Scandinavia and the Church of Hamburg, but was also lively in those areas attacked, conquered or colonized by Scandinavians. *De moribus et actis primorum Normanniae ducum*, written in the early eleventh century by Dudo (Lair, 1865) and William of Malmesbury's *Gesta Regum* (*EHD*, 8), written a century later, have been rich quarries for historians. It is, however, important to recognize that contemporary circumstances affected the interpretation of the past in all such works. It may perhaps be helpful to illustrate this aspect of our sources by discussing two that have been particularly influential; one Russian, the other Irish.

The *Russian Primary Chronicle*, often referred to by its opening words *Povest vremennykh let* (These are the tales of bygone years), was compiled in Kiev in the early twelfth century, drawing largely on eleventh-century material. It is yet another example of an attempt by a converted people to interpret their past. The Russians were converted by the Byzantines, and the chronicle tends to emphasize the links that existed between Kiev and Byzantium. It is also a dynastic chronicle, devoted to the princes of Kiev. Their descent is traced from Rurik, a Varangian (that is, a Scandinavian) who, together with his younger brothers, is said to have been invited by the peoples of north Russia, that is Chuds, Slavs, Krivichians and Ves, to rule over them. The list of tribes who made the invitation is significant, for it includes Finns and Balts as well as Slavs. Whatever lay behind this story, its function in the chronicle is clearly to reinforce the claim made by Rurik's successors to extensive authority throughout the region. Rurik's brothers were assigned to different areas: Sineus to Beloozero, in Finnish territory, Truvor to Izborsk, while Rurik himself had Novgorod, which is said to have been Slavonic. The omission of the Estonian Chuds from this fraternal arrangement is probably significant, for Rurik's successors in Kiev did not claim to rule that area until the eleventh century (Noonan, 1974). Rurik's brothers are abruptly dismissed in the chronicle:

After two years Sineus and his brother Truvor died and Rurik assumed sole authority. He assigned cities to his followers, Polotsk to one, Rostov to another and to another Beloozero . . . Rurik had dominion over all these districts. (Cross and Sherbowitz-Wetzor, 1953, p. 60)

The chronicle later asserts that sometime in the reign of the Emperor Basil (867–86) Rurik made a deathbed bequest of his realm to Oleg 'who belonged to his kin, and entrusted to Oleg's hands his son Igor, for he was very young'. Oleg immediately went south to conquer Smolensk and Lyubech, and then removed the rulers of Kiev, Askold and Dir, who were acknowledged to be Varangians but 'did not belong to Rurik's kin'. Oleg then 'set himself up as prince of Kiev and declared that it should be the mother of Russian cities'. Oleg ruled for thirty-three years and greatly extended his authority throughout Russia and even attacked Constantinople, concluding a treaty on favourable terms with the Byzantine emperor. He was succeeded by Rurik's putative son, Igor. With the birth of Igor's own son, apparently in 942, we enter a period of Russian history when independent evidence, especially Byzantine, begins to be available to check the *Russian Primary Chronicle*'s narrative. Its treatment of the earlier period is obviously suspect. Whatever lay behind the traditions it reports (see pp. 113–19), they have clearly been adapted to serve the compiler's purposes which reflected the political situation in Kiev in the early twelfth century. The main problem was the conflict between rival branches of the ruling dynasty, and the importance of brotherly co-operation between kings is therefore emphasized. Great weight is also put on the legitimacy of the princes of Kiev, and of their claim to an extensive authority that was not based initially on conquest but on choice, symbolized by the appeal to Rurik and his brothers (Lichačev, 1970).

The Irish text, *Cogadh Gaedhel re Gallaibh* (the War of the Irish with the Foreigners) is also a piece of dynastic propaganda, written in the twelfth century on behalf of the O'Brien kings of Ireland. It begins with an annalistic account of Viking attacks during the ninth and tenth centuries, and then develops into an heroic saga about two Munster kings, Mathgamain and his brother Brian Boru, from whom the O'Brien kings traced their descent. Brian's career is described in extravagant detail as he fought to make his authority accepted throughout Ireland, and the work culminates in a description of the Battle of Clontarf fought outside Dublin on Good Friday, 1014. In this battle Brian's forces defeated the Leinstermen who had rebelled against him, and had recruited Norsemen from many parts of the British Isles as allies. The battle was hard fought, and in the moment of victory Brian was killed in his tent by fleeing Norsemen. This battle had no significant effect on the position of the Norsemen in Ireland and its main result was the collapse of Munster supremacy over Ireland, later re-established with great ruthlessness by Brian's grandson, Turlough. The exaggerations about Brian are obvious enough, and many of his achievements, including his work as an ecclesiastical reformer, are plainly anachronistic, but the author of the *Cogadh* did not invent all the details. The battle of Clontarf grew in Norse and Irish traditions to become a heroic confrontation that was accompanied by many supernatural signs, and a detailed account is incorporated in the thirteenth-century Icelandic Saga of Njál (Goedheer, 1938). As time passed, many people throughout Scandinavia were proud to claim that an ancestor had fought at Clontarf, and in this way they contributed to the legend that Brian was opposed by the combined forces of the whole Viking world.

The preliminary annalistic section of the *Cogadh* is less straightforward than at first appears. It has been contrived to present the Vikings as opponents of extraordinary ferocity so that the achievement of the Munster kings can be made to appear even more remarkable than it was. This section includes an account of one Viking leader, Turgeis, presumably a form of the Norse name Thorgils. He is said to have arrived with a great fleet and assumed the sovereignty over all the Vikings in Ireland. He attacked Armagh, drove its abbot into exile and took the abbacy himself, and became sovereign in the north of Ireland in apparent fulfilment of a prophecy that is then quoted in the *Cogadh*:

> Gentiles shall come over the soft sea
> They shall confound the men of Erinn
> Of them there shall be an abbot over every church
> Of them there shall be a king over Erinn.

He later went to Lough Ree and, among other places, attacked Clonmacnoise, where his wife Ota is said to have uttered oracles (*huricle*) on the high altar. Finally, in 845, he was captured and drowned in Lough Owel (Todd, 1867, pp. 9–15).

As Donnchad Ó Corráin has pointed out (1972, pp. 91–2), the only historical fact in this 'farrago' that is attested by contemporary annals is the capture and drowning of a Viking leader, Turgesius, in 845. The rest is an imaginative portrayal of a super-hero who made a mockery of the great Irish king of his day. The author of the *Cogadh* probably did not invent the stories about Turgesius, but he did make skilful use of them to reinforce a remarkably successful propaganda work from which many persistent myths about the Vikings in Ireland are drawn.

The distortions and exaggerations of the *Cogadh* can be recognized thanks to the survival of annals from the ninth and tenth centuries. For many areas of Scandinavian activity – the Atlantic islands, Russia, and even Scandinavia itself – there is very little contemporary evidence against which the later traditions can be tested. The value of the texts written in the twelfth century or later as evidence for the Viking period is obviously affected by the reliability of the information available to the writers, most of which must have been transmitted by word of mouth through several generations. It is, however, no less important to consider in what ways writers were affected by the circumstances of their own times. They all had good reasons for writing; to please a patron by exalting his ancestors, to justify a claim to land or power, or to challenge the authority of a king. The purpose is rarely as clear as it is in Adam of Bremen's history of his own Church, and is sometimes concealed by an apparently simple interest in the past. Such appearances are deceptive. The compilers of *Landnámabók*, for example, were not simple antiquarians, and it is as necessary to understand why that text was produced as it is to recognize the motives of Saxo Grammaticus or the author of *Gutasagan*, if its value as evidence for the Age of the Vikings is to be properly assessed.

3

Contemporary sources

Writings of the twelfth century and later can, if used critically, yield important information about the Viking period, but contemporary sources are even more valuable. The fullest and most varied contemporary written evidence comes from ninth-century Frankia. Annals that were produced independently in different churches provide a chronological framework that can be supplemented by letters, lives of rulers and of churchmen, legislation, charters and accounts of the removal of relics to places of safety in the face of Viking attacks. This evidence makes it possible to trace the movements of some Viking bands in great detail, and to study the reactions of rulers and churchmen to the invaders (pp. 78–100). It also shows that the Franks were not exclusively preoccupied with the Vikings, but paid far more attention to political problems and to ecclesiastical disputes. It is clear that for many inhabitants of the Frankish empire the Vikings were a lesser threat than Slavs, Muslims or Bretons.

Sources for tenth-century Frankia are far less satisfactory. Annalists and historians, especially in west Frankia, at that time tended to have narrower interests and to be less well-informed than their predecessors. Our knowledge of tenth-century Viking raids and the Scandinavian occupation of the lower reaches of the Seine and Loire valleys has, therefore, largely to depend on incidental references, for example in charters, and these leave many details very uncertain.

For many parts of the British Isles there are virtually no contemporary sources for the ninth and tenth centuries. This is partly a result of Viking activity. The disruption of the religious communities in which annals, charters and other texts were produced and preserved has led to a dearth of evidence for many areas, especially those that were conquered and colonized by Scandinavians, from East Anglia to the Scottish islands. We are better informed about those parts of England that successfully resisted the Vikings, but that evidence tends to be rather one-sided. The main source, the *Anglo-Saxon Chronicle*, was initially compiled in response to the great invasion of 892 (Sawyer, 1971, pp. 16, 19) and for many years it is almost exclusively concerned with the West Saxon campaigns against Viking invaders. It is consequently difficult to avoid seeing English history in the ninth and tenth centuries through anything but West Saxon eyes. Independent annals were certainly produced elsewhere in England, but only small parts have been preserved as interpolations in later versions of the *Anglo-Saxon Chronicle*, or in compilations of the twelfth and thirteenth centuries (*EHD*, 3–4). One tenth-century Northumbrian text has survived, the *Historia de Sancto Cuthberto* (*EHD*, 6), and describes how Saint Cuthbert protected his patrimony against the Viking invaders, and in doing so shows that relations between the English and the Scandinavians were far more complicated, and could be much less hostile, than the West Saxon sources imply. Evidence for the final phase of attacks on England that began in Æthelred's reign is much more abundant and varied than for the earlier period, although the *Anglo-Saxon Chronicle*, which remains the main narrative source, is for most of Æthelred's reign violently and unfairly prejudiced against that king (Keynes, 1978). Our knowledge of the annals produced in Irish churches also depends on later compilations, but there are good reasons for believing that some of these, notably the fifteenth-century *Annals of Ulster*, incorporate reliable versions of large parts of the original texts (Ó Máille, 1910). We are, therefore, better able to study Viking activity throughout the ninth and tenth centuries in Ireland than in any other part of the British Isles.

These contemporary sources sometimes name Viking leaders, and it is therefore occasionally possible to trace the movements of Viking bands. There are the obvious difficulties that two or more leaders may have had the same name and that some of them acquired legendary reputations very early and were consequently credited with additional exploits. These complications are well illustrated by the supposed career of Hasting (or Hastein), who is reported in various independent sources as the leader of a fleet in the Loire, the Somme and the Thames between 882 and 892. According to Regino of Prüm, a leader of the Loire Vikings in 866 was also called Hasting. If Regino is right, and that is doubtful (Lot, 1915, p. 505 n. 1), it cannot be assumed that it was the same man who led his fleet to England in 892; it seems unlikely that one man can have been an effective commander for so long. The later claim, reported by Dudo of St Quentin among others, that Hasting was also a leader of the fleet that sailed into the Mediterranean in 859 and later attacked Luna in Italy, is clearly legendary (Lair, 1865, p. 38n.). Some later compilers generated even greater confusion by muddling references to different individuals. This happened, for example, in the so-called *Fragmentary Annals of Ireland* (Radner, 1978), in which two Viking rulers of Dublin, both called Olaf, have been confused (Hunter Blair, 1939).

Western sources also cast some light on early Viking Scandinavia. Ninth-century Frankish annals contain a little information about Denmark, and so too does the *Vita Anskarii*, written in about 875 by Rimbert, Anskar's pupil and successor as bishop of Hamburg-Bremen. Rimbert gives valuable glimpses of Birka, where he himself had worked, and also of the situation more generally in the Baltic in the mid-ninth century. Independent information about the Baltic is provided by an account of a voyage across it included in the English translation of Orosius made at the end of the ninth century (Bately, 1980, pp. 16–18). The virtual silence of western sources about Norway is broken by another of the additions to the English version of Orosius, an account of the activities of a Norwegian called Ohthere in English which probably represents the Norse name Óttar (Bately, 1980, pp. 13–16). He visited England and told King Alfred something about his life in northern Norway; he also described a voyage he had undertaken around North Cape as well as the route south to Hedeby. Western sources are less helpful in the tenth century, and even northern German writers such as Widukind, whose *Saxon Chronicle* was completed in about 968, have remarkably little to say about their Danish neighbours.

Scandinavian activities in the lands east of the Baltic are much less well documented than those in the west. The only contemporary texts come from Islamic and Byzantine writers, most of whom were remote from the *Rus*, as these Scandinavians were called in both Arabic and Byzantine Greek (pp. 114–17). The Islamic texts – geographical treatises, books of itineraries, and routes, as well as encyclopedias – are generally cumulative works with revisions and elaborations either by the original author or by later writers. So, for example, Ibn Hawkal, a widely travelled geographer, produced three editions of his great survey of the known world, the first before 967, the second in 977 and the definitive version in 988. The work was, however, itself a revision of an earlier geography by Istakhri. As A. Miqel has remarked (1971) 'no detail can be extracted from Ibn Hawkal's work, and no judgement pronounced on it before the origin of the passage in question has been determined'. It is an additional complication that many texts only survive in later copies in which modifications may have been made, deliberately or not.

Most of the Islamic texts were written far away from the parts of Russia they purport to describe – for example, central Iran is at least 2000 km from the middle Volga by the most direct route across the Caspian Sea, and some idea of the time this journey could take is given by the mission sent in 921 by the Caliph to Bulghar, on the middle Volga. They left Baghdad on 21 June 921 and travelled via Bukhara and Khwarizm by the Aral Sea to arrive at their destination on 12 May 922. They were obviously in no hurry, but we have no reason to believe that other travellers were much quicker.

It is, therefore, not surprising that many Islamic writers only had vague, and often muddled ideas of the situation in Russia. They depended on information that had passed through many hands or mouths, and sometimes they caused further complications by their attempts to interpret earlier 'authorities' and make them fit. This feature of these sources, and the resulting difficulties, was well stated by Barthold in commenting on the attempts that have been made to make sense of information given about the *Rus* in a late tenth-century treatise known as *Hudud al-'Alam* (the Regions of the World):

> It would hardly be expedient to attempt to analyse these hypotheses, founded as they are on the evidently insufficient and fragmentary information that has come down to us, especially in view of the fact that the author has blended together data belonging to different periods and in spite of the scarcity of his information, has tried, with illusory exactitude, to fix the geographical situation of the countries and towns which he enumerates. There are seemingly no contradictions in his system, but this system can hardly ever have corresponded to the actual facts. (trans. Minorsky, 1937, pp. 41–2)

We are, however, fortunate, in having at least one first-hand account of the *Rus* in the early tenth century, and it is preserved in a contemporary copy. It was written by Ibn Fadlan, an important member of the Islamic mission sent by Caliph al-Muktadir in 921 to the Bulghars, whose king had decided to convert to Islam (Canard, 1958). Ibn Fadlan was not the leader of the mission, that was a eunuch called Susan al-Rassi, but he did have important tasks: to read the Caliph's letter to the Bulghar king, to present the gifts, and to supervise the lawyers who had been sent to teach the Bulghars Islamic law. In 1923 a contemporary copy of this remarkable report was found at Mashhad in Iran. It is not the original, which was presumably sent to the chancellery in Baghdad, nor is it complete, for it lacks any account of the return journey (Canard, 1958, pp. 143–4). Ibn Fadlan was a learned man, with an eye for detail, but that does not necessarily mean that we should trust every detail. He presumably understood the Turkic language of the Bulghars, as is implied by his tasks on the mission, but he admits that he needed an interpreter to understand the *Rus* (Canard, 1958, p. 130). He certainly gives details about the funeral of a *Rus* chieftain that he cannot have seen himself, notably the description of the sacrifice of a slave girl which took place inside a tent, out of sight of onlookers. At this stage a number of men made a noise by beating their shields with sticks so that her screams would not be heard, and it is therefore improbable that her death, which he describes in some detail, was seen by any who were not directly involved (Canard, 1958, pp. 131–2). For his information about the Khazars he appears to have relied on the hostile witness of the Bulghars, who presented their overlords in a most unfavourable light (Dunlop, 1954, p. 110). He was, however, generally careful to distinguish between what he himself observed and what he heard from others. For example, the strange story about the dumb giant from the land of Gog and Magog, and the details of the fish diet of the inhabitants of that land were, as he explains, related to him by the Bulghar king (Canard, 1958, pp. 108–10). They can hardly be taken at face value, although they may reflect encounters with strangers from a distant region, probably around the White Sea. Ibn Fadlan's report is, therefore, a remarkably valuable source of information about one of the areas of Scandinavian activity in the early tenth century.

The only other contemporary evidence for the *Rus* of the ninth and tenth centuries, apart from one important reference in the *Annals of St Bertin* for 839 (pp. 116–17), comes from Byzantium (Obolensky, 1970). Constantinople was attacked by these northern barbarians in 860 and the first certain reference to them is in the homilies of the Patriarch Photius, one of which was preached in June 860 during that attack. Thereafter the Byzantines had regular dealings with the *Rus* of Kiev, concluded several treaties with them, recruited warriors with their help, and were eventually responsible for their conversion to Christianity. The diplomatic contacts had one remarkable result, a chapter about the *Rus* in the *De Administrando Imperio* written by Emperor Constantine Porphyrogenitus. It consists of two parts of which the first describes how the *Rus* of Kiev every spring gathered a fleet of ships from Novgorod, Smolensk and elsewhere and then, in June, travelled down the Dnieper to Byzantium. The second part is a short account of the annual tribute-collecting operations of the rulers of Kiev. It has been persuasively argued (Obolensky, 1962) that the first section was based on a description written by a Byzantine diplomat who used the imperial polo-ground and the Hippodrome as comparisons when describing the size of rapids and fords in the Dnieper. He may have been a diplomat who visited Kiev in 944 to negotiate the treaty agreed in that year. The second section appears to be a translation of a Slavonic account of the winter tribute-collection and may have been obtained at the same time. This chapter confirms the evidence of Ibn Fadlan that the *Rus* were of Scandinavian origin (p. 114), for it gives the names of several of the Dnieper rapids in the languages of both the Slavs and the *Rus*, and several of the latter forms are certainly Scandinavian (Obolensky, 1962, pp. 40–2; Sorlin, 1965, pp. 179–80). Byzantine diplomacy also resulted in the production of several treaties with the *Rus* of Kiev, in 907, 911, 944 and 971, that have been preserved in the *Russian Primary Chronicle*. There are significant differences between them in both language and diplomatic form, and there seems little doubt that they are genuine (Sorlin, 1961).

Fortunately, we are not entirely dependent on western Christians, Muslims or Byzantines for contemporary written evidence about Scandinavians in the Viking Age. Scandinavians were already familiar with the art of writing long before their conversion. Their script, using letters called runes, was formed by combining vertical and diagonal lines that were designed to be carved or scratched across the grain of wooden surfaces. A number of Viking period inscriptions on fragments of wood have been found in recent years, for example at Hedeby and Staraja Ladoga (Liestøl, 1958; 1973), but their preservation depends on suitable conditions, and they can easily be overlooked in an excavation. Runic inscriptions on bone or metal are more durable, and a number dateable to the Viking period are known. Most inscriptions of that time are, however, in stone, and are very unevenly distributed: roughly 2500 in modern Sweden, 220 in Denmark, but only fifty in Norway (Musset and Mossé, 1965, p. 241), while only about sixty are known from areas of Scandinavian settlement overseas, half of them from the Isle of Man (Page, 1980).

Some of these inscriptions were carved on earth-fast rock but most are on moveable blocks of stone many of which have disappeared, being used as building stone or in road-making. Their vulnerability is vividly illustrated by the stone at Randbøl in Jutland (plate II), which was lying on its face when a road worker began to cut mile-stones from it before realizing that it had an inscription. Fragments of rune stones are regularly discovered in the walls or floors of churches, and these are a reminder that many have been lost.

The interpretation of many inscriptions is uncertain, partly because of the limitations of an alphabet that only contains sixteen letters, but also because inscriptions are often damaged or partly illegible. The uncertainty is most obvious in the reading of early inscriptions for which there is little comparative material. There is, for example, great disagreement about the interpretation of the inscriptions from Rök and Sparlösa, both apparently from the beginning of the ninth century. Later inscriptions pose fewer problems but there is often uncertainty about particular words or phrases. To take one example, a stone at Järsta in Gästrikland (Gä 11; plate IIIa) has a clearly legible inscription which poses no problems except for the last eleven letters, immediately under the cross, *þasataimunt*. There is general agreement that the last six letters are a personal name, *Aimunt*, a form of Emund, but his function has been variously interpreted as the erector of the stone, the king in whose reign it was carved, and someone who was commemorated by it. This last seems most likely (Thompson, 1975, pp. 83–6) but the apparent reference to a king who is known to have ruled part of Sweden in the second quarter of the eleventh century has inevitably attracted a lot of attention and support.

Few, if any, inscriptions can be dated precisely. It is not even easy to establish a relative chronology, for stylistic arguments are hazardous (Lindqvist, 1922). Groups of stones that refer to related individuals can sometimes be arranged in chronological sequence, but the interval between different generations may have varied greatly. Some inscriptions name the men who carved them, but we do not know how long they lived, nor is it always clear in what order an individual's work was produced. One of the most prolific rune-masters was an Upplander called Asmund who is named as the carver, alone or with someone else, on at least nineteen stones, a claim that is supported by similarities of style that have, in turn made it possible to attribute a further thirty inscriptions to him, fifteen of them with considerable confidence (Thompson, 1975, pp. 82–152; cf. plate II and figure 3, p. 31). These forty-nine stones, and perhaps others, were therefore produced in one lifetime, but we do not know how long that was, or when it began or

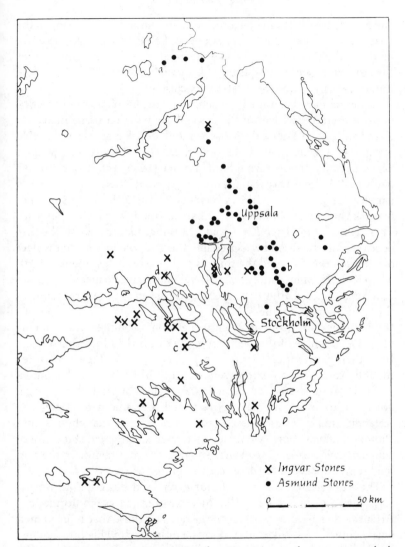

Figure 3   Rune stones in eastern Sweden. Two groups of stones are marked; those signed by, or attributed to Asmund (see p. 30), and those commemorating men who failed to return from Ingvar's expedition to the east (see p. 32). The stones illustrated in plates III and IV are marked as follows; *a* Järsta; *b* Yttergärde; *c* Gripsholm; *d* Svinnegarn kyrka.

ended. The best that can be claimed is that Asmund was working in the 1030s (Thompson, 1975, pp. 152–61). Some inscriptions refer to known individuals or events, like the great stone at Jelling (p. 138) or the cross commemorating Erling Skjalgsson (plate XVI) but that does not necessarily define their dates very closely.

Attempts have been made to determine the chronology of inscriptions in eastern Sweden on the basis of the few that name men who were paid geld in England (Wessén, 1960), but that still leaves a wide margin of uncertainty. Geld was collected by Knut and paid to Scandinavian warriors throughout his reign (1016–35). In one case it is likely that the geld of 1018 is meant. The stone at Yttergärde in Orkesta parish, Uppland (plate IIIb) in memory of Ulf of Bårresta says that he took three gelds in England: 'That was the first which Tosti paid. Then Torkel paid. Then Knut paid.' Nothing is known about the first occasion, but the second was probably the geld paid in 1012 to the fleet of Thorkell the Tall, and the third is most likely the payment of 1018 when Knut disbanded most of his fleet, but we have no means of telling how long Ulf lived after that: it could have been anything from one to thirty years; perhaps more.

One important group of twenty-five stones commemorates members of an unsuccessful expedition to the east, led by Ingvar. To judge from their distribution (figure 3, p. 30, and plate IV) Ingvar recruited his followers from an extensive area south of Mälaren and along its north-western shore. He became the subject of an Icelandic saga, according to which he died in 1041, and the same date is given in Icelandic annals. Elias Wessén (1960) has claimed that these stones should be dated some twenty years earlier, but the evidence cannot support such close dating. What is more, the coin hoards in the area lend some support to the date accepted in Iceland (p. 35).

These uncertainties do not, of course, render the inscriptions worthless. They are a rich and insufficiently explored quarry of information. Attention has naturally been concentrated on those that refer to men who went overseas, like Ulf of Bårresta or Ingvar and his companions, but it is worth emphasizing that those are only a small part of the material, about 150 inscriptions in all (Ruprecht, 1958; Liestøl, 1970). The stones commemorating men and women who stayed at home contain a great deal of information about such matters as family relationships, inheritance, landholding, communications, and the progress of Christianity (Musset and Mossé, 1965, pp. 239–88; 301–10).

Some runic inscriptions are in part poetic (cf. plates II, IVa) and a few incorporate whole stanzas, for example those from Rök and Karlevi (p. 53), but most of the poetry of the Viking Age is only preserved in the later writings of Icelanders. The antiquity of much of it is unquestioned, but there is a suspicion, at times amounting to certainty, that some verses were created in the twelfth century or later, and attributed to earlier poets. One verse, supposedly by the early tenth-century poet, Egil Skallagrímsson, describes an attack on the town of Lund, but there is no other evidence to support such an early date for Lund as a market of any importance (Blomqvist, 1951, p. 10). The historical value of the poetry that can be accepted as a reliable product of the Viking Age is, however, limited. It is, in the first place, often fiendishly obscure and its interpretation uncertain. There are many opportunities of misunderstanding and even the Icelanders did not always correctly interpret what they preserved (Frank, 1981). Most of the surviving poetry was written in praise of rulers or lords and as such can hardly be taken as a sober judgement, although the qualities that are singled out for praise do presumably reflect the standards of the circles in which this poetry was appreciated. The poems are also useful in revealing incidental details about, for example, ships (Foote, 1978; Hallberg, 1978), travel, or life in a lord's retinue (Frank, 1978), but they have little value as evidence for narrative history; the poets aimed rather 'at the artistic decoration of facts known to their hearers rather than at giving information' (Campbell, 1949, p. 66). There is also the difficulty that the original order of verses in a poem is rarely certain. *Víkingavísur*, by Sigvat Thórðarson, is an exception because it describes thirteen of the battles fought by St Olaf before he became king of Norway, referring to each by number. The first four were in different parts of the Baltic, the fifth may have been in Frisia, the next four in England, and the last four in France and Spain (Fell, 1981). This poem has been described as 'one of the best historical documents transmitted to us by the Scandinavian North' (Campbell, 1949, p. 76) but it gives hardly any significant details and the identification of some of the places mentioned is uncertain.

Coins are one of the most important sources of information about Viking Scandinavia and its external contacts. In the ninth and tenth centuries very large numbers of Islamic dirhams were imported into Scandinavia from across the Baltic, and towards the end of the tenth century a similarly large flow of German and English coins began to reach the north. Coins were also struck in Scandinavia, at Hedeby as early as the beginning of the ninth century, and by the end of the tenth century at several other places, including Sigtuna. These Scandinavian coins were generally modelled on western European types, at first Frankish *denarii* or *sceattas* from Frisia or England, but English pennies minted for Æthelred or his Danish successors were the pattern for many eleventh-century coins (Malmer, 1968).

Silver and gold were also imported in other forms – as ornaments, rings, and bars – but the coins are particularly instructive because their legends generally make clear when and where they were produced. Individual coins can therefore be important sources of information, and when they are found in hoards, they provide even more valuable evidence. Most of the coins imported into Viking Scandinavia have been found in treasure hoards, often with other objects of silver and, more rarely, gold. Coins included in a hoard are likely to represent what was available when the hoard was assembled, and the changing character of the coin stock in any area, or differences between areas, can be studied with their help. The ninth-century hoards, for example, show that there were then fairly large numbers of old coins in circulation, including some Sassanian coins minted before the Arab conquest of Iran, as well as others struck for Ummayyad caliphs before 750. It has been claimed that the discovery of such early coins as single finds or in graves proves that there were contacts between Iran and Scandinavia long before the ninth century (Linder Welin, 1974) but when they are found in Scandinavian or Russian hoards they are always found with later, ninth-century coins. Moreover, the Russian and Caucasian hoards show conclusively that these old coins formed part of the coin stock that began to be exported from Iran in the last quarter of the eighth century (Noonan, 1980a). The discovery of such coins at, for example, Paviken in Gotland (Lundström, 1981, pp. 104–08) cannot be taken as evidence for trading at that site before the ninth century. Similarly, eleventh-century hoards show that some early ninth-century coins were still in circulation. Sites or graves cannot therefore be dated to the ninth century on the basis of single finds of such coins.

The most recent coin in a hoard provides one date limit, the other may be uncertain. There are good reasons for thinking that in the tenth and eleventh centuries, when there was a fairly regular and substantial flow of coins into Scandinavia, a hoard is unlikely to be much younger than the most recent coin in it. This conclusion is supported by the fact that in many hoards with coins from different areas, the dates of the youngest coin from each area are often fairly close (Hårdh, 1976b, pp. 42–3). Unfortunately, the ninth-century hoards, which consist almost exclusively of oriental coins, cannot be checked in this way, as relatively few coins reached Scandinavia in that century and, the youngest coin in a hoard may be a misleading guide to the date of its deposit.

Hoards can show what wealth was available for hoarding; their absence cannot prove that there was no wealth. It seems likely that treasure was normally kept hidden, and some people may have preferred to conceal their wealth outside their houses in hiding places known only to them. As long as the hiding place was known, the hoard could be recovered, enlarged or reduced, but if the owner of a hoard died suddenly, or was forcibly removed, and no one shared his secret, the treasure was likely to remain hidden. Accidental discoveries of such hoards are still made from time to time. When a number of hoards, apparently of the same date, have been found in one area it may be the result of some violent disturbance. Violence did not, however, necessarily lead to the abandonment of hoards. England certainly suffered great violence from Viking armies in the reign of Æthelred but remarkably few coin hoards of that period have been found – far fewer than in the late ninth century (Dolley, 1966, pp. 48–52). This cannot have been because the English had no wealth to hide, and the probable explanation is that the Viking armies at that time were not so much interested in taking prisoners or killing people, their aim was rather to intimidate the English into paying tribute.

Treasure hoards might also be forgotten if their owners failed to return from a journey. A local concentration of hoards of the same date may therefore have been caused by an unlucky expedition, such as that led by Ingvar (p. 32). It is perhaps significant that more coin hoards have been found in the area of the Ingvar stones which have most recent coins dated 1034–40 than with most recent coins dating from the rest of the eleventh century (Hatz, 1974, nos. 192, 196, 228, 231, 244; cf. nos. 105, 149, 311, 330 with most recent coins dated 1002, 1021, 1060, 1079).

A hoard is sometimes recovered in the container in which it was concealed, but more commonly the container is broken and the contents scattered, for example by ploughing, before anything is found. This happened at Stenstuga farm in Alskog parish, Gotland where, in 1850 during the harvesting of rye, twenty-seven coins, a piece of silver and the bottom of a copper box were found. The main part of that hoard, 1311 coins, more silver and another part of the box were found three years later (*CNS*, 1.1.7). The recovery of some hoards has been even more protracted, and there is often doubt as to whether all the objects recovered in this way belong to one hoard or to several. It is also clear that some hoards have only been partly recovered. Even when an intact hoard has been found, the contents are too rarely available for modern study. Finders do not always hand over all their discoveries, and those that have safely reached museums have not always been preserved: museums have often exchanged coins with other collections, common or 'uninteresting' coins have been melted down, and that has even more frequently been the fate of fragments. The result of such cavalier treatment is, of course, that many hoards whose existence is known cannot be properly studied and, most serious, their dates cannot now be determined with any confidence. This is particularly serious for the dirham hoards, because they contain a large proportion of fragments and the youngest may well have been disposed of. Even if the fragments are preserved, they are not always easy to identify and date. One supposedly early Swedish hoard, from Väsby in Hammarby parish, Uppland contained thirty-one whole coins and 395 fragments, but 265 of the fragments were illegible. There is therefore no justification for dating that hoard on the basis of the youngest legible coin which was minted in 825 (Linder Welin, 1938, p. 124).

The evidence of coins and coin hoards is undoubtedly of very great value for the study of Viking Scandinavia. Unfortunately, it has too often been used uncritically. It is, for example, unreasonable to treat the hoard found at Valhall in Barkåkra parish, Skåne as an early ninth-century hoard on the basis of the two Islamic coins it contains that were minted in 749 and 810 (Hårdh 1976a no. 36). Many generalizations have been based on hoard evidence that is similarly unsatisfactory, and the reappraisal of this evidence means that many commonly accepted assumptions, particularly about the eastern contacts of Scandinavia in the ninth century, have to be challenged (pp. 124–6).

Place names can also provide valuable information about early Scandinavia. They can reveal much about the ways the landscape has been exploited in the past and, perhaps even more important, they can provide information about the grouping and regrouping of settlements for administrative or political purposes into units called different names in different parts of Scandinavia: hundreds, herreds, syssels or fylke. The early boundaries of such units are rarely known and may have changed greatly in the course of time, but some of their names are demonstrably old and can yield information about the early development of Scandinavian society (Kousgård Sørensen, 1978). Place names have also made a very important contribution to the study of Scandinavian colonization overseas (pp. 100–10).

The main advances in our knowledge of Scandinavia in the Viking period have, however, been made by archaeologists. Archaeological evidence of course poses many problems. Many sites have been completely, or partly, destroyed and what remains may not represent the original situation. Stone monuments and stone cairns, for example, are more likely to have been removed in areas in which stone is scarce or on arable land, than in areas where stone is abundant, or in woodland. Few sites have been systematically investigated, and distribution maps based on surviving monuments or on excavated material are notoriously misleading. The problem is obvious and would hardly need emphasizing were it not for a persistent tendency to interpret distribution maps with little regard for their inherent weaknesses.

The problems of interpreting archaeological material are well illustrated by the very thorough excavations that have been made for many years at Hedeby. Some 5 per cent of the town site has been totally excavated, and has yielded a vast quantity of material: over 250,000 individual animals, including 100,000 pigs, over 3400 pieces of soapstone weighing altogether 540 kg, and in one year's excavation alone, 1963–4, no fewer than 3390 antler burrs were found. The town site at Hedeby is, however, in effect a vast rubbish tip, in which few objects of any value have been found. The recent excavations in the harbour have underlined this because, although large quantities of refuse have also been found there, other more valuable objects, including sixty-nine coins, have also been recovered. One of the most remarkable discoveries in the harbour is a leather bag containing forty-two bronze matrices, or blanks, with which a jeweller could make a great variety of ornaments (plate V). In short, the town site contains what was thrown away, while the harbour has yielded more treasured objects whose loss in the water must often have been a source of great regret. The disturbed character of the town site is demonstrated by the fact that pieces broken from a single pot have been found up to 100 metres apart, and in layers that are separated horizontally by as much as 2 metres. It follows that little weight can be placed on the dating of objects from Hedeby that depend on stratigraphy. It is some compensation that large quantities of timber were found, much of which can be dated very precisely by the recognition of distinctive patterns formed by annual growth rings. It has therefore been possible to date the building and rebuilding of some of the houses very precisely (Eckstein and Schietzel, 1977).

Modern scientific techniques are indeed opening up many new possibilities of interpreting archaeological material. Ecological evidence is yielding information about diet, as well as the parasites that men and animals suffered from, while the analysis of pottery offers the hope of determining where the raw material came from, and therefore where it was made. Preliminary studies suggest that the shape of pottery, which has hitherto been the main guide to type and provenance, may be very misleading, for it appears that much of the so-called Slavonic pottery found in Sweden was made from local clay (Ohlsson, 1976, pp. 129–39).

The evidence for developments in pagan Scandinavia is obviously less satisfactory than for the Scandinavians who went overseas to raid, conquer and settle. Some knowledge of the former is, however, needed if that Viking activity is to be understood. In the next two chapters an attempt will therefore be made, first to show what we can hope to know about Scandinavian society in and before the Viking Age, and then to consider the contacts that did so much to change that society and create the conditions that made the Viking raids possible.

4

Scandinavian society

In Viking Scandinavia there were slaves and freemen, and an intermediate group consisting of freed slaves and their descendants. Slavery is well attested in early Scandinavia (Skyum-Nielsen, 1974): according to Rimbert there were many Christian captives in Birka in the ninth century, and one of Anskar's activities as bishop of Hamburg was to buy Danish and Slav boys so that they could be trained for 'God's service' (*VA*, 11;15). Adam of Bremen suggests that slaves were a familiar feature in Denmark and southern Sweden in the mid-eleventh century (iv.8), and as late as 1201 Absalon, archbishop of Lund, owned some. Adam also reports that pirates based on Sjælland paid tribute to the Danish king for licence to plunder their barbarian neighbours, but that they abused this privilege by attacking their own people: 'And as soon as one catches another, he mercilessly sells him into slavery either to one of his fellows or to a barbarian' (iv.6). It was possible for an individual, in time of need, voluntarily to surrender his freedom together with that of his family, but slaves could also be bought. Conflicts within Scandinavia or across the Baltic among Slavs, Balts and Finns, were probably the most important source of slaves until Viking raids enlarged the catchment area – the British Isles were apparently a source of the slaves who accompanied the first settlers in Iceland.

There is no reliable information about the number of slaves in individual households, or in the whole population of any area. Some households are described in thirteenth-century Icelandic sagas as having twelve, eighteen or even thirty slaves, but slavery had disappeared from Iceland by the twelfth century (p. 41) and it is improbable that these figures were accurately remembered for a century or more; they are perhaps based on the number of landless labourers and servants employed by great men in the thirteenth century.

Slaves were under the control of their owners but, according to the laws, had some legal protection, possibly, but not necessarily, thanks to

Christian influence. In pagan times a slave may sometimes have been killed and buried with his or her owner. Ibn Fadlan describes this custom among the *Rus* in the tenth century, and there are several references to similar practices in Icelandic sagas. This may indeed be the explanation for some of the double burials that have been found in Scandinavia and elsewhere, notably Russia (Ramskou, 1965). Slaves could be freed by their owners. A unique rune stone at Hørning in north Jutland, erected in the mid-eleventh century by a smith called Toki is in memory of his former owner, who had given him freedom. Toki appears to have been an unusual slave, and may even have been a goldsmith. This stone is the only runic inscription in Scandinavia that mentions slavery. The Church encouraged the liberation of slaves and forbade the enslavement or sale of Christians; but the liberation of slaves was not a Christian innovation. The Scandinavian term *leysingi*, which is used of a freedman in the twelfth century, was in use as early as the ninth century in England, where it was used to refer to the freedmen of the Danes. Slaves were also bought to be freed by churchmen like Anskar but their motive seems not so much to have been the slaves' liberation as recruitment of converts to work as missionaries. According to some laws slaves could buy their freedom, but that must have been a rare event, for the slave cannot often have had the necessary wealth.

The status of a freed slave had to be recognized in some way, especially if he or she remained in the same community. Some Swedish laws suggest that this involved a formal process in a public place, a *ting* or, perhaps later, a church, in which the newly-freed person was recognized as belonging to some free family (Modéer, 1976). Whatever the legal niceties of enfranchisement, in a world where status was largely determined by wealth, freed slaves and their descendants were obviously at a disadvantage and most joined the lowest ranks of society, becoming landless labourers or servants who, despite their legal freedom, were subject to many, often crippling, economic and social restraints (Schledermann *et al.*, 1975).

The compilations of laws made in the late twelfth and thirteenth centuries in several parts of Scandinavia and in Iceland contain a great deal of information about the rights and responsibilities of the different social classes, but the relevance of this information to conditions in pagan Scandinavia is uncertain. The laws doubtless contain archaic rules, but they are not easily recognized (p. 19). The collections are, in fact, more revealing about the period in which they were compiled than about a distant past. It is possible that one of the reasons for their production was to explain and justify the existence of a large group of people who were legally free but economically very dependent, even depressed. Few farmers in medieval Scandinavia owned the land they worked and most held it from the Crown, the Church or the nobility, with varying degrees of insecurity (Bjørkvik, 1965; Norborg, 1965; Rasmusson et al., 1962). Many Scandinavians nevertheless cherished the notion that their ancestors had enjoyed a greater degree of freedom and fuller control over their farms. One explanation for the supposed change, current in Norway and Iceland, was that kings, and in particular Harald Finehair, had tyrannically deprived many men of their ancestral rights. Thus, the compilers of the provincial laws made their own distinctive contribution to social history, for by suggesting that a large section of society was descended from slaves, and consequently had no right to inherit free land, the laws offered a convenient explanation for, and justification of, the control some exercised over others.

The law collections were not all fantasy. There is independent evidence for some of their provisions, particularly in matters of inheritance (Jansson 1962, pp. 76–8; U, 29) but the details on slaves and freedmen, which are most elaborate in the Norwegian and Icelandic laws, must have been at best no more than an oral tradition by the time they were compiled. In Iceland, for example, the only evidence for slaves is in the thirteenth-century collection of Icelandic laws known as Grágás, and in some sagas that purport to describe early conditions. The conclusion has reasonably been drawn that slavery had died out there by the twelfth century (Foote, 1975). No provision was made for slaves or freedmen in the laws introduced in Iceland in the thirteenth century after its submission to the Norwegian Crown, and in Norway itself slavery is virtually ignored in the Land Law of Magnus Lagabøter of 1274. It is remarkable that in Sweden, where slavery was not abolished until 1335, the provincial laws are very much less elaborate in their treatment of slaves and freedmen than are the Norwegian laws (Neveus, 1975).

The compilers of the Norwegian provincial laws used many archaic words for various stages of freedom, some of which are otherwise only known in poetry. There are grounds for suspecting that their meaning was not always well understood. The term frjálsgjafi, for example, was used in Iceland for the slave-owner who gave freedom, and that is the natural meaning of the word; in one set of Norwegian laws, however, the same word is used to describe the lowest grade of freed slave, who remained under some obligation to his former master (Bøe and Lárusson, 1965). A shift of meaning is conceivable, but as the word only occurs in that sense in these laws it seems more likely to have been a misunderstanding by the compilers. Many of the details in the Norwegian and Icelandic laws about slaves, freedmen, and the various stages of freedom they could hope to attain, are therefore very suspect. To the compilers the essential feature seems to have been that although the freed slaves, or their descendants, could one way or another hope to gain some degree of freedom and the right to work land for their own benefit, they could never aspire to the same status as men whose ancestry was unambiguously free.

That there were slaves, freedmen and different ranks of freemen need not be doubted; there is good independent evidence for them all. But the detailed classifications implied by the Norwegian laws probably owed more to the inventiveness of the compilers than to an accurate recollection of circumstances in the more or less distant past. The differences in terminology and substance between the various collections may reflect differences between areas, or be due to the social changes taking place in the twelfth and thirteenth centuries, but some are better explained as due simply to omissions. In the west Norwegian law, for example, two classes of freemen were recognized: the *hauldar*, owning inherited family land, and other men of free descent who farmed land that was not theirs by inheritance. The law of Trøndelag recognized these two classes, but also included a third, lower class of landless freemen. It has been suggested that these were a group peculiar to that area (Bjørkvik, 1969) but there must have been landless freemen in all parts of Norway and it seems best to assume that they were wrongly omitted from the other laws, or were included under some other category.

The status of a free person was, according to the laws, expressed in terms of the compensation which he was expected to pay if he committed an offence or that would be owed to him if, for example, he suffered injury at the hands of another (Hasselberg *et al.*, 1957). The most important of these was *mansbot*, the Scandinavian equivalent of the English *wergeld*, which is the price or compensation owed for a man's life. *Mansbot*, which can be translated as atonement price, was the legal value put on a man's life and was, in theory, the sum due to his kin if he were killed. In default of such a payment the family of the victim was free to take revenge on the killer and his family by feud

(Wallén 1962; 1966). The laws of Sweden, Denmark and south-east Norway suggest that freemen in any one district were undifferentiated, all having the same *mansbot*, although its value varied from region to region. In western Norway and Trøndelag freemen were divided into two or three grades, and in all the Norwegian laws freedmen are ranked below the fully free. According to the law of south-east Norway, this system of values was adopted by the Church and was used to determine such things as burial fees or the part of a churchyard in which a person might be buried. The detailed elaboration of these social classifications may owe much to the ingenuity of the lawyers who collected the laws, but there is no doubt that the society was hierarchical. The apparent uniformity of the free class in the greater part of Scandinavia may be somewhat deceptive. In both Swedish and Danish laws there is provision for unspecified payments in addition to *mansbot*, and this seems to leave the way open for adjustments to take account of the real status and power of individuals or families. Such payments were called *gørsum* in Danish, and *vängåva* in Swedish (Wallén *et al.*, 1966, 331; Petersson 1976).

The class of *hauldr* (plural *hauldar*), though well represented in Norway, does not occur in laws in other parts of Scandinavia, or in *Grágás*. It was, however, familiar to the English in the tenth century, who regarded *holdas* as men of very high status, leaders of Scandinavian armies, named with kings and earls. In an eleventh-century list of English wergelds the *hold* is ranked with the king's high-reeve as having half the wergeld of a bishop or ealdorman (*EHD*, 51b). The high status of such men is confirmed by the use of the word in the English place name Holderness – 'the headland of the *hold*' – to describe a large tract of land north of the Humber estuary. The fact that the word is also used in some Danish and Swedish place names shows that it had once been current there too (Hald, 1933). (The absence of *hauldar* in Iceland is surprising. The Icelanders came from that part of Norway in which the class was later well established, and Icelandic law is said to have been modelled on that of west Norway. What is more, when Icelanders visited Norway they were, for a while, entitled to be treated as *hauldar*.) The English evidence, and the place names in both England and Scandinavia, would suggest that in the early Viking period *hauldar* were a very superior class of freemen, and perhaps better described as aristocrats.

The evidence of the laws has led to the claim that the fundamental social institution in Viking Scandinavia was the family, effectively larger than the nuclear family of modern times (Johnsen, 1948), and one of its main functions was to protect its members. It was, indeed, the right and duty of the family to avenge a killing. However, a feud could be averted by the payment of an appropriate compensation, the *mansbot*. The provincial laws imply that the family group was, for this purpose, very large indeed, extending to fourth or even fifth cousins. This can best be seen in the elaborate regulations defining the responsibility for paying *mansbot*, and the right to receive it. The clearest example is a section found in one manuscript of *Grágás*, the *Baugatal*, (List of Rings) because the payments were expressed in terms of *baugar* (silver rings), of different weight which, together with supplementary payments, were due to be paid or received by different groups of kinsmen (Dennis, Foote and Perkins, 1980, pp. 175–83). The most valuable ring, weighing 48 ounces, was to be paid by the father, sons and brothers of a killer to the father, sons and brothers of his victim, while the fourth ring, weighing twelve ounces, was paid or received by the male first cousins. Additional payments are also prescribed for more distant relatives, as far as fourth cousins, who were jointly responsible for paying one ounce to the fourth cousins of the victim. However, as Bertha Phillpotts pointed out in 1913 (p. 14), neither the Sturlunga Saga, written in the thirteenth century about contemporary events, nor the sagas written at the same time about earlier times provide any evidence for the payment or receipt of wergelds as ordained by *Baugatal*. 'We never hear of any division of wergeld on *Baugatal* lines, between the various classes of kindred, nor of any dispute about wergeld shares either between kinsmen of the two opposing parties or among the recipients or payers themselves.' Medieval Icelandic history is full of violent disputes within families that end in killings, but there is no suggestion that these raised any problems over payment of wergeld, and the details given in the sagas correspond much more closely to the provisions of another section of *Grágás*, the *Vígslóði* (the consequences of slaying). This shows that compensation was due not to the whole kindred, but to the heir or heirs who had the right and responsibility to take legal action against the killer, if necessary by force (Dennis, Foote and Perkins, 1980, pp. 156 –8). The details of *Baugatal* must be considered fantasy, a good example of the artificiality and unreal systematization much loved by medieval lawyers.

Baugatal probably came from Norway where some of the law collections contain very complex – indeed incomprehensible – accounts of *mansbot* obligations of a very similar type (Phillpotts 1913, pp. 49 –65; 72–3). In one section the tariff of compensations extends to fifth cousins, as it also does in the Older Law of Västergötland. There is, however, no more sign in Norway or Sweden than in Iceland that these tariffs were ever applied, and the evidence in fact suggests that the kinsmen involved in feuds or reconciliations never extended beyond the immediate family (Johnsen, 1948, pp. 73–98).

Runic inscriptions confirm the narrow range of the family relationships that mattered. In Västergötland, for example, there are at least forty-five Viking-age inscriptions commemorating fathers, sons, husbands, wives or brothers, but only one raised to a cousin, and three for relations by marriage other than wives (Wideen, 1955, p. 131).

Runic inscriptions also confirm the later evidence of laws and charters that in Scandinavian society women could inherit as well as men. In such a society the families, however extensive, of two related individuals will inevitably be different (Fox 1967, p. 165). As Maitland pointed out, in commenting on the family as a blood-feud group in early English society, 'each set of brothers and sisters was the centre of a different group. From this it follows that the blood-feud group cannot be a permanently organized unit' (Pollock and Maitland, 1895, ii.239). The unique character of the relationship of any group of 'brothers and sisters' is underlined in both modern and medieval, Scandinavian languages, as well as in Old English, by the terms used to distinguish maternal and paternal relatives: grandfathers, for example, are either *morfar* or *farfar*.

Two features of later Scandinavian society have been adduced as evidence for the fundamental importance of the family in earlier times: the extended family and the right to challenge the alienation of family land. The right to challenge the alienation of family land (Hafström, 1957) was a feature of many European legal systems until the eighteenth century, its purpose being to prevent the disinheritance of kinsmen, especially heirs, by sale or gift. Joint- or extended families – that is, households including more than one married couple belonging to the same family – have been noted in several parts of post-medieval Scandinavia (Granlund, 1972) and it has been claimed that they were relics of an ancient system of family ownership of land (Olsen, 1928, pp. 43–55). This is most unlikely. Joint-families are naturally unstable; and so while members of a family may sometimes have found it in their common interest to co-operate, and even to live together, such family groups tend to disperse after one generation. The extended family is in fact fairly rare in most parts of Scandinavia (Winberg 1975, pp. 192–7) and tended to flourish in the remote areas of the north, and in Carelia, where labour was in short supply and many hands needed at critical times of the year. Moreover, it is possible to show that in some areas the number of such families increased rather than diminished after the sixteenth century (Tornberg, 1972). The extended families of eighteenth-century Scandinavia are therefore irrelevant to any discussion of Viking-age society from which they were separated by centuries of economic and social development, great changes in landownership, and such major upheavals as the Black Death and the late-medieval desertions and depopulation.

Individuals could, of course, expect or at least hope for the support of close relatives, and did so long after the Viking period, but late-medieval deeds of reconciliation after slayings show that normally it was a fairly limited group of kinsmen who were compensated (Phillpotts 1913; Grøtvedt, 1965). There are some examples of the participation of more distant relatives, but these generally involved the aristocracy, whose active family connections tended, then as now, to be more extensive than those of most people. The security of an individual and his family, therefore, depended not on the support of distant kinsmen, but on the protection that could be offered by lords or chieftains, whose importance in early Scandinavian society has been somewhat overshadowed by the myth of kindred solidarity.

Old Norse is very rich in terms for rulers, princes and other men of power, as the following incomplete list shows: *bragninr, dróttin, eorl, gœdingr, goði, gramr, harri, hildingr, hilmir, jǫfurr, konungr, lofðar, mildingr, ræsir, stillir, vísi, thióðann, thjóðkonungr, ǫðlingr*. Many of these words are only preserved in poetry in which many synonyms for ruler were needed because so much of it was written in royal courts for the praise of kings. Poets also needed many ways of referring to battles, ships and weapons but they tended to do this by devising metaphorical expressions called *kennings*. There are indeed some kennings for rulers, but it is significant that the poets could also draw on a very large, if archaic, vocabulary to serve their needs.

The existence of powerful and very wealthy people in many parts of post-Roman Scandinavia is confirmed by the evidence of graves. Some burials were covered by large mounds that remain impressive memorials a thousand or more years later. Some, like the three mounds at Old Uppsala, contain cremation burials but many were inhumations, commonly with the dead person placed in a ship or large chamber.

Huge mounds containing large quantities of grave goods of high quality can reasonably be interpreted as the burials of men or women of great power, well able to give protection or to demand obedience – in short, rulers. One of the most lavish finds, at Oseberg in Vestfold, was the tomb of a young woman, aged about twenty-five (Schreiner, 1927, pp. 107–8), and contained a most remarkable quantity of wood carving of the highest quality, and complex textiles that are, unfortunately, less well preserved. Individual items have often been reproduced as examples of fine craftsmanship, but the extraordinary volume and variety of this grave's contents ought to be emphasized (Sjøvold 1979, pp. 10–52). It contained not only an elegantly decorated ship over 21 metres long, but a cart and four sledges, three of them elaborately

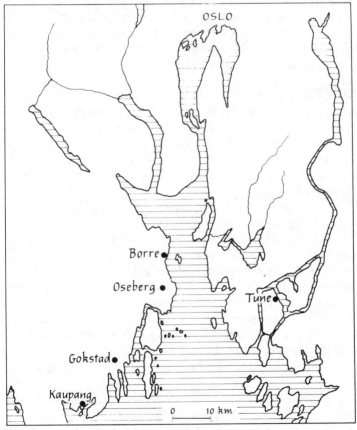

Figure 4 Oslo Fjord

carved like the cart, five wooden posts beautifully but strangely carved in the shape of animal heads, and a mass of household equipment, including buckets, pails, troughs, bowls, three cauldrons, a tripod, two lamps and a frying pan. There were three beds, a chair and three chests, one of them very handsome with iron bands and fine wrought-iron lock hasps. There were also four looms, other items used in making textiles, a variety of personal belongings, including combs and shoes, and a saddle. The grave was robbed, probably quite early, and badly disturbed. This probably explains the lack of personal ornaments, although the bronzes that remained are, like the other contents, of very high quality. The Oseberg find is not unique. Some 25 kilometres to the south, at Gokstad, a large mound was excavated in 1880 and found to contain a man buried in a ship that was larger and far more seaworthy than that discovered at Oseberg, together with a variety of other equipment, much like that of Oseberg, including three small boats, six beds, a sledge, and at least twelve horses, six dogs, and a peacock (Sjøvold 1979, pp. 53–68). At Borre, less than 10 kilometres north of Oseberg, and at Tune on the other side of Oslo Fjord, similar ship-burials were discovered earlier, but their contents have unfortunately not been so well preserved, although enough has survived to show that they were very similar to the Oseberg and Gokstad finds, and of the same period (Sjøvold, 1979, pp. 69–72). Such displays of extravagance are only explicable by the assumption that the dead had had great power and wealth, and were served by some of the finest craftsmen of the age.

Not all large mounds contain burials. One of the pair at Jelling in Jutland, for example, appears never to have contained a grave. Others contain very modestly furnished burials; many have not been excavated at all, and it would therefore be wrong to assume that all large mounds were raised over people of the highest rank. It does, however, seem reasonable to regard the largest mounds, and those with very rich contents, as the burials of unusual importance. Such mounds occur throughout Scandinavia, some standing alone, others having less prominent graves nearby; but in some places several mounds are grouped together – two at Jelling, three at Old Uppsala, and no fewer than nine, together with two huge cairns, at Borre (Plate VI and figure 5, p. 49).

Richly furnished boat- or chamber-graves that are unmarked by mounds are less easy to find, and a map showing the distribution of those that have been discovered would not be particularly informative.

There are, however, a number of cemeteries of this kind north of Mälaren that are of great interest (figure 6, p. 51) because very similar rites were followed in all of them, and each contains a regular sequence of burials: apparently one inhumation in each generation, with the other graves being cremations (Schönbäck, 1980). At Valsgärde there is a sequence of twenty-five male inhumations, fifteen of them in boats, from the fourth to the eleventh century, and about fifty cremations which, to judge by the remnants of the grave-goods, were mostly of women (figure 7, p. 52). The cemetery at Vendel shows much the same pattern, with fourteen boat-burials from about 600 to the mid-eleventh century. The finds from Tuna in Alsike are similar, although less complete, but in the cemetery at Tuna in Badelunda the roles were reversed: it was the men who were cremated and the women inhumed in chamber-graves or boats (plate VII; Stenberger 1956a; 1956b pp. 56–65).

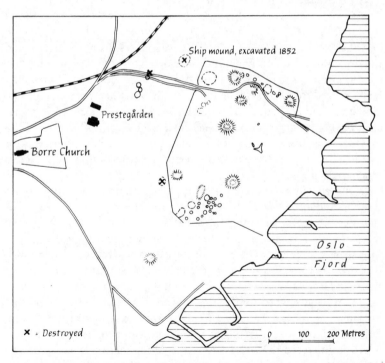

Figure 5 Grave mounds at Borre. The most prominent are hachured. Based on a map prepared for Universitets Oldsaksamling by Aslak Liestøl.

These rich boat-grave cemeteries of Mälardalen raise many questions about the status and functions of the people buried in them: what is the significance of the female inhumations at Tuna in Badelunda? Do the small helmet and the sword with a small hilt in one of the eighth-century graves at Vendel (no. xii) indicate the burial of a child, and if so what does that signify? Why does the quality of the grave-goods decline in the ninth century? Does the place name *Tuna*, which is also associated with Vendel, have any significant relationship with these places (Olsson, 1976)? Why do these cemeteries contain so few graves and apparently only one inhumation per generation? Satisfactory answers to these and many other questions cannot be offered at this stage, only speculations. If these cemeteries have a common origin, as seems likely, it must lie in the fourth century or earlier; their parallel development suggests close contact, but does not necessarily mean any form of central control. These cemeteries may have originated with a family or a group of leaders who were established, by invitation or otherwise, at key centres north of Mälaren in the fourth century, if not earlier. All but one of them lie very close to one of the main routes, by ridges and waterways, from the north, and the exception, Tuna in Badelunda, lies on a very similar route further west (figure 6, p. 51). The wealth displayed in these cemeteries may have derived from some form of tribute that was exacted from hunters, craftsmen and perhaps traders, taking such things as furs, antlers and, after the sixth century, iron to Mälardalen. The women buried in Tuna in Badelunda, and the possibility that one of the Vendel graves was for a child, suggest that the power of the people buried in these cemeteries was hereditary.

In the eleventh century the evidence for eastern Sweden becomes more abundant and varied, but many problems remain. There is, for example, the group of runic stones that commemorate men who died in the course of an expedition to the east led by Ingvar (figure 3, p. 31). Ingvar may have been the ruler of the extensive territory from which he drew his force, but he is, never described as a king, and does not figure in later royal genealogies, though that may be a consequence of the failure of his expedition. Kings who are named in the genealogies or king-lists do not appear in the Swedish inscriptions, apart from Håkon, who is said to have ordered the erection of a stone in memory of Tolir, who administered the royal estate of Adelsö, near Birka (*U*, 11). The difference between the two may indeed simply have been a result of the failure of Ingvar's expedition – he was forgotten, while others were

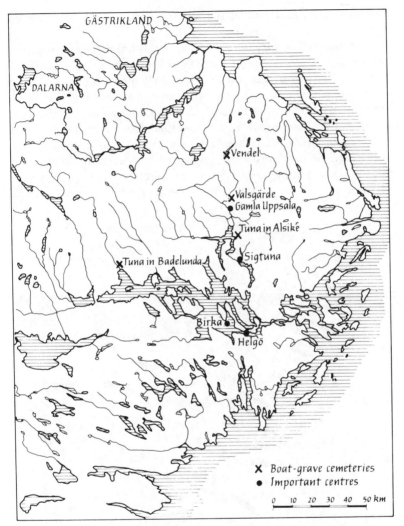

Figure 6 Boat-grave cemeteries north of Mälaren

remembered. Alternatively, it is possible that Ingvar was not a ruler but an adventurer, who attracted many men to join his enterprise as the Danish leader Knut had done earlier. But if a man who was not a king could attract so much support, and be named on so many memorials, the power and functions of the king must have been very limited indeed.

The most satisfactory interpretation of this unsatisfactory evidence seems to be that, as late as the eleventh century in many parts of Scandinavia, power was distributed among many rulers, including some women, whose authority rarely extended very far; they were indeed petty kings or queens. Some doubtless claimed, or hoped to win, a larger authority, and we may be sure that violent conflicts in pursuit of more resources and greater fame were a recurrent theme in pagan Scandinavia as they were, for example, in seventh-century England. In the eleventh century and later there were frequent and dramatic changes of fortune in the lands around the Baltic, and it seems

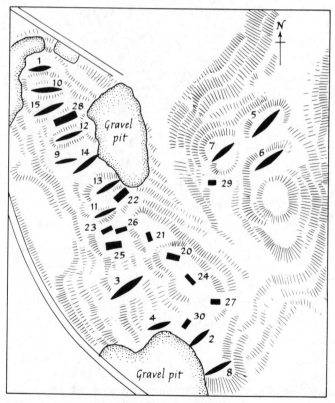

Figure 7 The boat and chamber graves at Valsgärde. The cremation burials are not marked. Based on Ardwidsson 1977.

reasonable to suppose that there were similar rapid fluctuations in the Viking Age and earlier.

Some, perhaps many, of these Scandinavian rulers are likely to have had poetry composed in their praise, but only fragments of these poems survive. Such verses were of little interest to the Icelanders whose sagas have preserved the poetry of the Viking Age. The surviving verses are mainly about Norwegian kings, and Swedish rulers only occur incidentally. We are, however, fortunate in having one stanza praising an otherwise unknown Danish ruler, Sibbi the Wise, son of Foldar. This was composed in about the year 1000 and is preserved in a runic inscription at Karlevi in Öland: 'A more righteous seafarer upon Endil's broad expanse [that is the sea, for Endil was a sea-god], one strong in battle, will not rule land in Denmark' (Frank, 1978, p. 121).

Frankish sources cast some light on the authority of Scandinavian rulers. The Franks were, naturally, mainly interested in their Danish neighbours, and we consequently know more about the kings of Jutland than about those from elsewhere. It has been suggested that the Danish kingdom included Skåne as early as the ninth century because one of the Danish representatives who confirmed a peace agreement with the Franks in 811 was called Osfrid of Skåne (*ARF*, 811); but the retinue of early medieval rulers commonly included men from far afield. There is indeed nothing to show that the kings with whom the Franks had dealings in the ninth century had any authority in the Danish islands. The only evidence of their activity outside Jutland is, in fact, the record of an expedition in 813 by two Danish kings to Vestfold 'whose princes and people refused to submit to them' (*ARF*, 813). This suggests that in the ninth century, as in the eleventh, the rulers either side of the Skagerrak attempted to extend their power across it. Two years later a Frankish army invaded Denmark and after seven days camped at an un-named place on the coast, unable to reach the Danish forces because 'they remained on an island three miles off the shore and did not dare engage them' (*ARF*, 815). That island has been assumed to be Fyn, and the conclusion has been drawn that Fyn was the heart of the Danish kingdom at that time (Randsborg, 1980, pp. 31–2). A Frankish army, however, is unlikely to have needed seven days to reach the coast opposite Fyn, a distance of at most 130 kilometres. The water that sheltered the Danes is more likely to have been Limfjord. According to Adam of Bremen (iv.1) it took between five and seven days to travel by land from Schleswig to Ålborg on

Limfjord. The Danish kings that Anskar, as bishop of Hamburg knew had authority in south Jutland, at least in the trading centres of Hedeby and Ribe, and churches were built in these centres with royal permission (p. 137). A leading opponent of the mission was Count Hovi, who ordered the church at Hedeby to be closed, but the king reversed the decision and expelled the count 'from Schleswig with the intention that he should never afterwards be able to return to his favour' (*VA*, 32). There is nothing in the *Vita Anskarii* to suggest that the kings Anskar knew had any power in the islands.

For information about ninth-century Sweden we are dependent on the *Vita Anskarii*, in which several kings are mentioned, but no information is given about the extent of their authority. There is however a fairly detailed account of the campaign in Kurland by which King *Olef* re-established an overlordship that had formerly existed but had lapsed (*VA*, 30). Rimbert does, however, provide some interesting details about the limitations of royal power. Although the king originally gave Anskar permission to stay in Birka and preach, after an outburst of popular opposition, during which one missionary was killed and the others fled, the decision to allow the work to be resumed could not be made by the king alone. He had to consult two assemblies, one in Birka, the other 'in another part of his kingdom', before he could give his full consent (*VA*, 27) for 'it is the custom among them that all public business is arranged rather by the wish of the whole people than by the king' (*VA*, 26). The favourable decisions in the assemblies appear to have been unanimous, and followed preliminary discussions with the 'chief men', in the course of which lots were cast. (There are several references to the casting of lots when crucial decisions were made, especially in military matters (*VA*, 19; 30).) A little more information is given about one of these chief men, Herigar, because he was an early convert. He is described as a counsellor of the king, and prefect of Birka. That is, of course, Rimbert's term, and we do not know what he was called in Swedish nor whether his position was owed to the king.

According to these Frankish sources, one of the main functions of both Danish and Swedish kings was to act as military leader. Very little is known about the way their armies or fleets were recruited or organized. The core of any force was probably the leader's personal retinue, his *lið*. (The Karlevi stone was raised in memory of Sibbe by his *lið*.) Such men shared a sense of comradeship – they were 'fellows' – and this word is used to describe warriors on some rune stones. One, at

Hedeby for example, was erected by Thorulv in memory of Erik, who was not only a warrior but the captain of a ship, a steersman, whom he described as his fellow, *filaga sin*. This feature of Viking armies is also mentioned in the *Annals of St Bertin*. In 861 the Vikings in the Seine agreed to leave, but because winter was approaching, they broke up into their *sodalitates* and were allocated to various places along the river: the word *sodalitas* is significant because it implies a brotherhood, a fellowship.

For larger undertakings more men would often be needed. When in the mid-ninth century a Swedish king, *Anound*, was exiled, he had eleven of his own ships but he recruited twenty-one Danish ships to help him regain his kingdom. The invasions of Æthelred's England required even larger forces, and the Danish armies included men from eastern Sweden, several of whom are commemorated on rune stones (plate IIIb). In areas where boats are essential, power must always have depended partly on the control of fleets, and locally recruited forces for defence or attack must have been partly naval. This was the case in the Hebridean kingdom of Dál Riata long before the Viking raids began (Bannerman, 1974, pp. 148–54). There can obviously be no direct evidence for such arrangements in early Scandinavia. The later system of naval levies that functioned in all parts of Scandinavia from the twelfth century (Bjørkvik *et al.*, 1965) may well have developed from earlier arrangements, but the details are irretrievably lost, and ingenious attempts to trace their evolution depend on too many untestable assumptions (Hafström, 1949).

However limited his functions, a king who ruled an extensive area, even for a short while, needed agents to look after his interests and act on his behalf. A permanently enlarged kingdom would also require centres in which revenues could be collected and royal power displayed. The Danish complexes at Trelleborg, Fyrkat, Aggersborg and Nonnebakken in Odense probably served such purposes in the late tenth century (Roesdahl, 1977, pp. 161–76). By the twelfth century there were widely scattered royal estates throughout Scandinavia, many called *Husaby*, implying a settlement distinguished from others in having several houses which served as bases for royal officials (Rosén, 1962b). In Sweden these agents were sometimes referred to by the term *husabyman*, but more commonly as *bryti* (in Denmark *bryde*) and they acted as stewards of such estates; they may be compared with the German *ministeriales*, some of whom gained great wealth and power. A rune stone at Randbøl in Jutland, erected by Tue *bryde* in memory of his wife (plate II) shows that such officials existed in Denmark in the eleventh century.

Kings also needed men of established authority in different parts of their kingdoms, like the Norwegian landed men who appear to have been the descendants of an ancient aristocracy with new functions as representatives of royal power (Bøe, 1965). When, in the thirteenth century, Norwegian kings were acknowledged in Iceland, the old aristocracy of chieftains, the *goðar*, became landed men. A similar process may well be the explanation of the disappearance of the *hersir* of western Norway in the eleventh century (Sogner, 1961). The entrance by local rulers into the service of more powerful kings must often have converted formerly independent areas of authority into units of royal administration. These later had a variety of names, *syssel* in Jutland; *herred* in the rest of Denmark and the greater part of southern Scandinavia, including southern Norway; *hundare* in Svealand; and *fylke* in western Norway. Many of these districts were physically well defined, with natural boundaries formed by coasts, mountains or forests and, in some, archaeological and place-name evidence confirms that they were distinct areas of early settlement, well separated from neighbouring groups (Christensen, 1969, pp. 80–8). Some are likely to have been independent units of lordship at some stage under the control of men or women with regalian powers; a few were even called kingdoms, *rike*: for example, Romerike, Raunrike (now Swedish Bohuslän), mentioned by Jordanes in the sixth century (Svensson, 1917), and Ringerike. This last is a particularly well defined unit, surrounded by forest and mountains, north-west of Oslo.

Our knowledge of Scandinavian society in the Viking Age is both slight and very patchy and we tend to be better informed about the upper classes. A more comprehensive impression can perhaps be glimpsed in Iceland (Jóhannesson, 1974), where the written evidence is relatively good from the twelfth century – better than for most areas of Scandinavia – and can be supplemented by archaeological investigations of sites that were abandoned at an early date. In the valley of Thjórsárdalur, for example, several farms were abandoned because they were smothered by tephra from an eruption of Mount Hekla that is dated in some Icelandic sources as 1104, and certainly happened at about that time (Stenberger, 1943; Thórarinsson, 1967). The excavated remains of these farms give a very vivid impression of the circumstances in which many Icelanders lived at that time (figure 8, p. 57). Other farms in the same area appear to have been abandoned even earlier, probably because the resources were found to be inadequate (Eldjárn, 1961). Such sites have the great advantage that they have not been disturbed by later occupation.

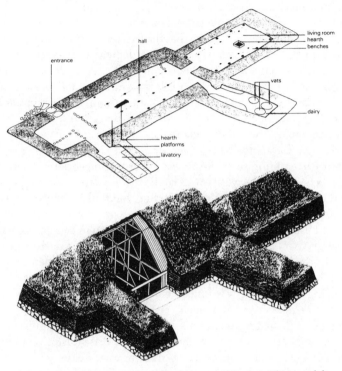

Figure 8 Reconstruction of the house at Stöng in Thjórsárdalur, Iceland. (From Graham-Campbell 1980b, p. 81, reproduced with permission from Frances Lincoln/Weidenfeld & Nicolson. Drawing by Ian Stewart after M. Stenberger.)

Iceland was colonized by Norwegians, the first settlers arriving in about 870. That at least is the date given by Ari Thorgilsson in *Íslendingabók* who also claimed that 'Iceland was fully settled in sixty winters, so that there was no further settlement made afterwards'. There are grounds for thinking that twelfth-century Iceland preserved some features of Viking society more faithfully than did twelfth-century Norway. In the first place, it was not a united kingdom; power was divided among many chieftains, *goðar*; and unlike Norway, its Church was not a royal institution, and, having adapted itself to the situation in Iceland, its organization reflected Icelandic society in various ways. The early bishops were in fact chieftains, and many landowners became priests. Bishops were chosen in assemblies that were dominated by chieftains, and it was in the same assemblies that offences against Church law were dealt with.

It seems reasonable to assume that the Icelandic settlers attempted to recreate in their new land patterns of settlement and social arrangements with which they had been familiar in their homeland. Later generations believed that their ancestors went to Iceland to escape the growing power of Norwegian kings. That tradition, however muddled it became, contains an essential truth and reflects the fundamental conservatism of the early Icelanders; they may have been rebels against new claims by Norwegian kings, but they were not revolutionaries attempting to create a new, experimental society. There are many echoes of Norway in Iceland: the settlers soon organized assemblies of freemen on Norwegian lines, and, like Norway, Iceland was divided into Quarters. The conservatism of the Icelanders is perhaps best represented by their language, which to this day remains far closer than the languages of continental Scandinavia to the Old Norse of the Viking Age. Their freedom to make arrangements which suited them was not limited by any earlier inhabitants, for they were colonizing a land that was effectively empty. There were no settlements to be taken over or avoided, and the social, economic and legal systems established by the colonists were unaffected by the presence of a native population. Elsewhere, notably in the British Isles, Scandinavian colonists had to accommodate to existing arrangements; in Iceland they did not. There they were free to organize their new homes as they liked, within the physical limits imposed by Iceland itself. We may therefore hope to discover many ancient features in Icelandic society, even if some appear in a thin Christian disguise.

Icelandic society was dominated by chieftains, *goðar*. This title, or rank, was known in Viking Scandinavia and occurs on three rune stones of the ninth and early tenth century on Fyn, where it is used to describe men of some importance. It also occurs in some Swedish place names. It is sometimes translated as priest, apparently because it is cognate with Gothic *gudja*, which does mean priest, but that association means only that in Iceland, as elsewhere, secular power had archaic religious roots. The authority of a *goði*, normally termed *goðorð*, was alternatively called *mannaforráð*, (rule over men), and in the thirteenth century its regalian character was even more clearly displayed by the use of the word *ríki*, (kingdom). The number of *goðar* at any one time is not known. The claim that there were originally thirty-six and that the number was later deliberately raised to thirty-nine is a late and suspect tradition (Sawyer, 1982). The number was certainly declining in the twelfth and thirteenth centuries – at one stage there were only five – as these men fought, often savagely, for increased power, much as the chieftains of Scandinavia had done for centuries and with similar results.

The men over whom the *goðar* had authority, their thingmen, are said to have had the right to change their allegiance, but they were normally bound together by a mutual need for support and protection, a reciprocal dependence that must have put severe limits on any statutory freedom of choice. Changes of allegiance certainly occurred, but not always voluntarily, and they reflected, or caused, fluctuations of power. *Goðar* were expected to support their men at law, if necessary by fighting. They sometimes paid wergelds that were owed by their men. They extended hospitality, especially at the annual assembly, the *Althing*, and expected to receive it in return. They convened assemblies and played a leading role in them. They did not, however, declare the law, which was the function of the lawspeaker. The division of power among many chieftains did not mean that Iceland was subject to a complexity of laws. It was, indeed, united by the acceptance of one, an ideal that was well expressed in the words attributed to the lawspeaker by whose decision the Icelanders accepted Christianity: 'Let all have one law and one faith, it will prove true if we break the law in pieces that we break the peace in pieces too.' There may have been many variations of practice among the local assemblies but at the annual Althing the unity of the country was symbolically expressed by the recitation of the law.

In 1096 a census was taken of the fully free population of Iceland and the total, recorded by Ari, was 4560. The total population of the island at that time has been estimated, on good grounds, to have been about 80,000 (Steffensen, 1968), rather more than in later times after erosion and volcanic eruptions had greatly reduced the available resources. The comparison of these two figures is a valuable reminder that, although freemen were undoubtedly important in Viking society, there were many less privileged men and women – tenants, labourers, servants, landless poor – whose contribution to society is sometimes obscured by the preoccupation of extant sources with the virtues and the rights of the fully free.

Our knowledge of the material conditions of the early Scandinavian colonists is being greatly enlarged by excavations in Iceland and in other Atlantic islands, but it is in Scandinavia itself that some of the most remarkable advances in settlement archaeology have recently been made. In Denmark a number of Viking-age villages have been found showing that nucleated settlements were a characteristic feature of Danish society long before the Viking period. At Sædding, near Esbjerg, about one hundred large houses and a similar number of smaller buildings of the Viking period have been found grouped around an undisturbed central area, apparently a green or common (Stoumann, 1979), while an even earlier example of the same arrangement has been found at Hodde, about 30 kilometres further north. Not all the buildings at Sædding were occupied at the same time. They represent a series of rebuildings, and it has not been possible to recognize individual units in that village, but at Vorbasse in the middle of Jutland, about 40 kilometres from Sædding, clear traces of boundary fences were found, separating groups of buildings (figure 9, p. 59).

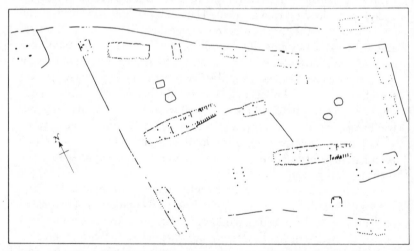

Figure 9   Part of the early Viking-period settlement at Vorbasse. Cf. fig. 11 (p. 69), phase 7. Based on Hvass 1979, p. 153.

These, and other Danish settlements of the Viking period, can be excavated because the sites were abandoned, apparently in the eleventh century, in favour of others nearby on which the medieval and modern villages stand. In earlier times it had been normal for Danish settlements to be moved from time to time. They never shifted far, normally less than 500 metres, and the inhabitants seem to have continued to exploit the same area. No satisfactory explanation can yet be offered either for the early instability of settlements or for the change to permanent sites towards the end of the Viking period (figure 11, p. 69; Grøngaard Jeppesen, 1981). The later villages often have early names which must either have been applied to the whole succession of settlements, or were in fact the names of the areas within which the successive settlements moved about rather than of the settlements themselves.

Viking period settlements have also been excavated in many parts of Scandinavia: Löddeköpinge and elsewhere in Skåne (Ohlsson, 1976; 1980; Strömberg 1961), Fjäle in Gotland (Carlsson, 1979), Ytre Moa in Sogn Fjord (Bakka, 1965), and recently a number of farm sites have been investigated in the far north of Norway, in Lofoten and even Troms (Sjövold, 1974). In most areas, however, it is necessary to trace the development of settlement by means of the grave-fields. The settlements themselves can rarely be located, perhaps because the sites are still occupied, but there are indications in Mälardalen that settlements moved around as they did in Denmark (Biörnstad, 1966; Arwidsson, 1978). The 250,000 known graves in Mälardalen, distributed over some 8500 cemeteries, provide unusually good opportunities for studying the development of settlement in that area, which can moreover be related to the changes in the shore line caused by a drop in the water level of about 5 metres since the ninth century. Very bold attempts have been made to base general studies of the whole region on this material and these have stimulated much research and discussion (Hyenstrand 1974; 1981) but detailed studies of small areas of the kind pioneered by Björn Ambrosiani (1964) still seem likely to yield the most valuable results. One very significant general conclusion, which must however be considered tentative until it has been tested by further studies, is that at the beginning of the Viking Age there were some 2000 farms in Mälardalen, and that in the eleventh century there were twice as many, with a total population of approximately 40,000. The area was not, however, over-populated and there were good opportunities for further expansion, quite apart from the new land rising from the sea.

One commodity that was essential in Viking Scandinavia was iron. It was needed for tools, weapons, household equipment and even ships – about 80 kg were needed for the rivets of the Gokstad ship alone.

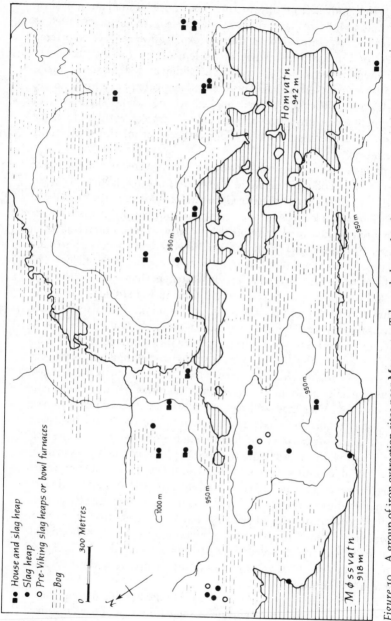

■ *House and slag heap*

● *Slag heap*

○ *Pre-Viking slag heaps or bowl furnaces*

||| *Bog*

300 Metres

0

N

1000 m

950 m

950 m

950 m

950 m

Homvatn
942 m

Møssvatn
918 m

Figure 10 A group of iron extraction sites near Møssvatn, Telemark, located and mapped by Irmelin Martens. Based on the official Norwegian Economic Map

Deposits of iron ore are widespread in Scandinavia and iron production began in the southern part of the region in the pre-Roman Iron Age. In the sixth century rich, although relatively remote, deposits in mountainous regions of Norway and in Dalarna began to be worked, and by the Viking period the quantity being produced must have been very large indeed (Clarke, 1979). One area that has been very systematically studied lies around Møssvatn, on the south-east edge of Hardangervidda, at a height of about 900 metres. Almost 200 iron-extraction sites of the period 600–1200 have been located and some small areas that have been closely investigated have as many as eight or nine furnaces and 100 charcoal pits in each square kilometre (figure 10, p. 62). Production grew rapidly in the Viking period and reached a peak in the tenth and eleventh centuries. The decline after that was probably due to the exhaustion of wood supplies. A very cautious attempt to estimate the total production of the whole area of Møsstrond, measuring some 275 square km, is that the annual production was about 4000 kg of iron, and perhaps more in the late Viking Age (Martens, 1981).

The work required skilled craftsmen, the temperature in the furnaces had to be carefully controlled otherwise the iron was of little value. Nothing is known about the origin of the men who did this work, nor of the way the iron was distributed. It appears to have been exported from the district in the form of the blooms that came from the furnaces, some of which have been found complete and weigh about 10 kg each. This raw material was then either worked into the tools, weapons and other equipment that was needed, or converted into rods or bars that could be used later or elsewhere, and are known as currency-bars. Hoards containing these currency-bars have been found in many parts of Scandinavia (Helgö, V:1; Martens, 1981). Powerful men who controlled the routes out of the area may have taken some of the iron produced at Møsstrand as tribute, and may even have organized its production. They needed iron themselves for equipment or to give to followers and allies, but they could also sell it at such places as Skien, which lies on the outlet of the main route from Telemark to the sea, and is now known to have been established in the Viking period (Myrvoll Lossius, 1979). The situation in eastern Sweden appears to have been very similar. The people buried at Vendel and similar cemeteries in that area probably owed their wealth partly to their control of the routes from Dalarna and Gästrikland to Lake Mälaren where iron was worked in such places as Helgö, or sold at Birka (p. 50). Markets for exchanges between different regions – highland and lowland, iron producing and iron consuming, the arctic north and southern Scandinavia – certainly existed in the Viking period. Some were probably very specialized and did not result in permanent settlements, but others were associated with local markets at which people living nearby could buy and sell their surplus produce. Traces of such markets have been found in many parts of Scandinavia: Valle in Setesdal (Larsen, 1980), Paviken on Gotland (Lundström, 1981), Skuldevig near the mouth of Roskilde Fjord (Crumlin-Pedersen, 1978b, pp. 67–9), and several are known in Skåne, Löddeköpinge, Ystad, Hagestad (Ohlsson 1976; 1980; Strömberg 1963; 1978). Craftsmen visited these places to make and sell their wares. At Löddeköpinge some of the workshops were seasonally, not permanently occupied and there are indications that other markets too were seasonal (Ambrosiani, 1981). Some were held in the winter which is the best time for collecting furs and for travelling over frozen rivers and lakes (plate X). Many of these markets were sited on rivers or lagoons a short distance inland, where they were accessible by boat but had some shelter from storms and raiders. Some were already active in the eighth century, or even earlier. There are, for example, clear signs of eighth-century activity at Ribe and Hedeby, but it was in the ninth and tenth centuries that most flourished and that new ones, such as Århus, were founded. The most important places like Birka, Hedeby and Kaupang attracted merchants and craftsmen from great distances largely because they were ideal centres for trading in furs, walrus ivory, antler and probably iron. The demand for these and other northern produce was certainly growing through the eighth and ninth centuries and the resulting commerce brought Scandinavia into closer contact with the outside world than it had been since the Roman Iron Age.

5

Scandinavia and Europe before 900

No part of Scandinavia was ever conquered by the Romans, but their influence nevertheless reached far into the north, and in Scandinavian archaeology the first four centuries AD are commonly called the Roman Iron Age. Imports from the Roman Empire have been found in many areas, especially in eastern Denmark, mostly as grave-goods but sometimes in what appear to have been votive offerings deposited in marshland. The artefacts that reached Scandinavia were generally luxury goods, made by craftsmen rather than mass produced. There are many glass bowls and beakers, cauldrons and other large bronze vessels, jugs, bowls, ladles of silver or bronze, jewellery, fine pottery and weapons. Some may have been brought back by people who had spent some time in the Empire as servants, soldiers, or even honoured guests, and it is likely that some of the best pieces were diplomatic gifts. There is, however, no reason to doubt that at least some reached Scandinavia by way of trade, in exchange for the northern goods such as amber and furs that were in demand in the Roman Empire. Pliny describes how a Roman knight, commissioned to obtain amber for a gladiatorial display, travelled to the Baltic from Carnuntum in Pannonia and collected 'so plentiful a supply that the nets used for keeping the beasts away from the parapet of the amphitheatre were knotted with pieces of amber, and the arms, biers [for the dead gladiators] and all the equipment used on one day, the display each day being varied, had amber fittings' (*Nat. Hist.* xxxvii.45). The largest piece was said to weigh 13 lb. This anecdote not only shows how Roman extravagance could create a demand for large quantities of such commodities, it also implies that direct contacts of that kind were unusual; the amber was collected by a knight not a merchant. The normal mechanism of trade seems to have been through a series of middle-men. That is certainly suggested by Jordanes who wrote, in the sixth century, that the Svear, 'famed for the dark beauty of their furs', sent 'sapphire-coloured skins through innumerable other tribes for Roman use' (Mierow, 1915, p. 56). The Roman conquest of Gaul and Britain opened the way for trade by ship, and the very large quantities of Roman material found in

Frisian settlements suggests that that area was already a key centre for contact between western Europe and the north (Eggers, 1951, karte 8).

The lands around the Baltic had much to offer the Empire. Amber, a fossilized resin with beautiful colours and remarkable electrostatic properties, is found in many parts of Europe, but the richest deposits are in the lands just south of the Baltic, particularly in Samland and Jutland. Much of the amber occurring in Bronze Age finds in the Mediterranean world has been shown by analysis to come from this area (Beck, 1970) and according to Pliny it was 'imported every day of our lives and floods the market' (*Nat. Hist.* xxxvii.41). There were also the furs mentioned by Jordanes, and probably slaves. The Roman army needed large quantities of leather for boots, shields, clothing and tents and some of this was probably supplied from the cattle-rearing areas of Scandinavia. It has been pointed out that the areas of Sweden that are rich in Roman imports also tend to have many graves that included leather-working tools among their equipment (Hagberg, 1967, pp. 115 –28). It is significant that among the few Latin words borrowed from the Germans, two are connected with cattle: *reno* (hide, skin) and *sapo* (soap). Other loan-words in Latin that suggest contact with the Baltic area are *ganta* (goose) and *glaesum* (amber) (Wilde, 1976). In return the Germans borrowed Latin words for 'trader' and one, *caupo*, is ultimately the source of such place names as Linköping and København.

Scandinavian burial customs were apparently influenced by contact with the Roman world. Cremation, formerly the universal custom, continued to be the most common form of burial, but inhumations began in the early Roman Iron Age. This first occurred in Denmark and later in other parts of Scandinavia, but it was not universal; in some remote areas cremation continued to be the only method of disposing of the dead. Some of the inhumations were very richly furnished, and they often contained Roman imports. Cremations were not necessarily poor; it is sometimes possible to show from fragments that survived the fire that the dead person had been lavishly equipped, and the ashes were sometimes placed in a fine Roman bowl rather than a clay pot. Towards the end of the Roman Iron Age there was a tendency for graves to be less elaborately furnished and there was also a decline in inhumation.

It would certainly be wrong to base any conclusions about the density or even the distribution of population solely on the graves that have been discovered; more reliable evidence is provided by settlements. Recent studies, especially in Denmark, have shown that during the Roman Iron Age the number and size of settlements grew in several areas and that where comparison is possible, houses and their enclosures were larger in the fourth century than in the first. At Vorbasse in mid-Jutland, for example, twenty enclosed plots of a fourth-century village have been excavated, with an average size of 2000 square metres, much larger than the enclosures on the same site three centuries earlier; the houses are also significantly larger (Hvass, 1978). In one area of about 500 square km in north Jutland there were at least forty-six settlements of the Roman Iron Age – that is one in every 2–3 square km (Jensen, 1976). New land was also being cultivated and it was at this time that the intensive exploitation of the marshes of west Jutland began. This activity naturally had its effect on the prevailing plant types as revealed by deposits of pollen. The forests were drastically reduced, as enormous quantities of wood were used for buildings or fuel, and the alder declined markedly, probably because the wet ground in which it flourished was cleared to grow hay. The grazing of cattle is also likely to have contributed to the reduction of woodland by inhibiting new growth. The Roman Iron Age was clearly a period of remarkable expansion in Denmark (Jensen, 1979, pp. 177–234). Similar developments have been recognized in many parts of Scandinavia, from Rogaland in south-west Norway to Gotland in the Baltic (Myhre, 1973; Stenberger, 1979, pp. 379–423).

Whatever the causes of this expansion, it is likely to have been accompanied by significant social and political changes, but here archaeology is a less satisfactory guide. In Denmark there seems to have been a shift in the main centre of wealth from Lolland to the eastern part of Sjælland during this period, and the remarkable concentration of very richly furnished, late Roman graves in the area of Stevns suggests that that area of Sjælland had become an important centre of power, – a 'chiefdom' – by then (Hedager, 1979).

The collapse of Roman imperial authority in the west, and the subsequent struggle for power throughout Europe, certainly had great effects, both direct and indirect, in Scandinavia as the demand for northern products declined. Imports from the Roman and Byzantine worlds, and from former Roman provinces, still reached Scandinavia but the quantities were much smaller in the fifth and sixth centuries. Large quantities of Roman gold, however, continued to reach Scandinavia and the lands south of the Baltic. By 1952, 281 Roman gold coins struck between 457 and 565 had been found on Öland and 245 on

Gotland, together with large numbers of gold objects which presumably also came from Rome (Stenberger, 1955, pp. 1161–72). This gold cannot have been a trading surplus and was probably originally paid to soldiers or to tribes on the frontier. Although the land routes across Europe were disrupted in the fifth and sixth centuries, the sea route from the west remained open, and in the fifth century an increasing number of western imports reached Jutland where they have been found in excavated settlements sites, and in Norway, where they have been found in graves (Bakka, 1971).

The apparent scarcity of imports in many parts of Scandinavia suggests that there was a significant decline in the prosperity of those areas. The change may be exaggerated by the tendency at that time to furnish graves more simply, but there are several indications that the sixth century was indeed a time of crisis. In Gotland, for example, large numbers of farms with massive stone foundations were abandoned, and similar desertions have been observed in Öland, Skåne and south-west Norway. There have been many attempts to explain this widespread phenomenon. Suggested causes include migration, climatic deterioration, soil exhaustion, deficiency diseases in cattle, violent invasion and internal conflicts. Some are more generally relevant than others, but it is possible that all played a part in varying degrees, in different areas. It has also been suggested that bubonic plague also affected Scandinavia at this time (Stenberger, 1955, pp. 1161–85; Gräslund, 1973).

It is possible that the changes were less dramatic than has sometimes been supposed. In most parts of Denmark it is now clear that Iron Age settlements did not normally remain on one site permanently, but moved from time to time within the neighbourhood from which the local resources could be exploited (Grøngaard Jeppesen, 1981). At Vorbasse the whole sequence of settlements from the first century BC to the modern village has now been traced (figure 11, p. 69). In Gotland the stone houses of the Roman Iron Age were sometimes replaced by wooden structures that are much more difficult to detect, and may occasionally have been overlooked (Carlsson, 1979). Very rich finds at Dankirke in south-west Jutland show this to have been an important place from the first to the fifth centuries, but it continued to be occupied until the eighth (Thorvildsen, 1972). The settlement of Helgö in Mälaren certainly flourished from the fifth century until the tenth (Holmqvist, 1979). Mälardalen seems, in fact, to have been relatively unaffected by the sixth-century decline (Hyenstrand, 1981). Many settlements in that area were continuously occupied from the Roman to the Viking period and it has even been claimed that there was a general increase in the number of settlements in that period. Continuity can be demonstrated in the boat-grave cemeteries at Vendel and Valsgärde (pp. 49–52).

Western Europe was also disrupted by the collapse of Roman power, but Gaul recovered quickly under its new Frankish rulers, who gained control of the markets attended by foreign merchants (Ganshof, 1962). Many of these markets had been founded or developed by the Romans but some appear to have been established by the Franks themselves.

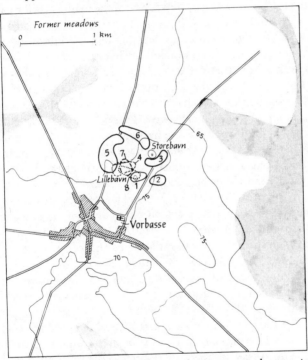

Figure 11   Vorbasse. The location of successive settlements is shown as follows:

1 1st century BC	**5** 4–5th centuries AD
2 1st century AD	**6** 6–7th centuries AD
3 2nd century AD	**7** 8–10th centuries AD
4 3rd century AD	**8** 11th century AD

The water meadows are taken from a map made in 1870 (Hvass 1979, p. 138). Based on information provided by Steen Hvass

Quentovic, in the estuary of the Canche, for example, was not the Roman port of that area, which was at Boulogne, but there may have been a Roman fort there (Dhondt, 1962). Military and economic considerations often led to the choice of the same site. The largest and most important of these northern Frankish markets was at Dorestad (van Es, 1969; van Es *et al.*, 1978) which lies in a fork between two branches of the Rhine, about 20 km south-east of Utrecht. It was well placed to control traffic along one of the main branches of the Rhine and it also had good access, thanks to a network of waterways, with both the Meuse and, through the *Almere*, with the north Frisian coast and Scandinavia (figure 12, p. 74). It was one of the main ports for journeys between the Continent and England. In 716 the English missionary Boniface sailed from London to Dorestad and the Frisian merchants who are mentioned at both London and York in the eighth century probably came from there. There had been a Roman fort at Dorestad, and in the seventh century the Franks established a market nearby which developed in the eighth century to become the largest and most active trading centre in north-west Europe. Modern development means that the full extent of the harbour cannot be determined, but there are indications that the river frontage was about two km long, and that at least parts of it were tightly packed with wharves or landing-stages (van Es and Verwers, 1980). It was a major craft centre. Ships were built or repaired there, weapons and jewellery were made, as was cloth, and there is abundant evidence of bone and amber working. Large quantities of imports from the Rhineland have been found, including high quality pottery, mill-stones and barrels that probably once contained wine. From Dorestad the produce of the Rhineland was shipped to other parts of Frankia, England and Scandinavia. Similar markets flourished at the same time in England, although none rivalled Dorestad in size (Sawyer, 1978, pp. 220–6). It was through these markets that goods were taken to and from Scandinavia. The trade was in the hands of Frisians who most probably used Dorestad as their main base. The *Vita Anskarii* shows clearly that in the first half of the ninth century Dorestad was the main port for people travelling between western Europe and Scandinavia.

The commodities imported into Europe from the north were probably much the same as they had been under the Romans – in particular furs – but there was now a demand for walrus ivory. The best ivory comes from elephant tusks and vast quantities were used in Roman times, among other things for the diptyches sent out in large numbers by newly-elected consuls. The collapse of the Empire reduced the supply and, although it never dried up completely, the fact that Roman ivories were re-used in Carolingian times shows that it was scarce. Walrus ivory was a less fine, but satisfactory substitute, and it was used for some prestigious objects, such as the eighth-century Gandersheim casket (Beckwith, 1972, no. 2). It was still used for major works of art, for example the Bury crucifix, as late as the twelfth century. Walrus ivory was only found in the Arctic, and before Greenland was colonized, western Europeans could only obtain it from northern Norway. Óttar's account of northern Norway confirms the importance of walrus hunting, for when he made his voyage round North Cape it was, he explained, in part to survey the land:

> But mainly for the walruses, because they have very fine ivory in their tusks [they brought some of these tusks to King Alfred] and their hide is excellent for ship-ropes. The walrus is much smaller than other whales, being not more than seven ells long.

Whaling was also important:

> The best whale hunting is in his own country [that is probably near the Island of Senja] where the whales are forty-eight ells long, the biggest fifty. He said that he and five others had killed sixty of these in two days.

Óttar also profited from the tribute paid to him by the natives of the mainland, the Lapps:

> Óttar was a very wealthy man in the property which constitutes their wealth, that is in wild animals. He had, at the time when he came to the king, 600 unsold tame deer, of the kind called reindeer, and six of these were decoy reindeer. These are very valuable among the Lapps for they use them to catch the wild reindeer. He was among the foremost men in the land, yet he did not have more than twenty cattle, twenty sheep and twenty pigs, and the little that he ploughed he ploughed with horses. But their wealth is mostly in the tribute which the Lapps pay them. That tribute is in the skins of beasts, in the feathers of birds, in whale-bone and in ship-ropes which are made from whale-hide and seal-hide. Each pays according to his rank. The highest has to pay fifteen marten skins, five reindeer skins, one bearskin, ten measures of feathers and a jacket of bearskin or otterskin, and two ship ropes. Each of these must be sixty ells long, one made from whale-hide the other from seal. (Ross, 1940, p. 21)

It is likely that much of this tribute eventually reached the royal and noble households, secular and religious, of western Europe. There must have been a great demand for furs and other skins, which were important for clothing. Fur-bearing animals are found throughout Europe, but the best come from the coldest regions, and in fourteenth-century London the highest prices were paid for the grey-backed skins of the winter squirrel imported from Novgorod (Veale, 1966, pp. 72–7, 223–9). Three centuries earlier, Adam of Bremen was well aware both of the abundance of furs in the lands beyond the Baltic, and of the high value put on them by his German contemporaries. He records that in Norway: 'There are black foxes and hares, white martens and bears of the same colour who live under the water' (iv.31). He also describes the *Sembi*, or *Pruzzi*, of Prussia as having:

> An abundance of strange furs, the odour of which has inoculated our world with the deadly poison of pride. These furs they regard as dung, to our shame, I believe, for right or wrong, we hanker after a marten-skin robe as much as for supreme happiness (iv.18). [While the Swedes] regard as nothing every means of vainglory: that is gold, silver, stately chargers, beaver and marten pelts, which make us lose our minds admiring them (iv.21).

Another export from the north may well have been iron, but there is no clear evidence that any of the abundant supplies of iron being produced in Norway and Sweden were sent overseas. A better attested export is amber, for although lumps can be found washed up on the shores of the British Isles, it seems more likely that the large quantities that were worked at Dorestad were imported from Jutland, if not further away.

We are fortunate in having rather better evidence for contacts with western Europe in the pagan burials of Scandinavia. Material excavated from graves and settlements suggests that there was a significant increase in imports from western Europe in the eighth century. This is best seen in the relative abundance of western glass, in the form of bowls and beakers, that was buried in the eighth-century Swedish boat-graves (Arwidsson, 1942, p. 120). The excavations at Ribe in south-west Jutland show that the *portus* described in the *Vita Anskarii* began at least a century before his time. In the first half of the eighth century craftsmen were active there, working with bronze, iron, antler, bone, leather, glass and amber (Bencard, 1979). Ribe's contacts with the west are evidenced not only by the glass, pottery and mill-stones, but also by the discovery there of thirty-two silver coins, called *sceattas*, some of which certainly came from Dorestad. These form part of a rapidly growing body of coin evidence for eighth-century contact between western Europe, especially Frisia, and western Denmark (Bendixen, 1981). Dankirke, a few kilometres south of Ribe has also yielded 13 eighth-century European coins, Merovingian, Frisian and English, together with other imports, including glass (Bendixen 1974). Eighth-century imports from western Europe have also been found at Helgo in Lake Malaren which, like Ribe and Dankirke, was a place in which craftsmen worked (Holmqvist 1979).

By the beginning of the ninth century there were several well attested centres for long distance trade in Scandinavia and the Baltic: Kaupang in Vestfold, Hedeby, Birka, Truso and Staraja Ladoga. In northern Europe, as in the west, any ruler able to control such markets could hope for increased wealth and prestige. According to the Frankish royal annals, the Danish king Godfred deliberately removed merchants from *Reric*, an unidentified site in Slav territory, to his own lands because the *Vectigalia* were of great benefit to his kingdom. That technical term may owe more to the interpretation of the Frankish writer than to a conscious adoption by a Danish king of imperial and post-imperial prerogatives but, taken together with the evidence of the *Vita Anskarii* that rulers were actively interested in Ribe, Hedeby and Birka, it does suggest that some Scandinavian kings by then had rights that were very similar to, and may even have been based on, those enjoyed by rulers in Christian Europe.

The Frankish annals associate Godfred's removal of the *Reric* merchants with the fortification of his kingdom,

> with a rampart, so that a protective bulwark would stretch from the eastern bay, called *Ostarsalt*, as far as the western sea, along the entire north bank of the river Eider and broken by a single gate through which waggons and horsemen would be able to leave and enter.

It has, until recently, been thought that the complex of fortifications protecting southern Jutland and known as the *Danevirke* originated in this way, but excavations have shown that Godfred was elaborating an earlier barrier that was constructed with timbers that have been shown by dendrochronology to have been cut down after the summer of 737 (Andersen, Madsen and Voss, 1976, pp. 90–1). This defensive structure may have been made necessary by Charles Martel's campaign against the Saxons in 738, but it also shows that whoever then had

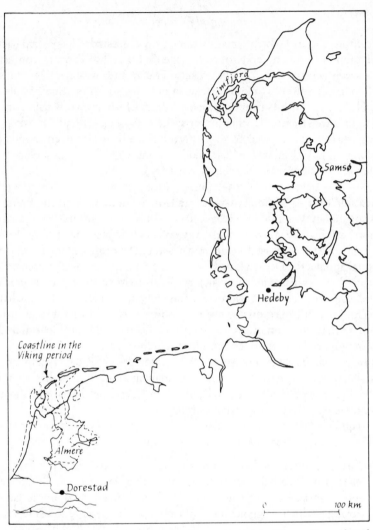

Figure 12 The route from Dorestad into the Baltic. The early medieval coastline of the Netherlands is based on a map prepared by Jan Besteman

power in south Jutland also had the resources to build such an elaborate barrier and judged it worth the effort.

The *Danevirke* was a defence against a land attack from the south, but there were also threats from the sea. Anskar was attacked by pirates on his first visit to Birka and his *Vita* contains several references to the growing threat of piracy to merchants travelling to Dorestad. The exact route these merchants took is not known. It has been claimed that it crossed south Jutland from Hollingsted on the river Treene to Hedeby, but there is no direct evidence for this, and the fact that no trace has yet been found of the western end of what must have been a busy route, together with the obvious disadvantage of unloading and loading, suggests that the normal route was by boat the whole way, and that Jutland was traversed by Limfjord. The early importance of that waterway, which was then open to the west, is confirmed by many signs of eighth-century activity along its shores, including the large cemetery at Lindholm Høje and the settlement at Aggersborg (Roesdahl, 1981; Ramskou, 1950). The route from Dorestad to the western end of Limfjord was well sheltered by islands, and could also make use of inland water (figure 12; plate XI), and from its eastern end the natural route was either through the Great or Little Belt: strong currents made the Öresund a difficult stretch of water. The entrance to the Belts is commanded by the island of Samsø, which is bisected by a canal which made it possible for ships to pass from one side to the other, whether the purpose was to collect tribute from passing vessels or to protect them. This canal has very recently been dated to the early eighth century and confirms the impression that great efforts were being made at that time to protect or control Jutland and its coastal waters.

The growing demand for northern goods in western Europe led some men to travel far in search of supplies. Óttar's hunt for walruses has been mentioned. In the eighth century Scandinavians appear to have been active in the lands east of the Baltic, presumably gathering amber, furs and slaves as tribute (Ozols, 1976). The archaeological evidence from Grobin and the nearby sites (Nerman, 1958) agrees well with the *Vita Anskarii*, which describes the *Cori*, (the inhabitants of Kurland) as having been formerly subject to the Swedes (*VA*, 30). Staraja Ladoga was established in the second half of the eighth century on the route leading to the rich fur areas of north Russia, and was certainly visited by Scandinavians at an early stage (p. 114). Later, in the ninth century, Scandinavians were drawn further into Russia in the search of furs and slaves to sell to Muslim merchants (p. 122) but the initial Scandinavian interest in north Russia was stimulated by the demands from the west, not the east.

The development of sailing ships in the Baltic and Scandinavia seems to have been a direct result of the trade between western and northern Europe. The Baltic and Scandinavian peoples had long been familiar with boats, but in the Roman period these depended on oar power: the contacts of the Scandinavians with the Romans who had sailing ships did not lead to the introduction of the sail into the north. Many ships of the Viking period are known but earlier ship finds are rare. Those that have been discovered, for example at Kvalsund in Norway or Grestedbro in Jutland, are too poorly preserved for it to be possible to determine whether they had sails or not (Crumlin–Pedersen, 1981). Large boat-houses have been found at several places along the Norwegian coast, some capable of housing boats of more than 20 metres, and one is even 37 metres long. They have been dated between the Roman period and the sixth century, but this evidence cannot show how these boats were propelled (Myhre, 1977). We are, therefore, dependent on the Gotland picture stones, which depict rowing boats in the sixth century and elaborate sailing ships in the eleventh (Lindqvist, 1941). Some eighth-century stones show ships with sails, but it is not possible to determine which are the earliest, or to date any of them very closely. It is therefore possible that sailing ships were already used in the Baltic in the seventh century. Whatever the date, the idea seems to have been derived from western Europe. The shape and construction of ships used in the Viking period are a direct development of a long-established Baltic tradition. The novelty lay in the addition of mast and sail. Ole Crumlin–Pedersen has pointed out that while the method of fixing the mast in Viking warships is unique, that used in cargo boats, such as the one found at Äskekärr in Göta Älv or Skuldelev 1 and 3 from Roskilde Fjord, is very similar to the western European method (1978a; 1981). It has also been pointed out that although most ships shown on the Gotland stones and on ninth-century Danish coins (plates XII, XIII) have the characteristic 'Viking' profile, some have a sharp angle between stem and keel, much like later depictions of 'cogs'. (Cogs were cargo boats that were certainly used widely in northern Europe from the eleventh century onwards, and probably had antecedents in the ninth century or even earlier.) Some significant differences between Danish and Frisian ships is implied by Alfred's decision to build ships for naval defence 'neither on the Frisian nor the Danish pattern' (*ASC*, 896). The fact that ships of the cog-type on ninth-century coins are never shown with shields displayed supports the suggestion that they represent cargo rather than warships, while their shape implies that they were not Scandinavian (Christensen, 1964). The Gotland stones support the suggestion that a new, probably western, type of ship was being used in the Baltic in or before the Viking Age. Western traders were then sailing in the Baltic, and circumstances encouraged technological change. For seafights, short journeys, or voyages through narrow waters, sometimes with strong tidal currents, rowing was an ideal method of propulsion but for cargo-carrying or long journeys like those undertaken in the ninth century by Óttar and Wulfstan, sails were an obvious advantage. The Scandinavians added masts and sails to their ships in the eighth century or earlier, not simply because they had then become familiar with the technique in western ships but because long voyages were needed to take goods from the far reaches of northern Norway or the Baltic to the markets of England and Frankia, or at least to Hedeby or Dorestad. Another powerful stimulus to such technological development must have been the competition between traders and pirates.

Commercial contacts between Scandinavia and western Europe, which were certainly developing greatly in the eighth century, not only encouraged piracy, they also increased the power of rulers who, like Godfred, were able to protect and control traders and trading places. The success of some rulers must often have driven their defeated rivals into exile. The *Vita Anskarii* contains a remarkable account of an attack on Birka by such an exile:

> About the same time a king of the Swedes whose name was *Anoundus* was driven from his kingdom and was living in exile among the Danes. He was keen to return to the territory of his former kingdom and he requested the help of the Danes, promising that, if they accompanied him, they would gain many gifts. He offered them Birka because there were many rich merchants there, an abundance of goods of every kind and much treasure. He promised that he would lead them to that town where, without loss to their own army, they might gain much that they wanted. Delighted by the promise of gifts and greedy to acquire treasure, to assist him they manned twenty-one ships with men equipped for battle and placed them at his disposal. *Anoundus* had eleven ships of his own. They left the land of the Danes and came to Birka unexpectedly (*VA*, 19).

In the end, the raiders were persuaded to attack the Slavs instead. Merchant ships crossing the Baltic and the market places they visited offered good opportunities for pirates – whether led by royal exiles or not – to gain both wealth and prestige, and it is hardly surprising that before the end of the eighth century some pirates had begun to seek victims outside the Baltic, in western Europe.

6

The raids in the west

Scandinavian pirates began attacking the coasts of western Europe some time before 800. In that year Charlemagne inspected defences that he had ordered for the protection of the north coast of Frankia as far west as the Seine, against pirates who, according to the contemporary Frankish annals, were infesting the Gallic Sea. In the years that followed a lot of attention was paid to these defences, and towards the end of his reign Charlemagne had fleets based in the estuaries of the Garonne and the Loire and, apparently in response to an attack on Frisia in 810, he ordered fleets to be built and stationed at Ghent and Boulogne. The signalling system was also improved. The fact that no attacks on that coast are recorded before 810 underlines the inadequacy of our knowledge of the earliest raids; the threat was serious enough to warrant Charlemagne's personal attention for several weeks in the spring of 800. Similar efforts were made in south-east England. A charter of 792, confirming the privileges of the Kentish churches, shows that King Offa was organizing defences against 'pagan seamen', and several early ninth-century Kentish charters specifically refer to pagan enemies. In two of these, dated 811 and 822, mention is made of the obligation to destroy forts built by the pagans (Brooks, 1971, pp. 79–80). In 804 the monastery of Lyminge, an exposed site just north of Romney Marsh, acquired a refuge inside the walls of Canterbury. In the years before and after 800 the Vikings were obviously a serious threat in both southern England and northern Frankia. In 809 they captured a member of the papal and imperial mission who was accompanying Eardwulf, king of Northumbria, back to England. He was taken to Britain and ransomed (*ARF*, 809). The first recorded attacks on western churches were on coastal monasteries in the north and west of the British Isles. Several famous shrines were raided before 800; St Cuthbert's on Lindisfarne in 793, St Columba's on Iona in 795, and in 799 St Philibert's on Noirmoutier. In 795 the remote communities on Inisbofin and Inismurray, islands off the west coast of Ireland, were attacked, and the church on Lambay Island near Dublin was burned. According to the *Anglo-Saxon Chronicle*, the first raid on Wessex occurred in the reign of King Brihtric, that is between 786 and 802, and was apparently aimed at a trading place rather than a church.

We are better informed about the attack on Lindisfarne than any other early raid thanks to five letters that were written about the event by Alcuin, a Northumbrian who was then living in Frankia and later became abbot of Tours. These letters were presumably written in response to one or more letters giving news of the raid, and from them we can gain some idea of what happened. The shrines were desecrated and 'the bodies of saints trampled like dung in the streets', ornaments were plundered, the blood of priests was shed and some members of the community were captured, at least one of whom was ransomed. In one passage that is often quoted he implied that the attack was unprecedented:

> It is nearly 350 years that we and our fathers have inhabited this most lovely land, and never before has such a terror appeared in Britain as we have now suffered from a pagan race, nor was it thought possible that such an inroad from the sea could be made. (*EHD*, 193)

This does not, however, prove that Lindisfarne was the first place to be raided in western Europe. It might mean that Alcuin thought it was the first attack on Britain, but what appears to have astonished him was that such a holy place was violated and, even more, that such a crossing of the sea (*navigium*) was possible. Attacks along the north coast of Frankia by Frisians, if not by Danes, were probably no novelty and could well have affected Kent, but a direct crossing of the North Sea was a much more alarming threat, giving little or no chance of a warning being sent by signals or messengers.

The early raiders came from both Denmark and Norway, but their victims must often have found it difficult to distinguish between them. Scandinavians naturally found it easier to distinguish between the different nationalities. Óttar, for example, distinguished between Norwegians, Swedes and Danes. He explained that there were mountains that took between six days and two weeks to cross lying between the long and narrow land of the Norwegians, *Northmonna land*, and the land of the Svear, *Sweoland*, while the Danes lived in the south, in what he called Denmark.

The sea between Jutland and Norway was no barrier to sailors and the many contacts, both friendly and hostile, between the people living either side of the Skagerrak must have greatly complicated the ethnic as well as the political situation. Most Scandinavians thought of themselves as coming from a district, such as Vestfold, Jutland or Óttar's *Halgoland*, and the bands that raided Europe must often have included men from more than one area. The armies that attacked England in the reign of Æthelred included men from eastern Sweden as well as from Norway and Denmark, but the English identified them by their leaders, as the armies of Olaf, Sven, Thorkel or Knut, and thought of them all as Danes. The smaller bands of the ninth century were similarly identified by their leaders, and when an Aquitanian chronicle described the raiders who attacked Nantes in 843 as *Westfaldingi*, it was probably the leaders who were identified as coming from Vestfold, west of Oslo Fjord.

There was, however, a general distinction between the main areas of Norwegian and Danish activity, at least in the first half of the ninth century. The Norwegian area was in the north and west of the British Isles together with western Frankia, while the Danes concentrated on the southern North Sea and the coasts of the Channel. The Danes first arrived in Ireland in 851 and were clearly distinguished in Irish annals from the Norwegians, with whom the Irish were by then very familiar (Smyth, 1976). The linguistic as well as archaeological evidence for Viking activity in Ireland and the Scottish islands confirms that Norwegians were predominant there, while in eastern England the settlers were mainly Danish. There were violent conflicts between the two groups in Ireland, a reminder that Vikings were not natural allies; their loyalties were to their leaders, and the plunder with which this loyalty was sustained could as well come from other Vikings as from Christians.

The first raids were on a small scale. The attack on Portland was by three ships, and in 820 a fleet of thirteen ships was repulsed from Flanders and the Seine before gathering booty on the west coast of Frankia. The attack on Frisia in 810 is said by the Frankish annalist to have been by 200 ships, but that is probably a gross exaggeration; if not, the individual shares of the £100 paid as tribute must have been so small as to be hardly worth the effort. It is, however, likely that coastal attacks from Denmark were on a larger scale than those made after long sea crossings. It would have been difficult, if not impossible, to keep a large fleet together during a voyage of several days and the attacks on Inisbofin and Inismurray may well have been by a single ship. When, in 837 and later, the Irish annals report larger attacks, by sixty or more ships, they probably came from bases that had by then been established in the Hebrides (p. 101). It was easier to mount larger attacks on northern Frankia or southern England because fleets could more easily keep together as they travelled along the Frankish coast or made the short crossing to England.

It may have been the small scale of the first attacks that contributed to the initial success of the defenders. The raiders who attacked Jarrow in 794 suffered casualties, and the Franks prevented the raiders of 820 from doing much damage until they reached the west coast. The Irish also had their successes – in 811 in Ulster, and in 812 in both Connaught and Kerry.

The situation changed when disputes arose about the division of the Frankish empire. This led to some neglect of the defences and when, in the autumn of 833, the emperor Louis the Pious was deposed by his sons, Vikings were quick to seize their chance. In the summer of 834 the great market of Dorestad, some 80 km from the open sea, was attacked for the first time, and a new phase of Viking activity in western Europe began. In 835 raiders returned to Dorestad; Sheppey, in the Thames estuary, was also attacked. In the following year Dorestad was raided for the third time, and so too were other coastal markets at Antwerp and *Witla* on the Meuse. The Vikings also grew bolder in the west and extensive raids are reported for the first time in the interior of Ireland in 836. The first raid in the Bristol Channel, also in 836, may have followed one of the Irish expeditions. The fact that the community of St Philibert abandoned Noirmoutier in 836 and sought shelter in the Loire valley suggests that they were now more seriously threatened and it was at about the same time, when Ecgred was bishop (830–45), that the relics of St Cuthbert were taken from Lindisfarne to Norham on the River Tweed (Sawyer, 1978b).

There is no direct evidence of any connection between the attacks on Dorestad and nearby targets, and the more extensive raiding in the western parts of the British Isles, but it is likely that once the feasibility and profitability of such attacks had been demonstrated at Dorestad in 834 the news spread far and fast and encouraged much greater boldness and more recruits.

Louis the Pious recovered power in 834 and was crowned again in February 835. But the damage had by then been done. When Dorestad was attacked in June 835, Louis was 'very angry and made arrangements for the effective defence of the coast', but the Vikings attacked

Frisia and Dorestad again in 836. That year they waited until September, and it may be that the defenders thought the danger had passed by then. Renewed efforts were made to put the defences of Frisia in order. It was probably at that time that the series of circular forts or encampments were constructed along the coast from Brokburg (Bourbourg) in Belgium, to Burg on Schouwen in the Rhine estuary, and perhaps even further north on Texel (van Werveke, 1965; plate XIV and figure 13). These structures have many features in common, and all have four regularly-placed gates. One of the forts on Walcheren, Ost-Soubourg has been partly excavated (Trimpe Burger, 1973); the earliest occupation cannot be dated more precisely than to the ninth century. The fact that they occur on both sides of the Scheldt estuary, which marked the boundary between two kingdoms after Louis' death in 840, suggests that they were built when the whole area was under one ruler, probably in Louis' last years. Thegan, in his life of Louis, states that in 837 he built forts at several places, and that the Danes successfully attacked one of them (Blok, 1979, p. 131). The *Annals of St Bertin* show that the attack that year was on Walcheren, that the

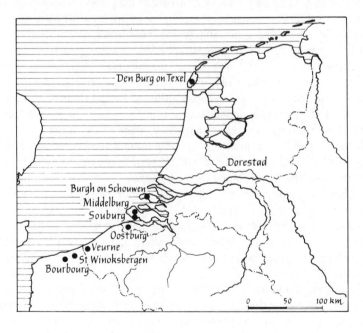

Figure 13   Frankish coastal forts, cf. plate XI

defenders were overcome, and that tribute was taken from Dorestad again. The raiders withdrew when Louis abandoned a visit to Rome and hurried to the nearby fort of Nijmegen. Then, according to the *Annals of St Bertin*:

> The Emperor summoned a general assembly, and held an inquiry in public with those magnates to whom he had delegated the task of guarding the coast. It became clear from the discussion that, partly through the sheer impossibility of the task, partly through the disobedience of certain men, it had not been possible for them to offer any resistance to the attackers. Energetic abbots and counts were therefore dispatched to suppress the insubordinate Frisians. Now too, so that from then on he would be better able to resist their incursions, he gave orders that the fleet should be made ready to go more speedily in pursuit in whatever direction might be required.

In the following year Louis took the additional precaution of staying at Nijmegen himself from May 'so that by his presence the sort of damage that occurred in previous years because of the pirates' savagery and our peoples' fecklessness might now be avoided. An assembly of loyal subjects was held and supplies were distributed around the coastal areas' (*AB*). It appears that the Danes nevertheless planned an attack, but that their fleet was destroyed by a sudden storm. Louis' efforts were rewarded. There was an attack on an unidentified part of Frisia in 839, but Dorestad seems to have escaped and Frankia remained free from raids for the rest of Louis' reign. It may indeed have been his strenuous efforts to restore and improve the defences that encouraged some Vikings to try their luck in the British Isles. In 840 thirty-three ships attacked *Hamwih*, and the same fleet could possibly have been responsible for the attack on Portland in Dorset reported in the same year. In 841 there were attacks on Romney Marsh and elsewhere in Kent, East Anglia and Lindsey. In 842 a fleet crossed the Channel from Quentovic to raid *Hamwih*, and in the same year both London and Rochester were attacked. In 844 the Northumbrians suffered a major defeat that was noted in Frankish annals but not in the West Saxon *Chronicle*, and in 851 Vikings wintered in England for the first time, on Thanet in the mouth of the Thames.

Ireland was also attacked in these years, and Vikings began to winter there earlier than in England. A fleet that had been operating on Lough Neagh in 840 did not withdraw at the end of that year, and in 841 the first Viking bases were established on the coast. The most famous was at Dublin, where, at Kilmainham west of the medieval city, a ninth-century cemetery with many richly-furnished warriors' graves provides the only clear archaeological evidence in western Europe for the Viking raiders of that period.

In the next few years the Irish annals report a large number of attacks throughout the country, apparently by several independent bands operating from inland bases, such as that established on Lough Ree, as well as from the more familiar coastal strongholds. News of the Viking onslaught on Ireland reached Frankia and, according to the *Annals of St Bertin*, in 847,

> The Irish, who had been attacked by the Northmen for a number of years, were made into regular tribute-payers. The Northmen also got control of the islands all round Ireland, and stayed there without encountering any resistance from anyone.

The Viking success in Ireland was short-lived. In the following year the same Frankish annals report a dramatic change of fortune and claim that: 'The Irish attacked the Northmen, won a victory with the aid of our Lord Jesus Christ, and drove them out of their land.' News of this success was presumably brought by the Irish envoys who visited the west Frankish king Charles, and requested permission for an Irish king to pass through Frankia on a pilgrimage to Rome. The Irish annals confirm that there were a number of major victories over the invaders in that year and thereafter the scale and extent of Viking raids in Ireland was greatly reduced. This is well illustrated by the number of Viking attacks on churches reported in each decade by the *Annals of Ulster*:

Decade beginning	Number of Viking raids on churches reported in the *Annals of Ulster*
820	8
830	25
840	10
850	2
860	2
870	1
880	1
890	1
900	0
910	2 (both in 919)

It may be that the need for raids was lessened as some churches agreed to pay tribute, but it is clear that there was a significant reduction in Viking activity in Ireland. One reason for the change of fortune was that the Viking bases were themselves vulnerable to attack. In 849 Dublin was raided, and in 866 all the Viking strongholds along the north coast were rooted out. There were also conflicts among the Vikings themselves, aggravated in 851 by the arrival of a Danish fleet to challenge the Norwegians. By the end of the century the Dublin Vikings had been so weakened by defections and disputes that in 902 they could be expelled. The Vikings had in fact become little more than an element in the complex of Irish politics, and even as early as 850 some native rulers had formed alliances with them.

The main reason for the early reduction of Viking activity in Ireland is, however, likely to have been that Frankia offered much better opportunities to accumulate wealth. As Irish monasteries did not possess large quantities of precious treasure (Lucas, 1966), the main plunder from them was in the form of slaves and cattle, but Frankish churches were exceedingly rich. This can be no more than a hypothesis. We know the names of very few early Viking leaders in Ireland and cannot trace their later careers, but the remarkable diminution of Viking raids in Ireland happened at much the same time as the number of Viking fleets in Frankia increased.

Louis had found it exceptionally difficult to prevent sudden raids on the exposed coast of Frisia or on such relatively vulnerable places as Dorestad, but the raiders did not go further up the Rhine in his reign, and the great river routes that led into the heart of Frankia, the Meuse, Seine and Loire apparently remained safe throughout his reign. The situation changed dramatically after his death on 20 June 840, with the outbreak of civil war among his sons. In 841 Vikings sailed up the Seine for the first time and attacked the abbey of Jumièges and other churches, as well as plundering Rouen. The civil war ended in 843 with an agreement to divide the empire into three, but by then the Vikings had discovered how vulnerable the churches and towns of Frankia were, and that the Franks were able and willing to pay very large amounts of silver for the sake of peace. In 841 towns along the Seine paid large sums to the raiders, and in the following year, when the market of Quentovic was raided, some buildings were spared in return for payment of money. We do not know how large these payments were, but in 845 an attack on Paris was prevented by the payment of 7000 lb of silver. Small wonder that the number and boldness of the raiders grew.

In the twenty years after the first attack on Paris every major river in western Frankia was exploited by one or more Viking fleets; even the Rhone was plundered by Vikings, who established a base in the Camargue in 859. As early as 843 there was a Viking base on Noirmoutier, and in 851 they wintered in the Seine for the first time. It was not long before several bands were operating for years at a time in the Loire, the Seine, and other large and easily navigable rivers of France. The growth of the Viking menace is well illustrated by what happened in the Loire valley. Nantes, like many other places on the west coast, had suffered several attacks before 850, but the raid of 853 was the prelude to a series of attacks that penetrated further up the valley, year by year. In 853 they moved from Nantes to Tours, which was attacked on 8 November just before the great feast of the patron saint, St Martin, when, presumably, large numbers of pilgrims and merchants were gathering in the city. The monks, forewarned, had managed to remove the relics of the saint to the abbey of Cormery and the treasures even further, to Orleans. The raiders then wintered in the Loire and in the next year attacked Blois but they turned back from Orleans, where defensive efforts had been made by the bishop, aided by the bishop of Chartres. In 855 the same band attempted to attack Poitiers, which meant leaving their ships and going cross-country; but they were beaten back. In 856 they returned to Orleans and, meeting no opposition, sacked it. In 857 Tours and Blois were both attacked again. There were then a few years of apparent peace, although Vikings were still based in the Loire, but in 865 they penetrated even further to Fleury, and on their return attacked Orleans and later that year, in alliance with Bretons, Le Mans.

Western Frankia was indeed the main area of Viking activity for some twenty-five years after Louis' death. It was particularly vulnerable because Louis' son Charles' position was weakened by disloyalty and rebellion, difficulties that his brother Louis, who had inherited eastern Frankia, tried to exploit. This rivalry culminated in 858 when Louis, invited by disaffected elements in Charles' kingdom, invaded at the very moment that Charles and his nephew Lothar were making a determined effort to reduce the Seine Vikings to submission. Abandoned by many of his men, he was forced to raise the siege and flee. His position was saved by the archbishop of Rheims, Hincmar, and other church leaders, and Louis had to withdraw in January 859.

The other Frankish kingdoms were also attacked, but less systematically than western Frankia. In the east, a large-scale raid in 845 led by the Danish king, Horik, resulted in the destruction of Hamburg. Peace was restored between the two rulers by negotiation in which Anskar took part, and the booty and prisoners were returned. In the following thirty-four years, apart from attacks on the Frisian coast that may have affected his territory, Louis' kingdom suffered only three Viking raids: in the Elbe, 851, at Bremen, 858, and unspecified disruption in 862. The middle kingdom, inherited by Louis the Pious' eldest son, Lothar, was also fortunate to escape attacks on the scale of those suffered in the west. The coast, from the mouth of the Scheldt to that of the Weser, certainly suffered, and Dorestad was frequently attacked, together with the nearby area, Batavia. The valleys of the Rhine and Meuse seem, however, to have been safe most of the time, apart from one major incursion in 863 when Xanten was attacked and the raiders reached Neuss, about 30 km downstream from Cologne, before they were persuaded to withdraw.

The reason for this relative security seems to have been that both Lothar and his son Lothar II, who inherited the northern part of the middle kingdom, were prepared to accept the presence of Vikings permanently established in the estuaries of these rivers. Even before the treaty of 843 the elder Lothar had granted the island of Walcheren, at the mouth of the Scheldt, to the exiled Danish leader Harald. The

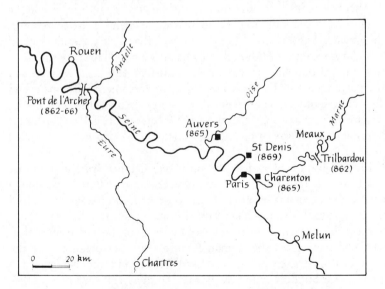

Figure 14   Defences constructed around Paris 862–9

author of the annals that report this may well have exaggerated Lothar's freedom of action, and nine years later the same writer reported that Lothar was forced to make a similar grant to Harald's nephew, Roric:

> Roric . . . who had recently defected from Lothar, raised whole armies of Northmen with a vast number of ships and laid waste Frisia and the island of *Batavum* and other places in that neighbourhood by sailing up the Rhine and the Waal. Lothar, since he could not crush Roric, received him into allegiance and granted him Dorestad and other counties. (*AB* 850)

Roric controlled this area until his death in the mid 870s except for intervals in which he attempted, unsuccessfully, to win power in Denmark. The arrangement, like that made later with Rollo in the Seine (pp. 98–9), made a major contribution to the security of both the middle and eastern kingdoms. It did not, of course, ensure complete immunity from attack, for Roric's loyalty could not be taken for granted. The main assault on the Rhine in 863 seems, in fact, to have been made either by Roric himself or with his agreement, for the withdrawal from Neuss is said to have been made 'on Roric's advice'.

The political problems that Charles faced made the organization of defences very difficult. A common solution was to pay tribute, and the raiders seem generally to have honoured the terms of the agreements they made. The *Annals of St Bertin* report that in 863 Vikings burned St Hilary of Poitiers 'although they had been bribed to spare the city'; this implies that such treachery was unusual. The main weakness of such arrangements was, of course, that an agreement with one group did not bind others. There were also attempts to make the Danish king 'restrain his own people from their attacks on the Christians' (*AB*, 847) but that required the co-operation of all the Frankish kings, and proved ineffective.

In the absence of a fleet the only real defence was to construct fortifications. It was, however, many years before Charles was able to devote the necessary effort to their construction, or even recognized the need. Frankish cities had fortified Roman walls that had been built to meet the very similar threat posed by bands of the barbarian raiders who had penetrated the Roman Empire's frontier defences. By the ninth century these walls were old and decayed and were being used as quarries for building-stone. As late as 859 the archbishop of Sens was given permission to take stones from the walls of Melun, a mere 50 km from Paris – an astonishing display of shortsightedness. Perhaps even at that stage the Franks thought the Vikings were a temporary menace, a judgement of God to be met by prayer and reform rather than stone walls. It was only in 862 that Charles began a systematic effort to fortify at least the heart of his kingdom, at first by building bridges to block the rivers. In that year he forced the surrender of one Viking group by following what Hincmar called 'indispensable good advice'. He blocked the Marne by building a bridge at Trilbardou and stationing forces at either end of it. Later that year he began to construct another across the Seine, below the point where it is joined by the Eure and Andelle. He also built forts nearer Paris. The Seine bridge, at Pont de l'Arche near the royal villa of Pîtres, was only completed after very great efforts, requiring resources from far afield, and the work was delayed by Viking attacks. There was also the problem of maintaining a garrison. Four years after the work began Vikings were still able to reach Paris and had to be bought off. After that group sailed down the river 'to await the payment due to them', 'Charles marched to the place called Pîtres with workmen and carts to complete the fortification so that the Northmen might never again be able to get up the Seine beyond that point' (*AB*, 866).

At last this defensive measure worked, although still requiring constant attention. In 868–9 it was reinforced by a fortress of stone and wood, and arrangements were made to man it permanently. One result was that the Paris region enjoyed some years of freedom from Viking attacks; the next fleet reported on the Seine, in 876, did not reach Paris. The success of these defences, and an attack on Orleans in 868, probably combined to encourage Charles to take similar precautions in the Loire valley. Le Mans, Tours and Orleans were all fortified, and a bridge was built across the river at Les Ponts de Cé near Angers. The upper Loire, like the upper Seine, was thus given some security, and the main operation against the Vikings in Charles' last years was his elaborate and successful siege of those who had occupied Angers in 873.

These defences meant, in effect, the abandonment of the lower reaches of the Seine and Loire and other coastal areas to the mercy of Viking raiders. Vikings remained in the lower Loire for many years and apparently considered that they had a right to tribute from the surrounding countryside. Their attitude is revealed in the *Annals of St Bertin* in connection with the fortification of Le Mans and Tours to serve as refuges for the local populations. 'When the Northmen heard about this, they demanded a great sum of silver and quantities of corn, wine and livestock from the local inhabitants, as the price of peace' (*AB*, 869). A natural consequence of this concentration on the defence of the region round Paris and Orleans was that most religious communities and leading ecclesiastics left the exposed areas to find greater safety elsewhere. The episcopal succession in Normandy was seriously disrupted in these years. No bishops are known for the sees of Avranches, Bayeux, Evreux and Lisieux for some time after the early 870s, and the bishop of Coutances sheltered in Rouen, where a Frankish count still retained some semblance of power. The bishop of Bordeaux fled to Poitiers and then, in 876, to Bourges, while Actardus left his see of Nantes in 868, first for Thérouanne and later for Tours.

In the years after 866 many Vikings, faced with improved defences and finding little left to plunder in the undefended areas, sought their fortunes elsewhere, especially in England. In the autumn of 865 a Viking army landed in East Anglia, and in the following year took advantage of a civil war in Northumbria to seize York. This happened on 1 November and it is likely that the army was reinforced during the summer by other groups, perhaps including some of the Vikings who had sailed away from the Seine in July. This force was described by the *Anglo-Saxon Chronicle* as a 'great army'. The term was probably justified, for the army was led by several kings. In the course of the

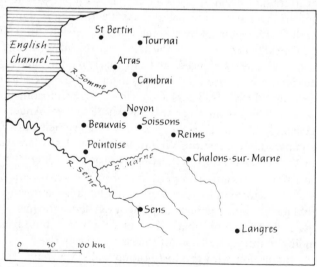

Figure 15   Places in northern Frankia that were fortified in the late ninth century (Vercauteren 1936)

next ten years no fewer than seven are named, but never more than four at any one time. In the spring of 867 the Vikings defeated an attempt to oust them from York, and were left free to establish a Scandinavian kingdom based on that city. They then proceeded to take over eastern Mercia, east of Watling Street, and East Anglia. Alfred successfully defied their efforts to conquer Wessex, and in 878 the remaining Viking leader, Guthrum, was forced to accept defeat and baptism. He then retired to rule East Anglia.

Alfred's success in stabilizing the situation in southern England coincided with a period of renewed weakness in Frankia. Charles the Bald died in 877 and his son two years later. This was followed by a period of political confusion, as claimants and their supporters competed for power. Once again the Vikings were quick to take advantage of dissension. An army assembled at Fulham on the Thames, and in the summer of 879 began a long series of campaigns on the continent. Some of the men who gathered at Fulham may have come direct from Scandinavia but some – perhaps many – had already been in western Europe for some time, either in England or Frankia. Like the 'great army' that campaigned in England, this was the result of a combined operation in which several Viking leaders joined. In 882, for example, Hastein (see page 25) brought his fleet from the Loire to the Somme to share in the enterprise. The composition of the force changed as groups joined or left as, for example, the 200 ships laden with prisoners and booty that are said to have returned home in 882 (*Annals of Fulda*).

The movements of this 'great army' can be traced in some detail, thanks to the relative abundance of independent sources from the plundered areas. The Vikings suffered several defeats, but found that they often had opportunity to plunder cities and churches before opposition could be mobilized, especially in Flanders and the lands between the Seine and Rhine. This area was particularly vulnerable, because the cities had not been fortified by Charles the Bald, partly because they had been protected by Roric's fief. Amiens, Arras, Beauvais, Cambrai, Corbie, Liège and Tongres were all attacked early on, and this phase of operations culminated in a great raid up the Rhine to Cologne and Trier in 882. One response was to grant what had been Roric's territory in Frisia to one of the leaders of the army, Godfred, in 882. Another, more effective one was to build fortifications. In the years after 880 many of the towns and great abbeys of this area were fortified, and in 885 the Vikings moved west to attack Paris, which had also been fortified. Here the defences held, and in the following year the raiders moved into the area beyond Paris for a while, before raiding in Brittany. They were defeated there in 890 and returned to their original area where they were defeated at Louvain in 891. They then re-equipped at Boulogne and sailed to England. For the next four years Frankish annals record no Viking activity in Frankia; there appears to have been little room for small-scale, private enterprises; large operations requiring the co-operation of many groups seem to have offered the best hope of good results.

They were, however, not very successful in England either. Alfred had learned the lesson of the campaigns in Frankia and had taken pains to construct a network of fortifications, some round former Roman cities, others to defend the new centres of royal government, and there were also some smaller forts. He also had a fleet of ships constructed and was therefore able to offer some opposition at sea. The campaigns of Alfred and his allies are described in great detail in the *Anglo-Saxon Chronicle*, which was compiled at this time. Its account is hardly impartial, but there is no denying the English success. In 896 the Vikings, having failed to gain any foothold in those areas of England not already under Scandinavian control, abandoned the attempt. In the words of the *Chronicle*: 'The Danish army divided, one force going into East Anglia and one into Northumbria; and those that were moneyless got themselves ships and went south across the sea to the Seine.'

Later developments in Frankia are unfortunately obscure, but it is at least clear that in 911 the west Frankish, or French, king granted Rouen and the surrounding territory to a Viking leader called Rollo in the hope that he would deny other raiders the passage of the Seine. Some relatively small-scale Viking activity continued around the Frankish coasts for a while. A Viking base was established at Nantes for some ten years after 927, and there were also Viking raiders in Normandy, especially after the murder of Rollo's son, William Longsword, in 942.

In the early years of the tenth century the opportunities for Viking activity in western Europe were greatly reduced. The most lucrative targets were well defended by fortifications, or by Scandinavians like Rollo. The rulers of Wessex and Mercia continued to defend their territory successfully. The land available for conquest or colonization had been taken, and in Iceland the first settlers had occupied the most desirable areas. Vikings who did not wish, or were unable, to take advantage of the rich opportunities then offered in the Baltic returned to Ireland. In 914 Viking fleets were again reported on the Irish coast, and Dublin was retaken by men who claimed to be descendants of a former king of Dublin, Ivar, who, on his death in 873, was described by the *Annals of Ulster* as 'King of all the Scandinavians of Ireland and Britain'. For a while Ireland was once again disrupted, and the *Annals* report many raids on Irish monasteries, but these had no more treasure then than a century before. The new rulers of Dublin coveted the greater wealth of Northumbria and tried to gain control of the Scandinavian kingdom of York. From time to time their efforts met with some success, but never for long. The English kings were too powerful, and after 945 the dynasty of Ivar had to be content with the kingship of Dublin. By then the Irish had recovered from the shock of the renewed attacks, and counter-attacked with growing success. The freedom of action of Viking leaders in Dublin, Limerick, Waterford and Cork was severely limited, and after the middle of the century they only played a minor role in Irish politics.

The Viking armies of the ninth and early tenth centuries were normally fairly small, numbering hundreds rather than thousands of men. Irish sources rarely attempt to estimate numbers, but on one occasion in 868, 'a great host of foreigners' is numbered as 900 or more, although another version of the same annals gives the figure as 300 or more. The number of dead is reported on several occasions, always in round hundreds, long or short, and the figures are usually small: 120, 240, 100. It is only in 847 and the year of the great victories, 848 (p. 84) that more extravagant figures are given: 500, 700 and three counts of 1200. As Kathleen Hughes remarked (1972, pp. 151–2) 'they are obviously round numbers, and there is a natural human tendency to exaggerate. Nevertheless, the numbers are commensurate with the losses given for pre-Viking age battles . . . The annalist regarded the Viking attacks as devastatingly violent, yet he quotes the slain in hundreds rather than thousands.' The scale of Viking armies is more usually indicated by the size of the fleets. The *Anglo-Saxon Chronicle* gives the number of ships in twelve ninth-century fleets – eight were thirty-five or fewer. The number of men who could be conveyed by one ship obviously depended on its size, and those used by the Vikings are unlikely to have been longer than about 25 metres, and so able to carry at most fifty men for short distances. If, as sometimes happened, the raiders travelled with their horses, the number of men that could be shipped was greatly reduced. In 1142 it took fifty-two ships to carry a force of less than 400 mounted knights across the Channel (Sawyer, 1971, p. 127).

The armies were therefore normally small. By the middle of the ninth century there were, however, many operating in different areas, and when they combined they could constitute a formidable force, well meriting the contemporary description 'great army'. Even small bands of violent men could be very destructive, and there is no doubt that the ninth-century Vikings caused enormous damage, particularly to the churches and rich religious communities that were naturally a prime target. The ecclesiastical buildings contained rich treasures that could be plundered, and housed men and women who could be captured and sold as slaves or, if important enough, ransomed, like the abbot of St Denis, Louis, and his brother Gauzlin, whose ransom required

> many church treasuries to be drained dry, at the king's command. But, even all this was far from being enough; to bring it up to the required amount, large sums were eagerly contributed also by the king, and by all the bishops, abbots, counts and other powerful people. (*AB*, 858; Grierson, 1981)

Precious objects could be ransomed too, such as the Canterbury Bible, now known as *Codex Aureus*, that ealdorman Alfred and his wife 'bought back from a heathen army with true money, that is with pure gold . . . because we are not willing that this holy book should remain any longer in heathen hands' (*EHD*, 98). Alternatively, churches were often persuaded to pay large sums as, in effect, protection money. Little wonder that the Vikings were regarded by the churchmen with particular horror and that their violence was sometimes exaggerated. There can be no doubt, however, that the fear was real and justified, and many communities sought safety in flight.

Contemporary sources, almost all written by ecclesiastics, naturally reflect the fear, even horror, felt by the victims of Viking atrocities but these atrocities were described in even more lurid terms in later sources. Alcuin's letters show that although the community of St Cuthbert on Lindisfarne was disrupted by the attack of 793 (p. 79) it survived, together with many of its treasures and manuscripts (ten of which, including the Lindisfarne Gospels, still exist) and the church, built in the seventh century by St Aidan, was not destroyed (Sawyer, 1978b, p. 5). Three hundred years later, Simeon of Durham asserted that the raiders of 793:

> Laid everything waste with grievous plundering, trampled the holy places with polluted steps, dug up the altars, seized all the treasures, killed some of the brothers, some taken away in fetters, many driven

out naked and loaded with insults, and some they drowned in the sea. (*EHD*, 3)

The Viking menace clearly grew with telling and, as in Ireland (pp. 21–2), by the twelfth century the elaborations had become very fanciful. These exaggerated and colourful accounts have, however, played a large part in forming modern ideas about the Vikings and the threat they posed to Christian civilization. That threat has been given particularly acute expression in accounts of the peculiar bestiality of the Vikings who are supposed to have practised what has been called the 'blood-eagle sacrifice'. This involved ripping open the rib-cage of a living victim and pulling his lungs out to form the shape of an eagle. The evidence for this practice is suspect, and at least some references to it are a result of misunderstanding poetic references to the eagle as a symbol of battle, waiting to claim its victims. Snorri Sturluson himself misunderstood a verse in this way in his Saga of Harald Finehair. Similar misunderstandings lie behind other references to this ritual (de Vries, 1928, pp. 161–2). These grisly sacrifices have an extraordinary fascination for some modern historians who, accepting that they really happened, seem to think that such practices show that Viking in-humanity was unique. This is, of course, absurd. The Franks, Irish and English of the ninth century, like the Romans before them, and men throughout the world in the twentieth century, have been capable of horrifying tortures, and lurid accounts of the 'blood-eagle sacrifice' should perhaps be considered together with the form of execution that the English retained for so long; that of hanging, drawing and quarter-ing, for which the evidence is very much better.

The significant question is not whether the Vikings were more violent and brutal than others, which seems unlikely, but rather what effect their violence had, directed as it was to somewhat different ends than that of their Christian contemporaries. It has, for example, been claimed that the Vikings were responsible for the transformation of Irish society, for what has been described as 'the passing of the old order' (Binchy, 1962). It has been argued that before the Vikings came 'Irish warfare followed a curiously ritual pattern' that was not re-spected or understood by the Vikings, who ignored such conventions as ending a battle when the king was killed. The Vikings have indeed been held responsible for undermining the Irish respect for the Church by showing that the spiritual power of the saints could safely be defied. But long before the first Viking raid the Irish attitude to the Church, or rather to the Churches of rival dynasties, was very much like that of their Frankish contemporaries. In 764, for example, there was a battle between the religious communities of Clonmacnoise and Durrow in which 200 men belonging to the latter were killed, and in 780 Donnchadh laid waste and burned churches in Leinster in the course of a war. The Viking attacks certainly made matters worse, and may even have accelerated changes taking place in Irish society, but they did not precipitate those changes (Lucas, 1967; Ó Corráin, 1972, pp. 82–9). There are in fact several indications that the old order was already passing in the early years of the eighth century (Byrne, 1971).

Many Irish monasteries survived the Viking attacks, but in England the Vikings have been held responsible for the widespread collapse of monasticism and the disruption of Church organization throughout the conquered areas. Episcopal successions were certainly interrupted or ended at Lindsey, Leicester, Dunwich and Elmham, but not at York. Some monasteries, like Whitby, appear to have disappeared completely, perhaps as a result of violence, while others suffered loss of treasures, books and lands, but the 'monastic desert' of early tenth-century England owes more to the changing standards of later generations than to Viking depredations. Later reformers looked back to an idealized past, compared it with a present that they knew was far from ideal, and found in the Vikings a convenient explanation for the change. Long before the attacks began, Bede deplored the many pseudo-monasteries, which he admitted served some spiritual functions (*EHD*, 170), and the situation was much the same in Alfred's day; his biographer Asser complained that there were many monasteries, 'but not properly observing the rule of this way of life' (*EHD*, 7, c.93). Many communities did indeed survive, but the only one in Northumbria or in Danish territory to have left much trace was the rich and influential community of St Cuthbert, which Bede would certainly not have considered a monastery (Sawyer, 1978a). There are hints of other survivals – Crayke, near York, where St Cuthbert sheltered on his travels after 876; Norham, one of whose abbots, Tilred, became a bishop of Chester-le-Street in 915; the 'glorious minster of Ripon, which St Wilfrid built' was burned by an English king in 948; Oundle, where St Wilfrid died, was the burial place of Wulfstan, Archbishop of York, in 956; Bardney, whence Edward the Elder collected the relics of St Oswald in 909, and which place name evidence suggests retained its lands better than most (pp. 103–4). Houses like these often survived until the eleventh century as small and poor colleges of secular canons, or even hermitages, and after the Norman Conquest served as the basis for newly-reformed monasteries.

In Frankia monasticism had more vitality. Although many houses were destroyed by Viking raiders, losing their libraries and treasures, many recovered in a remarkable way. Other communities were saved by flight. It is likely that the raiders also forced many laymen, especially landowners, into exile, but there is nothing to suggest that there was any significant displacement of whole populations. Bishops and their households, monastic communities and secular lords naturally took to flight, but that does not mean that the peasantry abandoned their lands. The recent claim that 'the population of the Périgord, and perhaps also of the Limousin, fled for refuge to Turenne in the Haut-Limousin. We do not know if, or when they returned' (Wallace Hadrill, 1975, p. 15), is based on evidence for the migration of the monks of Solignac to Turenne and a sermon of Adhemar of Chabannes (who died in 1034) that was itself based on an 'ancient' account of the translation of the relics of St Martial. Adhemar is a most unreliable source (Gillingham, 1981), and even if he were not that sermon hardly amounts to evidence for a migration by the whole pious population of Limoges. It is also worth remarking that the supposed areas of refuge show no traces of any such massive movements of people. The Loire valley certainly suffered much more persistent violence and disruption than the Périgord and the Limousin, but the Loire Vikings did not spend years living off a depopulated countryside. The fortification of such places as Le Mans and Tours are obvious signs of vitality and, as Lucien Musset (1974) has pointed out, it was the areas that suffered most from Viking depredations in the ninth century that appear most prosperous in the tenth. In England, too, there was rapid recovery, especially in areas conquered by the Danes. However destructive the Vikings were, they often made a very positive and significant contribution to the development of western Europe, especially as conquerors and colonists.

7

Conquests and settlements in the west

Most of the ninth-century bases in western Europe were established by force, but some native rulers were willing to form at least temporary alliances with the men who controlled them. Irish kings fought alongside the Dublin Vikings as well as against them, and the Loire Vikings were employed in conflicts between Franks and Bretons by both sides. Roric was granted land in the Rhine estuary because Lothar 'could not crush him', but his presence there did protect the Rhine and Meuse valleys from other raiders and when, in 882, another Dane, Godfred, was 'granted' the same territory it was presumably for the same purpose. In 911 the king of western Frankia, Charles the Simple, conceded Rouen and the lower Seine valley to Rollo 'for the protection of the kingdom' and a little later other Vikings, who controlled Nantes and the lower Loire, were acknowledged first by Count Robert, and in 927 by the west Frankish king.

Many of these bases were short-lived. Roric did not hold his fief continuously, and after Godfred was killed in 885 the experiment was not repeated. This ninth-century occupation has left little trace in the Netherlands. There is only one place name that may have a Scandinavian origin – Assendelft – but that is not necessarily ninth-century in origin (Blok, 1978). A few genuine Scandinavian artefacts have been found there, together with some fakes and several objects that are as likely to be Frankish as Scandinavian (van Regteren Altena and Heidinga, 1977). There are some coin hoards that could have been the accumulated wealth of Vikings but that cannot, of course, be proved (Sawyer, 1971, p. 245). The Viking occupation of Brittany did not last much longer. Alan of Brittany returned from England in 937 and expelled the Vikings from Nantes, but the most notable Scandinavian monument, a cremated ship-burial on the Île de Groix, appears to be later than that (Müller-Wille, 1978) and is presumably the tomb of some later Viking raider. In 902 the Irish forced the Vikings to leave Dublin, but when they returned twelve years later that occupation proved more permanent; Viking Dublin preserved some measure of independence until the Norman conquest of the twelfth century.

Rollo's fief lasted even longer, and owed its success in part to the support of those kings who still needed his protection from other Vikings. The rulers of Rouen also strengthened their position by extending their authority over Vikings who had settled further west around Bayeux and in the Cotentin. This peninsula, together with the neighbouring areas around Avranches and in western Maine, had been abandoned by the Franks to the Bretons, and Viking expansion at the expense of their traditional enemies cannot have been entirely unwelcome. The rulers of Normandy themselves were, however, sometimes a threat; in 925 they attacked the regions of Beauvais and Amiens, and in 961 a fierce war began that was only ended by the treaty of Gisors in 965 (Douglas, 1947, p. 107). Similar breakdowns of relations also happened between the French king and others of his vassals. They were, in fact, a recurrent theme of Norman history until the independence of the duchy was finally ended by Philip Augustus in the early thirteenth century.

Vikings were also sometimes welcomed in Britain. The Britons of Devon and Cornwall formed an alliance with them against their West Saxon enemies as early as 838. Later in that century Viking leaders in Northumbria not only found Englishmen willing to serve as kings 'under their domination', but also had the support of the Archbishop of York. The complexity of relations between the English and the Danish invaders is demonstrated by the career of the West Saxon prince Æthelwold. He was the son of Æthelred, Alfred's brother and predecessor as king of Wessex. When his hopes of succeeding Alfred had been frustrated by Alfred's own son, Edward, Æthelwold went to Northumbria and was accepted by the Danes of York as their king. He was not the only member of an English royal family to join forces with the invaders, for Brihtsige, son of Beornoth, described by the *Chronicle* as 'atheling' (that is the son of a king – probably of Mercia) was killed fighting on the side of the Vikings in 902.

In both England and Frankia Scandinavian conquests were acknowledged by treaties, for example that concluded between Alfred and Guthrum after the English recovery of London in 886, and one between Charles and Rollo in 911. Similar agreements with neighbouring native rulers were probably made by most of the Scandinavians who won land in the British Isles, although they may have been less necessary for those whose power lay in the islands of Orkney, Shetland, the Hebrides and Man.

The new rulers of Normandy recognized the west Frankish, or French, king from the start, but in England the Scandinavian kings were at first as independent as their English predecessors had been. In time, however, they were forced to acknowledge West Saxon overlordship, and in 954 the last Scandinavian king of York was expelled and later killed. This extension of West Saxon power did not mean that the Scandinavian settlers were dispossessed: some chose to leave, but most of those who remained were allowed to retain their lands. Men of Scandinavian descent, therefore, continued to play a prominent part in local affairs in many parts of eastern and northern England, the area later called the Danelaw.

The early history of these Scandinavian conquests and settlements is very obscure. There is little contemporary written evidence for any area, and virtually none for the northern and western Isles. In those islands archaeology offers some compensation, thanks to the excavation of several Scandinavian settlements, but in England there is surprisingly little archaeological evidence for the presence of Scandinavians outside the towns, and in Normandy virtually none at all, even for the towns. Discussion of Scandinavian colonization, therefore, depends largely on the study of their influence on place names. The interpretation of this evidence is not entirely straightforward, however. In the first place Scandinavian names cannot be dated very closely; they cannot be earlier than the conquests of the ninth century, but few were recorded before the compilation of Domesday Book in 1086, and many are first mentioned centuries later; there is, therefore, room for doubt about the date at which they were first used. A second difficulty is whether Scandinavian names refer to new settlements, or are simply new names for existing places. The Yorkshire name Baldersby, for example, could be a new Scandinavian name, but it could equally well be a Scandinavian form of the English name Balderton. It is, therefore, sometimes impossible, on the basis of the place name evidence alone, to determine what effect the Scandinavians had on patterns of settlement.

Their influence on the place names of an area was, of course, largely a result of their general effect on the language. In Orkney and Shetland the Scandinavians renamed virtually every feature of the landscape; almost the only pre-Scandinavian names to survive are a few island names such as Unst, Fetlar and Yell (Stewart 1965, p. 248). This was partly a result of the complete disappearance of the native speech and its replacement by a Scandinavian language, later known as Norn. (This was still spoken by a few people in the eighteenth century, although by then the main language was Anglo-Scots.) This linguistic change is, however, in itself insufficient to explain the disappearance of the former names, as there are many examples of names surviving similar linguistic revolutions elsewhere. The change in the place names of the northern Isles suggests that relatively few natives survived, and that those who did were reduced to a very inferior status. Scandinavian speech was similarly dominant in the Outer Hebrides, but it did not last so long and had been displaced by Gaelic early in the sixteenth century (Oftedal, 1962). In Lewis ninety-nine of the 126 village names are Scandinavian, and a further eleven are partly Scandinavian (Oftedal, 1954). Scandinavian influence is also clear in the Inner Hebrides, but decreases gradually from north to south. In the north-east of Skye, for example, about 66 per cent of the settlement names are pure Norse, but there are few in Arran (Gordon, 1963, p. 82; Oftedal, 1953, p. 107).

In most parts of the British Isles and in Normandy, the Scandinavian settlers, or their descendants, learned the native language – English, Irish or French – and in doing so affected the dialects in varying degrees. They left very slight traces on the speech of Normandy and Ireland, but their influence on English was very great. These differences were partly due to differences in the density of settlement, but linguistic factors were also important. The fact that English and Danish are closely related does not mean that in the ninth century Danes and Englishmen could communicate with each other immediately and without difficulty; Olof von Feilitzen is reported as doubting 'whether the English and the Vikings really could have communicated with each other except by means of ribald gestures and uncouth noises' (Fellows Jensen, 1980, p. 187). In England, as in Ireland and Normandy, communication initially depended on individuals who knew both languages. The influence one language has on another in such circumstances is affected by their relative status, and by the need to borrow words to describe new things, but the relationship between the two languages is also significant. The similarity between English and Danish meant that the English found it much easier to adopt Scandinavian loan words than did the French or the Irish, whose languages had little in common with Danish or Norwegian. Another factor was, of course, the length of time during which Scandinavian languages were spoken. Danish continued to be understood in western Normandy longer than around Rouen thanks to the arrival of new immigrants. In about 940 Rollo's grandson, the future Duke Richard I, had to be sent to Bayeux to learn Danish because he could not do so at Rouen (Lair, 1865, pp. 221–2). This explains why Scandinavian influence on the names of minor features in the landscape is greater in western than in eastern Normandy, although to judge by the names of settlements the density of Scandinavian colonization was originally much the same in both areas (Musset, 1958; 1975).

In England there were several groups of new Scandinavian colonists after the initial settlement; in 896 some members of the 'great army' settled in Northumbria and East Anglia, and about twenty years later Ragnald came from Ireland and seized some of the estates of St Cuthbert for his followers. Such new arrivals must have ensured that Scandinavian speech survived in some parts of England well into the tenth century. The dialects of the Danelaw were therefore deeply affected by Scandinavian speech, and this obviously had its effect on place names. Some pronunciations were modified – Shipton became Skipton, and the word kirk replaced church. This process continued long after the Norman Conquest. In the East Midlands, for example, there are at least thirty-nine names that show less Scandinavian influence in Domesday Book than in later sources, and twenty of these retain traces of that later Scandinavianization in their modern forms. As Gillian Fellows Jensen has remarked:

> Scandinavianization of English place names, both by the local people who used them and by scribes, can be shown to have been quite common in the twelfth century and to have continued to take place as late even as the sixteenth century. This means that caution must be shown when assessing the value of Scandinavianized names as evidence for Viking colonization in the early years of the settlement. They can only show that the local dialect had been strongly in-fluenced by Scandinavian' (1980, p. 191).

This applies particularly to field names which, in Normandy as in England, reflect the dialects of later times; they cannot be used to assess the scale or extent of the original settlement.

The Scandinavians were also responsible for many new names. In England the distinctively Scandinavian *bý* meaning farm or village, the equivalent to the English *tūn*, was particularly popular. So too was *thorp*, but that word or the closely related *throp*, had long been used by the English in the same sense of 'outlying or dependent settlement', and cannot be considered uniquely Scandinavian (Lund, 1976). In

England *bý* was not actively used in forming place names for long, except in the remoter areas of the north-west. In the heart of the Danelaw it is comparatively rarely combined with English or Norman personal names and seems to have been current as an active element for less than two centuries. This did not mean that all the names in *bý* were given by the first colonists in the ninth century. There are indeed indications that the main period of Scandinavian name production was in the early years of the tenth century. Scandinavian settlement names are rare in the parts of the Danelaw that were recovered by the English soon after 900. The main concentrations are in East Anglia and north of Northampton, in areas that long remained relatively remote from the main centres of English royal authority. In Cambridgeshire, for example, the Danes certainly occupied the land 'between the dykes and the Ouse, as far north as the fens' but they were driven from it in 903 (*ASC*) and have left no trace in the place names. Further north, evidence from the Peak District of Derbyshire confirms the impression that most Scandinavian names were formed in the tenth century. In 926 Athelstan confirmed to Uhtred land at Hope and Ashford that he had been ordered to buy from the pagans by King Edward and Æthelred, ruler of Mercia, that is between 899 and 911 (Sawyer, 1981, p. 129). The estate was large and assessed at sixty hides. In Domesday Book it is represented by the royal vills of Bakewell, Ashford and Hope, which between them had twenty-seven berewicks. These were farms or settlements that were considered part of the demesne for taxation and other purposes, although they might be physically detached from it. If, as seems likely, this was part of the land occupied and shared out by Healfdene in 876, it was under the lordship of Scandinavians for at least twenty years but, although the field names reflect their influence on the local dialect, only four of the Domesday berewicks had Scandinavian names – Holme, Rowsley, Rowland and Flagg. This area was kept firmly under the control of the king or his leading agents, and in 1066 was a royal estate. Even in the main areas of Scandinavian settlement there were some districts, or estates, with relatively few Scandinavian names. The Archbishop of York's estate of Sherburn, near York, included holdings in thirty-three places (Robertson, 1956, no. 84), almost all of which have English names, a few showing some Scandinavian influence, but there is only one unambiguously Scandinavian name, Lumby. (Selby is an adaptation of an English name (Fellows Jensen, 1972, pp. 36–7).) There are also three *thorps* and two hybrids combining a Scandinavian personal name with the English element *tūn*. The proportion of Scandinavian names on this estate (23 per cent) is therefore significantly lower than in Yorkshire as a whole (33 per cent), probably because the archbishops who collaborated with the Vikings retained control of their estates rather better than most landowners. This interpretation is supported by the archbishops' Domesday estates in the North Riding, where some 35 per cent of the Domesday names are Scandinavian. The archbishopric held land in thirty-two places, only nine of which had Scandinavian names, and four of these were acquired by Archbishop Oscytel after 956 (Robertson, 1956, no. 54). There are other areas in the Danelaw with unusually few Scandinavian names. There are, for example, very few round Bardney, east of Lincoln (figure 16a). This may well indicate that Bardney Abbey, whose survival is suggested by the fact that in 909 Edward collected the relics of St Oswald from it (*ASC*, 909), did not lose all its estates. The area round Whitby Abbey, which certainly disappeared during the Viking invasion, offers a remarkable contrast.

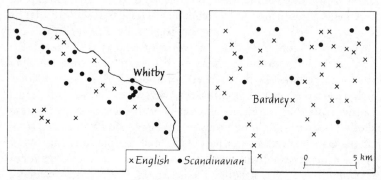

Figure 16   English and Scandinavian place names in the areas around Whitby and Bardney Abbeys

It therefore appears that areas recovered from the Scandinavians early in the tenth century, or retained by English landowners, have fewer Scandinavian place names than most parts of the Danelaw. This suggests that the Scandinavian names reflect the fragmentation of estates rather than settlement, and that this process of fragmentation did not begin until some time after the ninth-century conquests. This is hardly surprising. Settlement in most areas was not a haphazard affair, with individuals seizing land in a general free-for-all. The Viking army leaders naturally expected to receive tribute and services from the lands they had conquered, irrespective of whether these were provided by natives or by their own followers. Roger of Wendover's *Flores Historiarum*, a compilation made in the thirteenth century from various earlier annals, has an interesting entry for the year 876 that illuminates the process of settlement: 'Healfdene occupied North-umbria and divided it among himself and his thegns (*ministris*) and had it cultivated by his army' (*EHD*, 4). This variant on the familiar *Chronicle* text – 'Healfdene shared out the land of the Northumbrians, and they proceeded to plough and to support themselves' – probably derives from an early version, it can hardly have been Roger's own interpretation, and underlines a point that should, perhaps, be obvious: that the rank-and-file of the Viking armies were expected to cultivate the lands they had been given for the benefit of their leaders. Conquest did not mean that the cultivators, whether Scandinavian or native, were freed from the obligation to render tribute and service.

The estates that the Scandinavians took over were a characteristic feature of Britain at that time. The normal units of exploitation at that time were not individual villages or farms, but large estates that could produce all the food and raw materials that lords and their dependants needed. They usually included among their appurtenances woodland, arable, pasture, fisheries and, in coastal areas, saltpans. The woodland of the Kentish Weald, for example, belonged to estates whose centres lay in the richer land to the north and south, and many of these estates also had coastal rights for grazing on salt marshes, fishing and salt production. These varied resources were exploited from many settle-ments whose free inhabitants normally owed renders and services to the lord of the whole estate. The estates, called shires, lathes or sokes, although originally found in all parts of Britain, tended to survive longer in the north and west (Barrow 1973, pp. 7–68). There are many examples in Domesday Book. Some survived the Scandinavian con-quests and in Domesday Book's description of those in the Danelaw counties are called sokes or shires. Later texts show the varied rights that the lord of a soke had over it: he could expect payments, in money or kind, require services, including building work and a contribution to his military obligations, and he probably also held a court but, as Sir Frank Stenton pointed out, his rights 'were far from amounting to ownership' (Foster and Longley, 1924, p. xxiv). Lords did, however, retain more direct control over their own demesnes and berewicks. It is probably significant that in some areas with dense concentrations of Scandinavian settlement names Domesday Book records relatively few berewicks. In Cleveland, for example, several large sokes, including

Lofthouse, Hutton, Rudby and Stokesley, each had numerous soke-lands but no berewicks, and Whitby had only one. These sokes may be contrasted with the Bishop of Durham's estate of Howden, with eighteen berewicks (DB i. 305a-b; 302b; 331a).

Sokes and their centres tended to have English names. In Lincoln-shire the main medieval sokes were Bardney, Belchford, Bolingbroke, Caistor, Drayton, Folkingham, Gayton-le-Wold, Grantham, Greetham, West Halton, Horncastle, Kirton in Lindsey, Waltham and Wragby. Only two of these have names that are even partly Scandina-vian – Kirton and Wragby. Berewicks also tended to have English names, while sokelands and separate manors are more commonly Scandinavian. One striking example of the contrast is provided by the soke of Acklam in North Yorkshire, with sokeland in eight places, five of which have Scandinavian names: Coulby, Maltby, Thornaby, Stainsby and Cold Ingleby. Its one berewick is called *Englebi* in Domesday Book, the *by* of the English, and is now known as Ingleby Barwick (DB i., 305a).

In the first half of the tenth century the Scandinavian rulers of the Danelaw suffered a number of major defeats. The *Anglo-Saxon Chronicle* names two kings, two earls and at least five holds among the Danish dead after the battle of Tettenhall in 910, and records that at *Brunanburh*, in 937, the Scandinavians lost five young kings and seven earls. These battles, and many less famous skirmishes, must have greatly weakened the authority of the aristocracy in the Danelaw and so given many small landowners a chance to escape from at least some of their obligations, and to claim fuller rights of ownership over their holdings. This interpretation is consistent with the remarkable number of Scandinavian place names that incorporate a personal name. Well over half of the names in *by* and *thorp* include a personal name, normally a Scandinavian one (Fellows Jensen, 1978, pp. 276–86). The Danes did not bring this habit with them from Denmark, where combination of *by* with a personal name is rare (Pedersen, 1960). It was formerly thought that these place names preserved the names of the Scandinavians who colonized the places named after them, and that the place names that include the English *tūn* and a Scandinavian personal name were English villages taken over by the invaders at an early stage of the conquest. However, it is more likely that most of these names mark a change in the status of the settlements rather than new colonization or a change of ownership. Many were already settlements before the ninth century, but the men who held them, although free, were not free to dispose of them by gift or sale. They belonged to the estates to which tribute and services were due. In all parts of England after the ninth century, individuals were acquiring the right to sell, lease, give or bequeath their land, and sometimes the names of those who gained such enlarged rights have become part of the place names. Woolstone in Berkshire, for example, is the *tūn* of Wulfric, who was granted full rights over it in the tenth century, and Alverstoke in Hampshire was called *Stoce* in 948, while its present name incorporates that of Ælfwaru, who owned it a few years later, and was able to give it to Winchester Cathedral (Sawyer, 1978a, pp. 153–6). The disasters of the early tenth century facilitated similar developments in the Dane-law.

The effect of this process can be illustrated by comparing the Yorkshire Wolds with the Kentish Weald. Both were areas that were exploited by, and considered to belong to, estates with centres else-where. In Kent many of those estates remained remarkably intact long after the Norman Conquest and are therefore well documented, but the Yorkshire Wolds had been broken up into many small units of private ownership before 1066. The name *thorp* was very appropriate for such outlying components of estates, and it is significant that the largest concentrations of *thorp* names in Yorkshire are in the Wolds. Similar concentrations elsewhere, for example in the coastal marshes of Lin-colnshire, are likely to have a similar origin.

The fragmentation of old estates also explains the remarkable number, and small size, of Danelaw parishes. A parish was, in effect, the religious equivalent of a private estate. A man could build a church on his own land, but it did not have parochial status in the eleventh century unless that land was completely free and at the disposal of its owner. The large number of parishes in east Yorkshire, Lincolnshire and other parts of the Danelaw is a good indication of the progress of this fragmentation. Some very large parishes survived in the heart of the Danelaw, for example Horncastle and Grantham in Lincolnshire, or Pickering and Beverley in Yorkshire, but these were under royal or episcopal control and were exceptional; in the twelfth century most parishes in the Danelaw were small (Owen, 1971, pp. 1–12; Morris, 1982).

This process was facilitated by the growth of the markets. The tenth and eleventh centuries saw a remarkable increase in the number and size of such markets in many parts of England, but some of the largest and most prosperous were in the Danelaw. Their early growth can only be traced through archaeological investigations, but these have shown that both Lincoln and York expanded greatly in the tenth century, and that some streets were first established shortly before or after the year 900 (Hall, 1981). It is likely that these developments were stimulated by the presence of a prosperous local population, part of which had gained great wealth through plunder or tribute.

The early Scandinavian settlements in the British Isles served as bases for the colonization of other areas later. Some, perhaps many, of the Icelandic settlers came from the British Isles, and the Faroes also show signs of British influence (Craigie 1897; Pálsson, 1952; 1953; Dahl, 1970, p. 60). Some of the Scandinavian colonists who settled around the Solway Firth and in north-west England came from the Hebrides, while others came across the Pennines from the Danelaw (Fellows Jensen, forthcoming, a), and the Scandinavian settlers in the Wirral peninsula of Cheshire and in south-west Lancashire may have come from the Isle of Man (Fellows Jensen, forthcoming, b).

Normandy drew settlers from several areas of earlier Scandinavian activity. At least two armies were involved in the settlement (Musset, 1970, pp. 102–03). In addition to Rollo's occupation of the lower Seine, there was an army based on Bayeux which, to judge by the place names in that region, came from England. This might have been the army of Earl Thurcetel who left England in 916 and 'went across the sea to France, along with the men who were willing to serve him' (*ASC*). Further west, the Cotentin was settled by Scandinavians from the Celtic regions of the British Isles, some of whom were called Duncan, Murdoch or Kenneth (Musset, 1978).

There are few purely Scandinavian settlement names in Normandy. *Bý* only occurs twice, but *thorp* is rather more common. The Scandinavians did, however, introduce a large number of personal names, and their main effect on place names in Normandy was to form hybrids in which these names were combined with *ville*, as in Mondeville or Auberville, from the personal names Ámundi or Ásbjörn (Adigard des Gautries, 1954, pp. 256–61). In this respect Normandy is closest to East Anglia, where hybrids in *tūn* are common, but names in *bý* are generally rare.

The settlers in Normandy did not speak a Scandinavian language for long. There is no trace of Scandinavian influence on the pronunciation of Norman names, and they had little effect on the dialect except in matters concerning ships and the sea, especially whaling. In middle and western Normandy, however, a number of agricultural terms, includ-

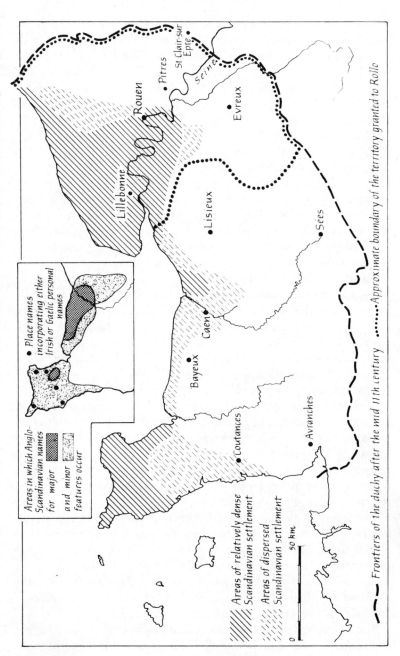

Figure 17 Normandy

Areas in which Anglo-Scandinavian names

for major and minor features occur

• Place names incorporating either Irish or Gaelic personal names

Areas of relatively dense Scandinavian settlement

Areas of dispersed Scandinavian settlement

— — — Frontiers of the duchy after the mid 11th century ⋯⋯⋯ Approximate boundary of the territory granted to Rollo

St Clair-sur-Epte

Pitres

Rouen

Lillebonne

Seine

Evreux

Lisieux

Sees

Caen

Bayeux

Coutances

Avranches

50 km
0

ing some from England, were used for minor features of the landscape and divisions of fields. The word *acre*, for example, is evidenced as early as 1006, well before Norman involvement in England, and there are many examples of *bekkr, haugr, lúndr* and *thveit* (brook, mound, grove and clearing) (Musset, 1959). In Normandy, as in England, Scandinavians not only occupied the land, they also took part in its cultivation.

The Scandinavians who conquered and colonized England and Normandy were not innovators, nor were those who settled in the northern Isles, the Hebrides and Man in the ninth century. Continuity of settlement in many places in those islands is only to be expected, for the number of suitable sites is limited. The evidence of the place names and some archaeological excavations has suggested that in many areas the natives were overwhelmed and that the survivors were reduced to a very inferior status (Crawford, 1981). That may often have been so, but there are indications that the later administrative divisions of the Scottish islands for taxation purposes had not been introduced by Scandinavians, but were an adaptation of arrangements that already existed before their arrival. Later charters and other texts show that the unit of assessment in the Hebrides was the ounce-land – *tír-unge* in Gaelic – and that this was commonly divided into quarters, or into twentieth parts known as penny-lands (McKerral, 1951). The name penny-land cannot have been introduced by the first settlers for they had no coinage. They could have organized assessments based on ounces of silver or gold, but that is also unlikely, as such assessments are not known in Norway or Iceland. The sub-division into twenty parts suggests that the system was that already current in Dál Riata (now Argyll) long before the Viking invasions, and described in a text known as *Senchus fer nAlban*. According to this, each group of twenty houses was responsible for providing two ships, each of seven benches, for military expeditions (Bannerman, 1974, pp. 49, 140–1). There is no evidence for the pre-Scandinavian system of assessment in the northern Hebrides, but it is possible that the later ounce-lands in those islands were based on an old Pictish unit, the *davach*. The two are in fact identified in a charter of 1505 from North Uist (Marwick, 1949). That may, of course, be the interpretation of a late medieval clerk, but it confirms the similarity of the units, both of which were commonly divided into quarters (Bannerman, 1974, pp. 140–1).

The ounce-land was also an assessment unit in Orkney and Shetland and called *Eyrisland* or *Urisland*, but it was divided there into four *skatlands*, or alternatively eighteen penny-lands (Marwick, 1949). These divisions must represent the combination of two different systems, for a skatland of 4½ penny-lands is unlikely to be the result of a deliberate plan. Skatlands were the units of assessment used when Orkney and Shetland were under the Norwegian Crown, as they were until the fifteenth century. The similarity of the other units to those found in the Hebrides strongly suggests that in the northern Isles, as elsewhere, the Scandinavians took over and adapted a native system of assessment. There is certainly no good reason for believing that the ounce-land and the penny-land were introduced by Harald Finehair after his conquest of these islands in the late ninth or early tenth centuries. (That conquest is probably apocryphal (p. 13).)

Harald Finehair may never have reached the Isle of Man, but many Scandinavians did during the ninth century and later. Some settled and farmed, while others found it an ideal base for raiding the lands around the Irish Sea. These settlers have left their mark in the form of pagan graves (Wilson, 1974), runic inscriptions (Page, 1980) as well as place names (Fellows Jensen, forthcoming, b) which make it possible to see how the newcomers took over existing estates and farms (Megaw, 1978, pp. 281–5). There are many indications that the native population continued to play a significant role in the island. The runic inscriptions of the tenth and eleventh centuries commemorate a number of men and women with Gaelic names, and show that there was intermarriage between natives and Norsemen. It is even more revealing that although the Norse kings of Man had Scandinavian forenames, several of them had Gaelic by-names. The first king was known as Godred Crovan, apparently from a Gaelic word meaning white-handed, and a later king, Godred, was called Don, from the Gaelic *donn* – brown, brown hair (Megaw, 1978, pp. 276–7).

The Kingdom of Man was in fact established by Godred Crovan, who was a survivor of the defeat at Stamford Bridge in 1066. For two centuries his successors claimed to have authority throughout the Hebrides under the distant overlordship of Norwegian kings. The extent of their kingdom is shown by the bounds of the diocese that was created for it – the bishopric of Sodor and Man. The independence of this kingdom was ended in 1266 by the treaty of Perth which transferred Man and the Western Isles to the kingdom of the Scots. This was almost the last stage in the absorption of the conquests and colonies of the Viking Age by the kingdoms of western Europe, a process in which Norwegian kings also shared. The kings of Norway had never had as much real authority in Man and the Hebrides as they had in Orkney and the Shetlands and it was presumably some compensation for them that four years before they were forced to surrender their claim to rule Man and the Isles, their authority had been acknowledged, however reluctantly, by the Icelanders.

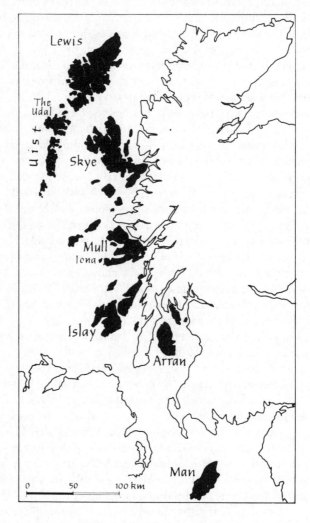

Figure 18   The Hebrides, showing the territory belonging to the kingdom of Man and the Isles.

8

The Baltic and beyond

Scandinavians were certainly active in the ninth and tenth centuries in the lands east of the Baltic. Unfortunately, the evidence leaves much room for doubt about their role there. Archaeological finds demonstrate contact between the two areas at that time, but the import of jewellery, weapons or even coins from one area to the other does not prove that the contacts were direct. Such objects could have been the personal possessions of a traveller or migrant, but they might equally have been stolen, received as gifts, or traded. The import of very large numbers of coins to Scandinavia from north Russia in the ninth and tenth centuries is often assumed to demonstrate trade, but they could as well have been plunder, tribute extorted by force, or the pay of mercenaries, as some other coin imports certainly were. The best archaeological indication that Scandinavians lived – or rather died – in Russia is provided by graves of a distinctively Scandinavian type, in particular boat-burials (Stalsberg, 1979). This custom of burial was at that time only practised in Scandinavia, including the Åland islands, and in areas of Scandinavian settlement overseas (Müller-Wille, 1970). The ten burials of this kind found at Plakun, near Ladoga (Korkukhina, 1971) are good evidence for the presence there of Scandinavians, probably of fairly high social standing. Some of the boat-burials found at Gnezdovo, near Smolensk, however, appear to be more recent and are a local adaptation of the Scandinavian custom (Bulkin, 1975). Such finds do not, of course, show whether the people buried were members of a ruling, perhaps conquering, group, or were warriors recruited by native rulers or merchants. The large group of burials at Plakun suggests that the Scandinavians were a settled group there, and this is confirmed by the fact that one of the burials was that of a woman.

There is a great deal of written evidence for Scandinavians in Russia in the period 850–1050, but most of it was composed in either Scandinavia or Russia long after that time (pp. 20–1). Some of the information given in these late texts may have been based on traditions that were current in the twelfth and thirteenth centuries, but traditions are not necessarily reliable and there was certainly much invention. The hundred runic inscriptions in Sweden that commemorate men who died in the east (Ruprecht, 1958) are good contemporary evidence that Swedes went there, but the purpose of their journeys is rarely indicated and most of these inscriptions date from the eleventh century. A few runic inscriptions have also been found in Russia. One of these, a metrical text in a Nordic language, was carved on a piece of wood that was found in an early ninth-century level at Staraja Ladoga. As Aslak Liestøl has pointed out (1970), the cultural background of this inscription is solidly Nordic, but that does not prove that there was a permanent Scandinavian colony there.

There are several references in tenth-century Islamic texts to the *Rus* as traders who brought furs and slaves to the markets of Khazaria and Bulghar and, according to one ninth-century report, they sometimes travelled to the south shore of the Caspian, and even as far as Baghdad (Pritsak, 1970). The best evidence is, however, provided by Ibn Fadlan. The *Rus* he encountered in Bulghar in 922 observed the Scandinavian custom of cremating their dead, even the poor, in boats, but they had been away from their homeland long enough to acquire alien habits of dress, for the silk tunic that was specially made for the dead *Rus* chieftain had buttons, which were not then used in Scandinavian costume. Ibn Fadlan describes the *Rus* as traders who offered slave girls and furs for sale. A fuller list of the exports of Bulghar, compiled at the end of the tenth century by al-Mukaddisi, includes several other commodities that the *Rus* may also have traded in: amber, arrows, swords, armour, falcons, wax and honey (Lewicki, 1962, p. 8). He also lists fish teeth, presumably meaning walrus tusks. These were certainly exported from Russia to Iran and India in the twelfth century and later (Abrahamowicz, 1970; Ettinghausen, 1950, pp. 120–36). The twelfth-century Persian writer Marvazi mentions that in the Arctic Sea there was a 'fish whose tooth is used for hafting knives, swords and suchlike' (Minorsky, 1942, p. 35). Walrus tusks were probably brought to Bulghar by Finns as well as *Rus* traders. Slaves figure prominently in all accounts and were certainly an important export from Russia to the Caliphate. They were in such demand in the ninth century that their price rose greatly and they were sometimes valued at as much as 600,000 dirhams. A century later there seems to have been a glut, thanks to the success of the Samanids in taking prisoners, and in

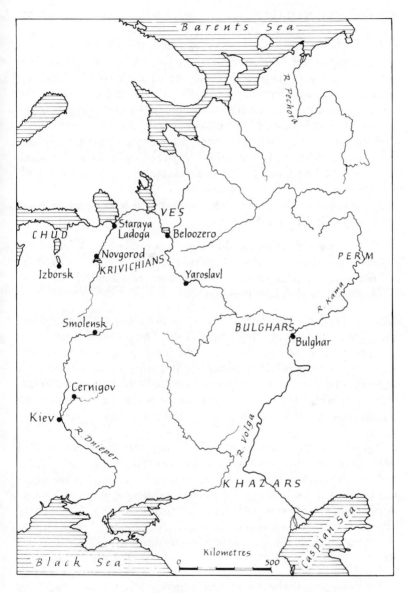

Figure 19   Russia

985 they are reported to have been sold for as little as 20 or 30 dirhams each (Frye, 1975, pp. 99, 150).

Most Islamic writers only had a vague idea that the *Rus* came from the region beyond Bulghar, from the Upper Volga. Ibn Rusta, who wrote before 913, claimed that they sailed their ships to raid the Sakaliba and take captives, but that is a very vague term for the white-skinned inhabitants of eastern Europe (Dunlop, 1954, p. 205n) and could mean Finns and Balts as well as Slavs, and might even include Gotlanders and other Scandinavians. His description of the *Rus* homeland or base as a marshy and unhealthy island, or peninsula, in a lake 'covered with forest and brush which it takes three days to walk round' is unspecific and probably fanciful.

According to Istakhri, who wrote in the middle of the tenth century, some of the *Rus* lived in Kiev:

> The *Rus* are of three kinds. The king of those nearest to Bulghar lives in the city called Kiev. It is larger than Bulghar. Another kind farther off than these is called *Slawiyah* and there is a kind called *Arthaniyah*, whose king lives in *Artha*.

Much research has been lavished on the identification of the second and third groups (Minorsky, 1937, pp. 434–6). The favoured suggestions seem to be that the second refers to the Slavs, perhaps of Novgorod, while the *Arthaniyah* have been identified with the *Erz'a*, a Finnish tribe who lived by the River Soura, a right-bank tributary of the Volga, west of Bulghar. There is, however, no doubt about the first of these *Rus* groups, and this was the normal meaning of *Rus* in later Islamic texts.

It was this same group of Kievan *Rus* with whom the Byzantines had dealings in the tenth and eleventh centuries (pp. 28–9). There is also good evidence that the *Rus* were known in Byzantium in the ninth century but the sources give no indication where they came from. Apart from the references in the sermons of Photius (p. 28), there is also the remarkable account in the *Annals of St Bertin* of the arrival in 839 at the Frankish court of a Byzantine mission, accompanied by some *Rus*.

> He also sent with the envoys some men whom his people called *Rhos* and who had been sent to him by their king (his name was *Chaganus*) so they said, for the sake of friendship. Theophilus [that is the Byzantine emperor] requested in his letter that the emperor

[Louis] in his goodness might grant them safe-conducts to travel through the Empire, as well as any help or practical assistance they needed to return home for the route by which they had reached Constantinople had taken them through the most fierce and savage primitive tribes, and Theophilus did not wish them to return that way in case some disaster might befall them. When the emperor investigated more closely the reason for their coming here, he discovered that they belonged to the tribe of the *Sueones* [Swedes]. Suspecting that they had really been sent as spies to this kingdom of ours, rather than seekers of our friendship, he decided to keep them with him until he could find out for certain whether or not they had come in good faith. He lost no time in sending a letter to Theophilus, through the same envoys, to tell him all this, and to add that he had received them willingly for the sake of his friendship for Theophilus, and that if they were found to be genuine, he would give them the means to return to their own country without any risk of danger, and send them home with every assistance, but if not, he would send them with our envoys back to Theophilus for him to deal with as he might think fit.

The outcome is, unfortunately, not known.

The written evidence from Islam, Byzantium and Frankia is remarkably consistent. Scandinavians, known as *Rus*, established themselves in Russia in the first half of the ninth century, apparently attracted by the prospect of gathering furs and slaves, as well as other produce of the forests and the Arctic to sell in the flourishing markets on the Volga. Some *Rus* reached Constantinople by 839, but they did not begin trading with the Byzantines until later in the century; they were still regarded as strangers from the north when they attacked the city in 860. By the beginning of the tenth century *Rus* had gained control of Kiev and traditions about that dynasty of Kievan princes, tracing its descent from Rurik, were later recorded in the *Russian Primary Chronicle* (pp. 20–1). Many of the dates given in that chronicle are unreliable, but the account is reasonably coherent and agrees well with the other evidence, particularly from Byzantium. By the middle of the ninth century the *Rus* had bases in several parts of northern Russia, at Izborsk, Beloozero and Novgorod, which was under Rurik's control. One group, led by Askold and Dir, went south and seized Kiev. They were possibly responsible for the attack on Constantinople in 860. Rurik died in about 880 and was succeeded by a kinsman, Oleg, who overthrew Askold and Dir, and established himself as prince of Kiev. He extended his authority to some of the neighbouring Slavonic tribes and forced them to pay tribute. He also attacked Constantinople in 907 and concluded a treaty with the Byzantine government that gave *Rus* merchants trading privileges. He was succeeded in 913 by Igor, supposedly a direct descendant of Rurik, who continued the expansionist policy and attacked the Byzantines, but with less success. He was killed in about 945 while trying to suppress a rebellion by one of the tributary Slavonic tribes. His son, Sviatoslav, was too young to succeed, so for twenty years the Kiev *Rus* were ruled by his mother, Olga. By the end of the century the Kiev *Rus* were extracting tribute from a very large area of Russia, from Finns and Balts as well as Slavs. Sviatoslav was especially ambitious and attacked both the Khazars and the Bulghars. He was, however, less successful against the Byzantines, and in 971 was forced to make concessions in a treaty under which he was obliged to supply the Byzantine emperor with mercenaries, known as Varangians. The Kiev princes also recruited Varangians to support them both in internal conflicts and in wars against Poles and Pechenegs. Varangians were recruited from many areas, but a major element came from Scandinavia, and the most famous and well-documented Varangian to serve in Byzantium was Harald, known as Hardrada, later king of Norway. Their contacts with Byzantium also introduced the Kiev *Rus* to Christianity, and when Sviatoslav's son, Vladimir, formally accepted Orthodox Christianity the opportunities for Byzantine influence in Kiev grew (Shepard, 1974).

The archaeological evidence is consistent with this general picture. The main concentration of Scandinavian imports is in and around Staraja Ladoga, the earliest levels of which, built on undisturbed natural soil, have now been dated by dendrochronology to the period 760–840 (information from Olga Davidan). Large timber houses with hearths were constructed, and some appear to have served as workshops for craftsmen working with glass, bronze and antler. Most of the material from the earliest levels is native – that is predominantly Finnish – with some Slavonic imports, and there are also a few Scandinavian objects, including an early type of oval brooch (Davidan, 1970). Combs were made there, apparently by itinerant craftsmen who worked at other markets in the Baltic (Ambrosiani, 1981, pp. 48–50). The number of Scandinavian finds increases significantly in the middle years of the ninth century, and include the rune-stick mentioned above (p. 114). The Scandinavian grave-field at nearby Plakun has been dated to the late ninth and early tenth centuries. Staraja Ladoga was destroyed by fire in about 860 but was soon rebuilt and fortified with a stone wall before the end of the century, possibly as a defence against attacks from the Baltic. Elsewhere in Russia, especially in cemeteries associated with important centres like Beloozero, Jaroslavl, Pskov, Novgorod and Gnezdovo, small concentrations of Scandinavian objects or ornaments made locally in Scandinavian style, have been found, together with some graves that can be identified as Scandinavian (Stalsberg, 1979). These graves were neither particularly rich nor isolated from other burials in which a variety of rites – Finnish, Balt, and Slav – were observed (Bulkin, 1973). These Scandinavians were therefore one, relatively small, element in a very mixed population, and seem to have been regarded as ordinary settled members of communities. It is possible that some were warriors who had been recruited by native rulers to defend their territory against Scandinavian and other raiders; others were probably traders. It must, of course, often have been difficult to distinguish between warriors and traders: to the people from whom tribute was extorted or who suffered from slave-raiding, the traders must have appeared as raiders. The *Rus* encountered by Ibn Fadlan were traders bringing furs and slaves, but they were also warriors. He reports that the king of the *Rus* had a personal retinue of 400 men who he implies were warriors, and he says that each of them had two slave girls (Canard, 1958, pp. 134–5).

Trade in Russia was not begun by Scandinavians. The riches of the north, especially of the Arctic, had attracted traders long before the ninth century, and their activity had led to the precocious development of some areas of Russia. The valley of the River Kama, that joins the Volga in Bulghar, was relatively rich in the sixth and seventh centuries with a settled population, large grave-fields and hill forts. Sassanian and Byzantine silver has been found there, presumably imported in exchange for furs and perhaps even Arctic produce, for there are indications that the Arctic valley of the Pechora was at that time being exploited by men from the Kama region in much the same way as it was at a later period (Tallgren, 1934; Lewicki, 1962, p. 10). The southern end of this trade route passed through the territory of the Khazars, who controlled the lower Volga and the Caucasus and gathered tribute from a vast area north of the Black and Caspian Seas (Dunlop, 1954).

These early contacts between the Byzantine and Persian empires and the far north were disrupted in the mid-seventh century by the expansion of Islam. After their conquest of Iran, the caliphs attempted, with great violence but without success, to bring the Khazars under their control, and as a result the traffic that passed through that region was interrupted. Byzantine and Sassanian coins, which until then had been fairly common in the Caucasus, disappeared from circulation in the course of the seventh century and by 700 the area was virtually coinless (Noonan, 1980a). In 749–50 there was a dynastic revolution in the caliphate in which the Abbasids overthrew the Umayyads and relations between the new dynasty of caliphs and the Khazars gradually improved; and by 770 coins were once again in circulation, and by the end of the century were being exported further north into Russia, where a number of dirham hoards have been found that appear to have been hidden in the early years of the ninth century (Noonan 1980a; 1981). The earliest, consisting of thirty-one dirhams minted between 749 and 787, was found at Staraja Ladoga. A detailed comparison of these early hoards with those found in the Caucasus and in the caliphate strongly suggests that the hoards reaching Russia came from Iran, and were probably taken directly by Muslim merchants to the Khazar markets on the Volga, where the goods they wanted could be bought either from northern merchants or from the Khazars who gathered tribute from their subject peoples, Slavs, Finns and Bulghars. The Khazars appear to have welcomed traders from all quarters and themselves profited by imposing a toll. Some Muslim merchants may have travelled further afield, for the Khazars do not seem to have objected to traders passing through their territory so long as they paid toll; the *Rus* were later able to sail down the Volga to trade and raid in the Caspian Sea.

At the end of the ninth century the situation was changed by the discovery of huge silver deposits in Afghanistan. As a result Transoxania suddenly became very rich and, in 893, its Samanid rulers began to mint vast quantities of unusually large coins of high quality at Tashkent, Samarkand, Balkh, Bukhara and elsewhere. Much of this silver was exported to Russia, where hundreds of thousands of Samanid coins have been found in hoards that indicate that the coins began to reach Russia by about 910.

For merchants from Transoxania the territory of the Bulghars on the middle Volga was much more convenient than the markets on the lower Volga in Khazaria. As a result, Bulghar began to develop very rapidly as a trading centre in the early years of the tenth century, rivalling, and perhaps even eclipsing, the markets of the Khazars (Hrbek, 1960). The Bulghars also began minting their own coinage, modelled on Samanid dirhams (Noonan, 1980b). The mission described by Ibn Fadlan was in fact a response to this new situation, as the caliph sought to ensure good relations with the Bulghars. They had to take a very circuitous route, presumably because of the hostility of the Khazars to this development. They would naturally be reluctant to allow their tributaries to achieve independence.

Ibn Fadlan shows that the *Rus* were not the only suppliers of northern goods in Bulghar. He also mentions the *Ves*, a Finnish tribe living to the east of Lake Onega, as suppliers of marten and black fox fur (Canard 1958, p. 107). Later Islamic writers give more details about the northern neighbours of Bulghar. According to Marvazi, a Persian who wrote in the early twelfth century:

> At a distance of twenty days from Bulghar, towards the Pole, is a land called *Isu* [that is, of the *Ves*] and beyond this a people called *Yura*; these are a savage people, living in forests and not mixing with other men, for they fear that they may be harmed by them. The people of Bulghar journey to them taking wares, such as clothes, salt and other things, in contrivances drawn by dogs over the heaped snows, which never clears away. It is impossible for a man to go over these snows, unless he binds on to his feet the thigh-bones of oxen, and takes in his hands a pair of javelins which he thrusts backwards into the ice, so that his feet slide over the surface of the ice; with a favourable wind he will travel a great distance in a day. The people of *Yura* trade by means of signs and dumb show, for they are wild and afraid of men. From them are imported excellent sable and other fine furs; they hunt these animals, feeding on their flesh and wearing their skins. (Minorsky, 1942, p. 34)

There was also trade with the Arctic region. Ibn Fadlan does not mention this directly, but his strange story about the dumb giant from the land of Gog and Magog (see p. 28) probably reflects contacts with the peoples living round the White Sea. Marvazi particularly mentions the walrus and its tusks in his otherwise fantastic account of people who lived on the Arctic coast (Minorsky, 1942, p. 35).

Carelian traders who collected produce in the Kola peninsula were encountered by Óttar (see p. 71). They are called *Beormas* in the Old English text representing Old Norse *Bjarmar*, which derives from the Finnish word *perm* used for travelling merchants (Vilkuna, 1956). The same word was also used for another group of traders who operated further east, between Bulghar and the Arctic, and has consequently been applied to their territory and survives as the name of a Russian province, *Perm*. There were other groups exploiting the Arctic, including Finns called *Kvenir* (Vilkuna, 1969). Óttar mentions them, and emphasized their conflicts with the Norwegians:

> The *Cwenas* sometimes make attacks on the Norwegians across the mountains, at other times the Norwegians attack them. Throughout the mountains there are very large fresh-water lakes; the *Cwenas* carry their boats overland to these lakes, and from there they attack the Norwegians; they have very small and light boats. (Ross, 1940, p. 23)

The traders may themselves have hunted but they probably relied for most of their supplies on extracting tribute from the natives of the region, the Lapps, as Óttar himself did. Icelandic sagas preserve some echoes of contacts between Norwegians and the Bjarmar, Kvenir and other traders, and with the Lapps, for example in the story in St Olaf's Saga and elsewhere (Chesnutt, 1981, pp. 76–7) about a trading expedition to the Dvina that ended with the sanctuary of the Bjarmar being plundered and their god, Jomali, destroyed. There is also a story in Egil's Saga about an alliance between Norwegians and Kvenir against Carelians.

In the ninth and tenth centuries Scandinavians, Finns, Bulghars and Slavs were eager to obtain furs, slaves and other goods to sell to rich Muslim merchants or their agents. Some were doubtless obtained by fair trading, but much must have been gathered as tribute exacted under the threat of violence, or as straightforward plunder. Ibn Rusta said that the *Rus* raided for slaves, and the *Russian Primary Chronicle* has many references to the collection of tribute and the resistance this provoked. Igor was killed when he attempted to extract extra tribute from the Derevlianians. Constantine Porphyrogenitus described the 'rounds' made every winter by the chiefs and all the *Rus* to collect tribute from their Slav subjects, and how this was brought to Kiev in April and later shipped down the Dnieper.

Constantine's account of the Kiev *Rus* and the treaties preserved in the *Russian Primary Chronicle* show that there was an active trade between Kiev and Constantinople in the tenth century. We have no information about its scale, and very little about the goods involved. The remarkable rarity of Byzantine coins of this period in Russia (Noonan, 1980c) suggests that the *Rus* preferred to take silk and other cloth, metal and glassware and wines, rather than cash. The few

Byzantine coins that have been found in Russia occur in hoards that were deposited after 950, which suggests that they left the empire as the pay of Varangians rather than as the profit of merchants (Rasmusson *et al.*, 1957; Shepard, 1979). The coin evidence clearly shows that the trade between Russia and Islam was on a much larger scale than that with Byzantium. Islamic goods were certainly imported into Russia and some reached Scandinavia, but the demand in the caliphate for Russian produce appears to have been so much greater than the reciprocal Russian demand for Islamic goods that the balance was paid in silver, which for many of those involved was acceptable and may even have been preferred.

Some Islamic coins were exported from Russia to neighbouring parts of Europe and large numbers have been found in Scandinavia. Some very early, even Sassanian, coins have been found, but the hoard evidence shows that they were not imported before the ninth century (p. 34). When found singly, for example in graves, they cannot be assumed to be very early imports, and they are often found together with ninth- or tenth-century objects, and appear to have been part of the stock of coins in circulation in the caliphate that was exported to Russia in the ninth century.

Dirhams began reaching Scandinavia in the ninth century, but the evidence for the date of the earliest imports is unsatisfactory. The earliest hoards, in which the most recent coins were struck before 800, contain too few coins – sometimes only two or three – to provide reliable evidence. Some larger hoards that have been confidently claimed as early ninth century are in fact of uncertain date (see p. 36). The three earliest hoards listed in the first two volumes of the *Corpus* of Gotlandic coins, supposedly with most recent coins of 819, 823 and 843, were found at Björke on no fewer than fourteen occasions between 1896 and 1904. Their allocation into three hoards is an arbitrary exercise that also requires the exclusion of one coin dated 911 as a stray from another, undiscovered, find (*CNS*, 1.2.8–10).

The hoard evidence improves after about 850, and we can then be fairly confident that Islamic coins were reaching Gotland and Sweden, if not the more westerly parts of Scandinavia. These imports were, however, on a small scale. Only twenty Gotlandic hoards have been dated earlier than 890, and these only contain 10 per cent of the dirhams found on the island (Linder Welin, 1956). It is probable that coins found on Gotland came from the nearest part of the Baltic coast, Latvia, where the hoard evidence suggests that Islamic coins began to arrive in the mid-ninth century (Noonan, 1977–8). This is supported by the discovery of Gotlandic material in Latvia but not further east near Novgorod or Ladoga (Kivikoski, 1937). Many of the ninth-century coins found in Gotland are fragmentary and have generally been neatly cut into fairly regular halves or quarters (plate XVa). This is also true of many of the coins found in Russia and eastern Europe, and it is probable that these fragments formed a significant part of the coin stock exported from the caliphate. The ninth-century hoard found at Susa in Iran contained 475 such fragments together with 655 whole coins (Miles, 1960). The early Islamic hoards found in mainland Sweden also contain many fragments but these are often irregular and appear to have been crudely broken rather than cut. The contrast is brought out very clearly in plate XV. This suggests that the Islamic coins found in Sweden did not come from the same source as those found in Gotland. They may possibly have come from the area of Ladoga.

Samanid dirhams had begun circulating in Russia by about 910 (Ianin, 1956, Table 2) and soon after that there was a dramatic increase in the quantity of Islamic coins reaching Scandinavia, where they spread further west than in the ninth century. This relative flood of silver, mostly from Samanid mints, continued until sometime after 965, when the number of coins being imported dropped so sharply that it has been claimed that there must have been a complete cessation of imports for about twenty years (Linder Welin, 1956). After 983, when small quantities of Islamic coins again reached Scandinavia, they tended to come from mints in the central provinces of the caliphate rather than from the Samanid territory in central Asia. By 1015 the flow of Islamic coins to both Russia and Scandinavia stopped altogether.

A central question for any understanding of the Viking period is how the Islamic silver reached the Baltic and Scandinavia. It has often been assumed to be the result of an active trade between Scandinavia and Russia. Birka has been described as a transit market between the rich centres in Russia and western Europe. When Birka ceased to function as a market, its place is said to have been taken by Gotland which then became the centre for the trans-Baltic trade (Yrwing, 1969). It has even been argued (Sawyer, 1971, pp. 197–9) that Birka's disappearance was a result in the drop in silver imports to the north. There are, however, difficulties with this interpretation. What was being bought with this silver? And by whom? We can hardly suppose that merchants from north Russia came to Birka and other Baltic markets to buy slaves and furs for sale in Russia, as one of the richest areas in the world for furs was, and is, Carelia, and north Russia had an abundance of potential slaves. It is possible that Scandinavians and others, who had in various ways made themselves rich in Russia, travelled to Birka to buy luxury goods imported from the west – fine cloth, glass, high quality pottery, wine, or the tools and weapons made by craftsmen there. There is however, little evidence for any substantial flow of such imports into Russia and, besides, such goods could as well, perhaps better, be obtained from Islamic merchants. If the oriental silver imported to Scandinavia was due to a favourable balance of trade, it is difficult to understand the reason for the cessation of those imports after 965; Islamic coins continued to reach Russia and eastern Europe (Ianin, 1956, Table 1), if in smaller quantities than before, but for twenty years little or none reached Scandinavia.

A more satisfactory explanation for the import of oriental silver into Scandinavia is that it was gained by violence, as plunder or tribute. The *Vita Anskarii* shows Swedes attacking the Baltic coast in the ninth century, and in the tenth the opportunities to gather silver were greatly improved thanks to the larger quantities that were then reaching Russia from Transoxania. Native rulers must have made efforts to protect their territory and are likely to have recruited Scandinavian warriors – Varangians – for this purpose, much as other Scandinavians had been recruited by western European rulers. The traditions recorded in the *Russian Primary Chronicle* are consistent with this hypothesis, as is the fact that Staraja Ladoga was strongly fortified in the second half of the ninth century.

Improved defences offer the best explanation for the interruption in the flow of oriental silver to Scandinavia after 965. The evidence of the Gotlandic coin hoards is consistent with this suggestion, for more hoards appear to have been deposited there in the middle years of the tenth century than earlier. That could indicate increased disturbance or even raids on the island, but these hoards could alternatively have been hidden by men who took part in expeditions that failed to return, as Ingvar's did at a later date (see p. 35). These hoards are now being systematically catalogued, and the 130 finds made in the parishes whose names begin with the letters A to F, provide a reasonable basis for a preliminary analysis of hoard frequencies. They are listed in the first four volumes of the *Corpus Nummorum Saeculorum IX–XI*, two of which have now been published. If the hoards containing ten or more coins are grouped by decades according to their most recent coins, the following results are obtained for the tenth century:

Decade beginning	Number of hoards
900	0
910	2
920	1
930	3
940	4
950	8
960	2
970	2
980	2
990	6

The decline in imports after 965 may have exaggerated the peak, for if few coins were being added to the stock in circulation it is unlikely that hoards concealed after 965 would have contained more recent coins. This may explain the relatively smaller peak of hoards that appear to have been concealed in southern Sweden in the 950s (Hårdh, 1976b, p. 44) but it cannot be the full explanation of the Gotlandic hoards, for they began to be more frequent before 950 when new coins were still arriving in large numbers. This increase in the number of hoards deposited in Gotland cannot prove that the Gotlanders were finding it more difficult to plunder their neighbours, but it is consistent with the hypothesis.

The import of silver from Russia into Scandinavia in the tenth century cannot, therefore, be taken as evidence of trade between the two regions. That does not, of course mean that there was no trade. Scandinavians imported many things from Russia and the lands beyond during the ninth and tenth centuries – cornelian beads, rock crystal, silver rings made in Bulghar and nearby, together with Slavonic, Finnish and Baltic ornaments. Large concentrations of these have been found at Birka, where many of the dead were buried in oriental dress, and traces of linen and silk, both imported from the east, have been found there (Hägg, 1974). Contacts between Sweden and Russia continued after 965. There were, in fact, fairly close links with Kiev and traders probably also went to Bulghar, but not beyond, for the Bulghars did not encourage through-traffic (Noonan, 1978).

When the oriental silver imports began to decline some Scandinavians started looking elsewhere for supplies, and by the end of the tenth century large quantities of silver coins from both England and Germany were reaching Scandinavia. The English coins were at first tribute that was extorted by violence, but after the Danes conquered England Knut and his successors continued to pay their warriors with English coins, many of which reached Scandinavia. Well over 50,000 English coins, almost all of the period 980–1051, have been found in Scandinavia. These date limits are significant because they show that this money had nothing to do with trade, for in 1051 Edward the Confessor disbanded his Scandinavian fleet and immediately increased the weight of the coinage. These heavier coins did not reach Scandinavia. Many of the coins were taken to Scandinavia directly, and some reached Finland without being circulated (Stewart, 1981). Once in Scandinavia they were passed from hand to hand, and in the process were sometimes tested to make sure they were genuine. This was done by bending the coin and scratching the surface with a sharp instrument to ensure that it was not a copper flan covered with a thin coating of silver. This was not necessary in England because their reliability was assured by the authority of the king, and the threat of dire penalties for false moneyers. But when the coins changed hands in Scandinavia that assurance counted for little, and sensible men tested coins they were given. These marks are therefore an indication that the coins had circulated outside the area in which they were produced. The number of pecks gives some idea of the number of times a coin changed hands

Analysis of peck marks on English coins in Myrände hoard (see p. 128)

Number of pecks per coin	Percentage of English coins in each category of pecking			
	Crux long cross 991–1003	Helmet small cross 1003–17	Quatrefoil 1017–23	Pointed helmet 1023–9
0	5	6	5	8
1–5	38	47	63	81
6–10	29	25	22	11
11–20	22	21	10	0
21–30	6	1	0	0
Number of determinable coins in each group of types	55	77	68	64

and therefore reflects how long it was in circulation. A study of this by Brita Malmer (1981a) has confirmed that the degree of testing varies with the age of the coin. This is shown very clearly by the 264 English coins found in a hoard at Myrände in Atlingbo parish, Gotland, which was deposited some time after 1036 (*CNS* 1.1.19): see table on p. 127.

German coins began to reach Scandinavia in the mid-tenth century; the earliest known hoard was hidden some time after 948 (Hatz, 1974, no. 3). A few hoards of the 960s contain single German coins, and the trickle gradually increased. In the next two decades, fourteen Swedish hoards are dated by the German coins that occur in small numbers in them, but after 991 the volume increased enormously and a total of at least 100,000 German coins of the late tenth and eleventh centuries have been found in Scandinavia. It has been widely accepted that they reached Scandinavia by trade (Ilisch, 1981). It has been claimed that a large proportion of these came from the mints along, or close to the Rhine, the main artery of German overseas trade. But scepticism about this claim is raised by the observation that German coins tend to have more peck marks than English coins minted at the same time (Malmer, 1981a). The difference is brought out by a comparison of the hoard from Myrände, discussed above, with one that was found at Hemängen in Ethelhem parish, also in Gotland (*CNS*, 1.3.34). This was possibly deposited a little earlier than the Myrände hoard, and contains 375 German coins. Some of these had more than forty pecks per coin and only a quarter had less than five. The contrast is brought out very well in a recent study of the Igelösa hoard from Skåne (Malmer, 1981b). This contained about 1850 English coins, mostly minted between 991 and 1003, and 133 German coins, the most recent being struck some time after 1005. The maximum number of pecks on any English coin is nine, while on the German coins there are up to nineteen. It is also significant that about three-quarters of the most recent type of English coin in that hoard have no pecks at all. The explanation for this contrast seems to be, as Malmer has suggested, that while the English coins arrived in Scandinavia unpecked, the German coins did not. This must mean that they had circulated somewhere outside Germany, possibly in the lands south of the Baltic, before reaching Scandinavia. It is, of course, possible that they were used by traders visiting Slav markets such as that at Wollin, but it seems more likely that they are not the result of trading surplus but, like the English coins, were obtained by force. There were many opportunities to do so in the wars and raids that were a regular feature of that region in the late tenth and eleventh centuries.

These silver imports, however they were obtained, had significant economic effects. As in western Europe, Scandinavians with silver to spend stimulated commerce. Merchants were encouraged to travel, and craftsmen to produce useful as well as ornamental goods. Comb-makers, glassbead-makers, bronze smiths, shoemakers, woodworkers and others were active in the markets that flourished in Scandinavia and around the Baltic at that time. The peck marks show that some coins passed through many hands, and in the late tenth century silver bars, rings and other objects were being cut into tiny pieces, often as little as 1 g, presumably to obtain the small amounts needed for relatively minor transactions (Hårdh, 1978). Adam of Bremen has many references to traders and in one, somewhat neglected passage, he describes Mälaren as 'the most secure haven in the maritime regions of Sweden in which all the ships of the Danes, and Northmen, as well as those of the Slavs and Sembi [that is Prussians] and other Scythian people, meet at stated' times for the diverse necessities of trade' (i.60).

There is also good evidence that merchants from western Europe were visiting Novgorod in the twelfth century and earlier. In the early twelfth century entry into its merchant guild of St Ivar required the payment of 50 lb of silver and a cloth of Ypres (Eck, 1933, p. 477) – remarkable testimony to the close links that then existed between Novgorod and Flanders. There is no doubt that merchants from Germany, Frisia and Flanders were travelling to Novgorod in the eleventh century to obtain furs, and that they paid for these partly in cloth, called *faldones* by Adam of Bremen (iv.18), and partly in silver, which was available in abundance thanks largely to the silver mines discovered in the 960s in the Harz mountains. The silver imports to the region of Novgorod and Ladoga from Germany replaced the earlier abundance from Islamic sources, and the silver ornaments of Carelia are larger and heavier than those from other areas in the eleventh century. Gotlanders may possibly have had some small part in this traffic, but most seems to have by-passed the island, for the proportion of German coins that come from Frisian mints is significantly lower in Gotland and mainland Sweden than in the area east of the Gulf of Finland (Hatz, 1974; Ilisch, 1981; Kluge, 1978; Metcalf, 1981, pp. 336–7, 369–71). The German coins found in Russia are, therefore, un-likely to have circulated in Sweden before being taken further east. This conclusion is supported by the observation that the German coins found in Russia tend to have fewer pecks than those in Swedish hoards (Peter Ilisch, personal communication). The coins must have been taken directly by merchants from Frisia and elsewhere to Novgorod. There are also some English coins in the Novgorod region minted in the late eleventh century; and even later examples are known from Estonia (Kluge, 1981). There is, therefore, little reason to assume that the wealth of Gotland in the eleventh century was based on trade between Russia and western Europe, and is more likely to have been gathered by piracy. The Gotlanders were noted for this later, and the picture stones of that island certainly do not give an impression of peaceful traders – the ships are normally filled with warriors.

Birka disappeared, not because of violence, or because its role was taken over by Gotland. Its successor was Sigtuna, in which coins were apparently being minted before the end of the tenth century, and where there are several archaeological indications of an overlap with Birka (Douglas, 1978). The establishment of a bishopric in the eleventh century suggests that it was under royal control, as to some extent Birka had been. It is, therefore, possible that the move was organized by a king, much as Godfred had earlier moved the merchants of *Reric* (see p. 73). The move may have been made necessary by changing water levels in Mälaren. Adam of Bremen has a curious passage in which he suggests that the inhabitants of Birka deliberately made the approaches to the island difficult for pirates by building underwater obstacles of rock. They may have done so, for underwater defences of the Viking period are known elsewhere in Scandinavia (Roesdahl, 1980, pp. 175–7), but the lowering water level of the lake must also have created new hazards. As Adam remarked 'the passage was as perilous for themselves as for the pirates' (i.60).

There may have been another reason for the move. The iron, which seems to have been an important element in the wealth of this region, came mainly from Dalarna in the north, and for that traffic Sigtuna was better placed than Birka. The merchants who came to Mälaren, whether to Birka or to Sigtuna, were, of course, interested in more than iron: they could also hope to obtain furs and other northern produce, brought south from the hunting grounds of the north to the mid-winter fair, later known as *Disting* (Granlund, 1958). Svealand may have had little significance as a transit market between Russia and western Europe, but it was an alternative source for some of the things that Europeans wanted in the eleventh century just as it had been in the eighth.

9

Pagans and Christians

Pagan Scandinavians seem to have worshipped the same gods as other Germanic peoples and in much the same ways. Place names suggest that different gods were worshipped in different areas. Thus Ti occurs in Denmark, but not Ull, while in Sweden the reverse is true. Thor is common throughout Scandinavia, except in Trøndelag, and Odin is well represented in Danish and in Swedish names, but is rare in Norway and Iceland. Some of these differences are probably much older than the Viking Age, but others involve gods who were certainly worshipped on the eve of Christian conversion, notably Odin and Thor. It has been suggested that Thor was a popular god, while Odin, as the chief god, was more appropriate for warriors, kings and their *skalds*, and it has even been claimed that the contrast between Denmark and Iceland reflects fundamental differences in the development of royal authority, and that the popularity of Thor in Norway, as in Iceland, is an indication of the relative weakness of Norwegian kings. It is, however, more likely that these contrasts are not so much of substance as of names. Odin, who was later said to have 170 names, was certainly identified with many other gods, some of whom were no less warlike than he was, and also had claims to primacy. Hierarchical societies naturally tended to have divine hierarchies and there were other chief gods before, and contemporary with Odin. Thor himself was cast in that role, and Ull also had very similar functions. Ull was commonly used in kennings for warriors, and in Sweden there are no fewer than eighteen early place names of the type *Ullevi* that indicate temples or sanctuaries devoted to his worship (Wessén, 1930).

Our knowledge of these gods, their attributes, and the myths in which they figured, depends almost entirely on poetry preserved in Icelandic manuscripts of the thirteenth century or later. Some of these poems were probably composed in pagan times and a few may be as early as the ninth century, but the date of many is very uncertain. *Rígsthula*, for example, which deals with the mythological basis of the social hierarchy from slave to king has been variously dated from the ninth to the thirteenth century, and many poems show signs of Christian influence. Some of these myths also served as themes for pictures, which can often be dated with rather more confidence than the poems, and they illustrate how some stories changed. Thus, in accounts of Ragnarök, when the gods were overthrown and destroyed, the wolf, Fenrir, either had its jaws broken, or it was killed by Odin's sword. A tenth-century stone-carving at Gosforth in Cumberland depicts the former and apparently earlier version, and shows that it was current at that date (Bailey, 1980, p. 236).

One of the most interesting of the poems that may be early is *Ragnarsdrápa*, which is believed to have been composed by a Norwegian, Bragi, probably in the ninth century, and describes scenes painted on Ragnar's shield. One scene – Thor's encounter with the world serpent – seems to have been popular, and is depicted in stone carvings from Altuna in Uppland, Hørdum in north Jutland, and Gosforth in Cumberland. The poem has many other allusions to the mythology of Thor, including of course his hammer, and his encounter with the giants.

Poems and pictures in stone, wood, metal and cloth show that stories drawn from the pagan past had a continuing fascination, at least for artists and presumably their patrons. They are often related with skilful displays of verbal or visual virtuosity, and learned or ingenious men, from Snorri Sturluson to Georges Dumézil, have found deep significance in them, without necessarily understanding them correctly (Page, 1979; Frank, 1981). What they can in fact reveal about the thoughts, beliefs and ideals of men and women in the Viking Age is, inevitably, a matter of dispute. It is, however, beyond doubt that these stories were not immutable, and it is also certain that in the form in which most of them are now studied, they have been deeply influenced by Christian ideas and the riches of the Bible. They clearly offer remarkable opportunities for scholarship, but what they, or the learning they have generated, can contribute to a better understanding of the Scandinavians in the ninth and tenth centuries is more doubtful.

We are on firmer, if less exciting ground in recognizing a general preoccupation with fertility and with divine approval or disapproval, whether this was discovered in advance by omens or the casting of lots, or revealed later by events.

Gods were placated or thanked by sacrifices, and these could be extravagant and could even include human beings. Small private offerings of the kind described by Ibn Fadlan were probably common, but larger votive deposits have been found in many parts of northern Europe and are best preserved when made in lakes or marshes (Hagberg, 1967). The custom seems to have declined in southern Scandinavia before the Viking Age but it did not die out altogether; Viking-age offerings are known from Gotland, and some contain treasure. The custom certainly flourished throughout the Middle Ages among the Lapps, and their offerings also included coins (Serning, 1956).

The most abundant evidence for the religious beliefs of pagan Scandinavians is provided by the graves, which make it possible to study the burial rituals and how they changed. The main contrast is between cremation and inhumation, but both could be practised in the same place and at the same time, as the cemeteries at Valsgärde and Birka show, and traces that survived some cremations suggest that they could be as richly furnished as any inhumation, with boats, fine jewellery, weapons and other equipment. Burials sometimes contained animals that appear to have been sacrificed, and it may be that funerals were occasionally accompanied by rituals that included feasting. The equipment buried in a grave can reasonably be interpreted as provision for the after-life and many Viking graves contained travelling gear, commonly a boat.

Pagan burials were in some respects sacrifices to honour, and perhaps placate, the dead; there may have been a fear that dishonoured dead would not rest, but return to haunt the living. Rich burials imply that some of the dead were greatly honoured, and some may even have been deified. Rimbert reports that some Swedes had begun to build temples and make offerings to a former king, Eric, and that it was even claimed that the gods, 'who owned the land' were prepared to elect him to their company (*VA*, 26). A great mound covering a rich burial, often prominently placed in the landscape, does not prove ancestor worship, but it does suggest some special respect for the dead person, who may well have been claimed as an ancestor by those who later held power in that locality. Title to land was commonly derived from ancestors, and it was not a big step to treat a royal ancestor as one of the gods 'who owned the land'.

Contact with Christianity began to have some effect on Scandinavian paganism long before the conversion was complete. Later runic inscriptions, invoking the blessing of Thor for example, seem to reflect Christian influence and pagan rituals may also have been modified. Icelandic sagas cannot be expected to provide reliable information about paganism; the temples they describe seem to have been modelled on Christian churches and their references to hierarchies of pagan priests and to temple taxes are similarly suspect. Virtually nothing is known about pagan temples beyond the fact that they existed. One has been found at Mære in Trøndelag under the church, but little more can be said about it than that there was a scattering of small pressed-gold plates that look like votive offerings, around four posts which could have supported idols, although they have been interpreted as the base of a 'high-seat'. It is not clear whether there was any building enclosing this place (Lidén, Holmqvist and Olsen, 1969). There is nothing to suggest that temples were large or elaborate structures until the very eve of the Christian conversion. Adam of Bremen's account of the temple at Uppsala is, at best, based on hearsay, and cannot be relied on for detail but it should not be dismissed as pure fantasy; it may be that in the eleventh century some pagans tried to make their temples more magnificent in response to the challenge posed by the Christians and their new churches. At Uppsala the challenge must have been abundantly clear when Adam was writing, for the runic inscriptions in that area show that most, if not all, the landowners were by then Christian.

The first Christian missionary known to have visited Scandinavia was Willibrord, an Englishman who worked mainly in Frisia. Some time about 700 he visited the Danish king, Ongendus but, having no success, returned 'hastily' taking with him thirty boys whom he instructed and baptized. He may have hoped to train them for missionary work among their own people, but for the next century the main preoccupation of the Franks who had supported Willibrord was with their immediate neighbours, the Frisians and the Germans across the Rhine. There may have been some contact between Scandinavians and Christians in the course of trade as early as the eighth century, as there was later, but if so it has left no trace. It was the Frankish conquest of Saxony, completed by 800, that opened the way for direct contact with the Danes, but these contacts were initially military and diplomatic. Charlemagne did not encourage missionary activity beyond the new frontier. It was left to his son, Louis the Pious, to begin the work of conversion as part of his efforts to gain more influence over his turbulent northern neighbours.

The lead was taken by Ebo, archbishop of Rheims, who was appointed legate among the peoples of the north by Pope Paschal II. In 822 he personally undertook missionary work in that part of Denmark controlled by the Frankish protégé, Harald. Harald's later expulsion from Denmark and his failure to re-establish himself there despite Frankish help, was a serious setback, but in compensation a new opportunity was offered in 829, when the emperor received a message from a Swedish king asking for preachers to come to Birka 'because there were many who desired to embrace the Christian faith' (*VA*, 9). Anskar, who had spent two or three years in Harald's entourage, was chosen for the task and travelled to Birka with a companion. They returned after about eighteen months, and were able to report a good beginning, their greatest success being the conversion of Herigar, described as the prefect of Birka, who had not only been baptized, but had also built a church on his own land. Ebo then provided for the continuation of the work in Birka by sending a relative called Gauzbert as bishop, while Anskar was rewarded with a newly-created bishopric at Hamburg. He was also granted a share of Ebo's legatine powers 'among the Swedes, the Danes, the Slavs and other peoples that inhabit the regions of the north' (*VA*, 13).

Anskar's see was poor and exposed to attacks by both Danes and Slavs. His position must have been weakened in 834 when Ebo was deprived of his see, and disgraced for his part in the deposition of Louis in 833. It is therefore not surprising that Anskar at first had little success as a missionary. He does not even seem to have visited the Danish king before 845; perhaps he could not afford to make the kind of generous gifts that such visits demanded (*VA*, 24). All that Rimbert can report from this period is that Anskar,

> Diligently executed the office that had been committed to him in the diocese and the country of the Danes, and by the example of his good life he incited many to embrace the faith. He also began to buy Danish and Slav boys and to redeem them from captivity so that he might train them for God's service. (*VA*, 15)

The year 845 appears to have been disastrous for the missionary effort in the north. Hamburg was attacked by a large fleet led by King Horik, and Anskar's church was destroyed. At about the same time opposition to the mission in Birka flared up violently; one member of the party was killed, and Gauzbert fled to find a safer post as bishop of Osnabrück.

The disasters in fact strengthened Anskar's position; he was granted the bishopric of Bremen in plurality and, with larger resources from that see, was able to embark on a more vigorous mission in Denmark, succeeding in having churches built at Hedeby and Ribe. As Gauzbert refused to return to Birka, Anskar went himself and persuaded the Swedes to allow the mission to continue. He remained on good terms with Ebo, who held the see of Hildesheim from 846 until his death in 851, and some of the priests Anskar later sent to Birka came from Ebo's circle. After Gauzbert's death in 859 he had sole responsibility for missionary activity in the north, and the last known missionary priest sent to work in Birka was, in fact, Anskar's pupil, biographer and successor, Rimbert, although Adam of Bremen reports that Archbishop Unni visited Birka in 936, and died there (i.61–2).

The ninth-century Frankish missions had little or no long-term effect, apart from creating precedents that were important when Scandinavia was finally converted. The claims of the see of Hamburg to primacy throughout the north derived from Anskar's time, and the episcopal sees of Schleswig and Ribe were in places in which Anskar built churches, although not on the same sites. These early missions are, however, better recorded than the later successful ones, and the *Vita Anskarii* in particular provides a remarkable glimpse of the methods of the missionaries, as well as of the Scandinavian world in which they worked.

The claims made by Rimbert are all the more credible for being so modest. No king ruling in ninth-century Scandinavia was converted – Harald never regained power in Denmark after his baptism in 826 – and Anskar's exhortations to King Horic brought him favours, but not the king's conversion. The missionaries in fact had a very limited field of activity, and their only recorded achievements were in the market places of Hedeby, Ribe and Birka. After Ebo's early visit to Denmark, when he is said, perhaps with some exaggeration, to have baptized many converts (*ARF*, 823), there is no evidence of any attempt to evangelize beyond these markets, which were certainly the most promising centres for missionary effort, as they contained Christian slaves and, even more important, merchants who had been converted on their travels. At Hedeby there were 'many who were already Christians and who had been baptized at Dorestad or in Hamburg; some of these were regarded as the leading men of the town; all were delighted that the opportunity had been given to them to practise their Christianity' (*VA*, 24). One of the participants in the debate at Birka about Anskar's request to renew the mission is reported as saying, 'Formerly some of us went to Dorestad and, taking the view that the rule of this religion would benefit us, adopted it of our own free will' (*VA*, 27). The missionaries may have been eager to minister to such people and to convert others, but their royal sponsors seem to have had rather different aims. It was in their interest to encourage Christian merchants to visit their markets and the existence of a church, served by Christian priests, gave visiting Christians some assurance of security. As Rimbert remarked after the church had been built at Hedeby, there was great joy there because,

> People of this race [Saxons] as well as merchants from this district and from Dorestad made for the place readily and without any fear – something which was not possible previously – and at that time there was an abundant supply of goods of every kind. (*VA*, 24)

This may indeed have been the reason for the original invitation to send preachers to Birka. The Danish and Swedish kings with whom Anskar dealt were prepared, even eager, to have Christian churches in their markets, but the *Vita Anskarii* gives no hint of any enthusiasm for a more general mission.

The first conversion of large numbers of Scandinavians was in western Europe. Most of the Scandinavians who settled there in the ninth century, whether as conquerors, colonists or merchants, were soon converted. When Viking leaders came to terms with Christian rulers, they normally accepted baptism, but their conversion was not always permanent. Hincmar complained that converts who reverted to pagan ways were behaving 'like typical Northmen' (*AB*, 876); some were suspected of deliberate insincerity. Weland and his family, for example, were baptized in 862 but he was later accused by two of his men of trickery and he was killed in the duel by which he tried to prove his innocence (*AB*, 863). Viking leaders who were permanently established in Frankia and the British Isles seem to have been converted rather more firmly. One of the early Viking rulers of York, Guthfrith, was not only buried in York Minster, he even gave the community of St Cuthbert the estate at Chester-le-Street on which they lived for more than a century. Guthfrith was indeed regarded by the guardians of St Cuthbert with more favour than the last native kings of Northumbria. The remarkable rarity of Viking burials in England is probably due to their habit of burying their dead in Christian churchyards, but that does not necessarily mean that those Vikings were converted. In Ireland there seems to have been a general change among the invaders, reflected in the words used by contemporary annalists to describe them. In the first half of the ninth century they are commonly called pagans or gentiles, but after 850 such descriptions are rare. There was a resurgence of paganism among the leaders who reconquered Dublin in the early tenth century, but they were in effect a new group. They seem to have been proud to display pagan motifs on the coins they struck in England, but most of them readily co-operated with the archbishops of York, and within thirty years at least three of them had been baptized. Olaf Cuaran, who ruled Dublin from 941 to 980, was not only converted but ended his life at Iona. The situation in Normandy was very similar: Rollo was converted, and soon began to endow churches. Later pagan revolts were led by new arrivals who tried to take advantage of the confusion following the death of William Longsword in 942.

The conversion of Scandinavians who lived in Christian Europe may have had some effect in Scandinavia. Converts returning home might well have lapsed 'like typical Northmen', but their experiences are likely to have left a mark, if only on their pagan beliefs. There is, however, no evidence that a significant number of Scandinavian settlers returned to their homeland. One Norwegian king, Harald Finehair's son Håkon, sometimes called Athelstan's foster-son, had a Christian education in England and there may be some truth in the later tradition that he invited English missionaries to Norway (Birkeli, 1961) but he must have abandoned the new faith for the poem composed in his honour, *Hákonarmál*, treats him as a pagan king.

The first area of Scandinavia to be effectively converted was Denmark. The event is proudly proclaimed on the great stone at Jelling church: 'King Harald had this monument made in memory of his father Gorm and his mother Thyri; this was the Harald who won for himself all Denmark and Norway, and made the Danes Christians.' Harald's own conversion is surrounded in legend (Demidoff, 1973). Ruotger in his *Life of Archbishop Bruno* indicates that it took place between 953 and 965, and Widukind reports that it was the work of a priest called Poppo, later a bishop, who proved the superior power of Christ by carrying a red-hot iron in his bare hand, suffering no harm. Different versions of this miracle appear in various sources, including Adam of Bremen, who makes Poppo convert Eric of Sweden, and Saxo, by whose time a Poppo cult appears to have developed in Denmark. The seven gold plates portraying scenes of this conversion from the altar at Tamdrup in Jutland were made at about that time and probably came from a shrine (Christiansen, 1968). It is at least clear that Harald's conversion was not due to any initiative on the part of the archbishops of Hamburg, otherwise Adam would have been better informed.

German pressure was, however, indirectly responsible. A synod at Ingelheim in 948 was attended, among others, by the bishops of Schleswig, Ribe and Århus, and in 965 Otto I issued a charter freeing the Danish lands of these bishoprics from royal tributes and services. Although Harald was regarded as a tributary king of the Germans, there is no evidence that these bishops ever occupied their sees. Otto's privilege appears to have been intended to safeguard the interests of Hamburg, and these bishoprics were probably created to provide the archbishop with the number of suffragans he needed to maintain his metropolitan status. Bishops who never visited their sees were not unknown at that time. Adam condemns several, but he is still careful to report the fact that they were appointed and consecrated by the archbishop.

Harald was certainly aware of these German moves, and his conversion was probably intended in part to deprive his German overlord of a pretext to invade (Bolin, 1931). Harald also built a church at Jelling and appears to have removed his father's remains from the neighbouring mound and to have interred them there. He also built a church at Roskilde, in which he was probably buried. Harald was overthrown (and probably killed) in a revolt led by his son, Sven Forkbeard. These events, and the history of Sven's reign, are very obscure but through all the confusions the newly-established Church seems to have been securely based, and by the beginning of the eleventh century there were bishoprics in Odense, Roskilde and Lund as well as in Jutland.

Other parts of Scandinavia were less vulnerable to external pressure, but their conversion to Christianity was not much later than that of Denmark. In all areas the lead was taken by rulers; there is no evidence that conversion was ever the result of popular demand. In later tradition three kings are particularly credited with the conversion of Norway and Sweden – in Norway, Olaf Tryggvason and Olaf Haraldsson, later Saint Olaf, and in Sweden, Olaf Skötkonung. The Norwegian Olafs were converted and baptized in western Europe, after careers as Viking leaders, and then returned to Norway with enhanced reputations and great wealth. They had discovered what great advantages Christianity could confer on kings, and only that can explain the extraordinary ferocity with which they evangelized. Their reputation as the men who converted Norway was established very early. Ari Thorgilsson claimed that 'Olaf *rex* Tryggvason brought Christianity to Norway', and Olaf Haraldsson was recognized as a saint throughout the Viking world very soon after his death at Stikklestad in 1030

(Dickins, 1939). The fact that Olaf won his sanctity fighting the forces of Knut, king of the Danes and the English, who was not only a Christian but had been to Rome to pray at the shrines of the Apostles, should serve as a warning that the situation was not a straightforward confrontation between Christians and pagans. It is perhaps even more significant that some of Olaf's opponents in Norway were themselves as devout Christians as himself. One of them, Erling Skjalgsson, a kinsman of Olaf Tryggvason, was described by Snorri as 'the noblest and most powerful of men in Norway, excepting only those of princely rank' and ruled the west of Norway from Sogn Fjord to Lindisness, the southern tip of the country. He joined forces with Knut in 1028 to oppose Olaf, but was defeated in battle and surrendered. He was then struck down by one of Olaf's companions. Snorri put these prophetic words in Olaf's mouth: 'With that blow you have struck Norway out of my hand.' He was right, for Olaf's flight and exile to Russia were the result. Erling's fame and fate were commemorated by a skald, Sigvat, but a more revealing memorial is a runic cross that formerly stood in the heart of his kingdom, close to Stavanger (plate XVI). It was erected by a priest, who called Erling his lord, *dróttin sin* (*NIYR*, 252). Erling, and men like him, played as important a part in the conversion of Norway as did Olaf, and it was indeed in Erling's territory that most of the early Christian crosses were erected (Birkeli, 1973). Olaf owed his sanctity to his death, not to his life, and had Christianity not been so deeply rooted, his merits as a saint would not have been so quickly or so widely recognized.

Erling, like Olaf, may have learned about Christianity during Viking campaigns. Unlike the earlier generation of Vikings, many of these men returned home taking with them some knowledge of the new faith as well as the wealth of England. Ulf of Bårresta is commemorated by the rune stone at Yttergärde as a man who took three gelds in England. It is perhaps more significant that he was a Christian (plate IIIb).

Some of these new Christians realized that they needed priests, and many of these were naturally recruited in England where many conversions had taken place. As a result, towards the end of the tenth century, a number of English missionaries reached Scandinavia, and after Knut's conquest of England there were even more, much to Adam of Bremen's disgust. Many had no permanent base, and even those who were ordained as bishops had no fixed sees at first. The archbishop of Hamburg did his best to assert his metropolitan rights, but he did not always succeed. The extraordinary mobility of these individuals and the difficulty of exercising any control over them is well illustrated by the career of Osmund, an Anglo-Danish priest who died shortly before 1071, and was buried in Ely Abbey. Adam of Bremen gives a fairly full, if hostile, account of his career. He was sent by a Norwegian bishop, Sigfrid, himself an Englishman, to the school at Bremen but 'forgot these kindnesses' and went to Rome for consecration, which was refused. He finally secured consecration from an archbishop of *Polonia*. (This could mean Poland, but is more likely to refer to the land of the Polianians, the territory of Kiev (Arne, 1947).) He then went to Sweden, where he boasted that he had been consecrated archbishop for those parts, but Adam insists that he was *acephalus*, ('headless', that is, without authority). When the archbishop of Hamburg sent legates to the Swedish king 'they found this same vagabond Osmund there, having the cross borne before him after the manner of an archbishop'. They also heard that 'he had by his unsound teaching of our faith corrupted the barbarians, who were still neophytes'. He then persuaded the king not to receive Hamburg's legates on the grounds that they were not apostolically accredited (iii.15). The most satisfactory explanation for Osmund's conduct, and for Adam's attitude to him, seems to be that suggested by Toni Schmid (1934, pp. 61–6) that his Christianity was Byzantine, and that the Swedish king, like Jaroslav of Kiev, was attempting to create a 'national' Church.

Byzantine influence on later Church art, especially on Gotland (Pilz, 1981) is obviously due to the close links that then existed with Russia. There had been direct contact with Byzantium earlier thanks to the Scandinavians who served there in the Varangian guard, and there were also dynastic links between Scandinavian rulers and Kievan princes. The graves of Birka also show clear indications of Byzantine, or at least Kievan, influence (Hägg, 1974), and it may be that Byzantine missionaries played a larger part in the conversion of eastern Scandinavia than is generally recognized. It is even possible that some of them reached Iceland. That is at least one interpretation of Ari's statement that the foreign bishops in Iceland included three *ermskirmen*, apparently meaning Armenians, called Peter, Abraham and Stephen (Fell, 1973).

The conversion of Iceland poses many problems. According to Ari it was brought about by pressure from Olaf Tryggvason on Icelanders visiting Norway. This seems to exaggerate Olaf's power in Norway, and it is not easy to see why Icelanders needed to put themselves at his mercy. There is no reason to doubt that the Icelandic leaders agreed at a meeting of the Althing to accept Christianity, while still allowing some pagan practices, in about the year 1000. The change was made easier because some of the original settlers, perhaps many, had some experience of Christianity, having spent some time in the British Isles before making the journey to Iceland, and it is also possible that some Icelanders took part in the Viking raids of Æthelred's reign. The situation in Iceland was probably very similar to that in other parts of Scandinavia at that time, with missionaries from various places invited by different chieftains. Ari names twelve foreign bishops, or men who 'called themselves bishops'. His claim that all but one of them visited Iceland after the conversion may be correct, but he also insists that several chieftains were baptized before that date, although he does not say by whom. Ari's family and friends dominated the Icelandic Church in his own day and he was naturally eager to emphasize the importance of their ancestors in the conversion. This, combined with his confessed interest in Norwegian kings (p. 14), must have affected his interpretation of those events, and we may reasonably suspect that this interpretation is far from the whole truth.

Christian conversion seems to have led to a drastic reduction in the quantity and variety of grave furnishings, and the fact that there are very few pagan burials with grave goods in southern Norway after the middle of the tenth century may well be a sign of growing Christian influence. There are exceptions, like the little group containing the bodies of a man and two children by a farm near Grimstad in Aust-Agder. Among the grave goods there was a coin of Otto III but such a find only serves to emphasize the general change that had taken place in that area (Rolfsen, 1981).

In eastern Norway and some parts of Sweden pagan customs survived until late into the eleventh century, and perhaps even into the twelfth. Runic inscriptions provide independent information about the spread of the new faith, for many of them commemorate Christians, but only a few refer specifically to the conversion. One of these, on the island of Kuli, in Møre and Romsdal, is decorated with a cross and bears the inscription, 'Raised twelve winters after Christianity was in Norway' (*NIYR*, 449). What date is meant by that is unclear. Another explicit reference to conversion is on a stone from Frösö in Jämtland: 'Östman, Gudfast's son, had this stone raised, and this bridge made, and he had Jämtland Christianized' (von Friesen, 1928, p. 66). Some of the Christian stones are decorated with crosses or include such formulae as 'God and God's mother help his soul in light' or more simply,

'God help his soul'. Some of these stones stood near farms, in old pagan cemeteries or by the side of roads and must have been raised in memory of people who were buried elsewhere in consecrated ground. Old habits died hard and such memorials served as links with the past. Pagan myths and stories about heroes continued to be told, and some that were well adapted to illustrate Christian doctrine were used in decorating churches; the legend of Sigurd, for example, was extraordinarily popular.

The early history of the Church in Scandinavia, especially in Sweden, is, and probably always will be, hidden by a dense growth of legend. It is, however, clear that in all parts of Scandinavia the eleventh century saw the establishment of regular bishoprics, one of which, at Lund, was raised to metropolitan status in 1104. Through these bishoprics a beginning was made with the integration of these missionary churches into the wider structure of western Christendom and canon law. There were, however, no monasteries there before the twelfth century. In the countryside churches were built by landowners and chieftains, sometimes on sites of local importance or even sanctity. Many Scandinavian churches are in fact placed close to prominent burial mounds and at Hørning in Denmark a church was built in the eleventh century on top of a mound that had been raised only a century before (Krogh and Voss, 1961). In such ways the Christian Church adapted itself to, and so preserved, patterns inherited from the pagan past.

10

Conclusion:
kings and pirates

Towards the end of the tenth century our evidence for events in Scandinavia and the Baltic improves. German and English chronicles, runic inscriptions, skaldic poetry and Scandinavian coinages then make it possible to test and supplement the traditions reported by Adam of Bremen and, later, by Icelanders and Norwegians. These sources reveal a confusion of alliances and conflicts involving Slavs as well as Danes, Götar, Norwegians, Swedes and, after 1016, the English as well. The details are often unclear and the evidence contradictory, but there is no doubt that in the century after 950 there were very large fluctuations of power as northern rulers competed to enlarge their resources by placing their neighbours under tribute.

This was not a new pattern. Ninth-century Frankish sources show Danish kings campaigning to assert their power in Norway, other Danes plundering Slavs, and Swedes gathering tribute from Kurland (see pp. 53–4, 77). The power of a ruler depended in large measure on his ability to reward his followers; the loyalty due to an ancient line of kings would not alone sustain a dynasty in power for long. Some ninth-century Scandinavian rulers, such as Godfred, were well placed to take advantage of the trade that passed through their territory and to profit from merchants and market places (p. 73) but for most of them, in the ninth and in the eleventh century, the main source of the wealth they needed came from raids or conquests. As Tacitus remarked, the open-handed generosity of chieftains must have war and plunder to feed it.

It is possible that there were fewer independent rulers in the year 1000 than there had been two centuries earlier, and that some kingdoms had grown larger. That at least appears to have been true in Denmark, where Harald Gormsson's claim to have won all Denmark and Norway is supported, as far as Denmark is concerned, by the imposing structures that he had built at the end of his reign to serve as symbols and centres of royal power at key points in Fyn and Sjælland as well as in Jutland (p. 55). In the early eleventh century there were other symbols of Denmark's unification – royal coins minted at such places as Ribe, Orbæk, Viborg, Roskilde and Lund.

There were other differences between the early and late Viking Age. In the late tenth and eleventh centuries Scandinavian kings led Viking raids, their ninth-century predecessors did not. It also appears that the men who did lead early Viking fleets were unable to gain recognition as rulers in their homelands. Roric and Godfred returned to Denmark in 855 'in the hope of gaining royal power but without success' (*AB*). They, and most other Viking leaders at that time, appear to have been exiles who had to be content with what they could win in Christian Europe or in Russia. Olaf Tryggvason and Olaf Haraldsson were more fortunate, and both became kings of Norway after careers as Viking raiders overseas.

Another important difference was that by the end of the tenth century Scandinavians were no longer able to plunder the riches of Russia. They had been astonishingly successful for a while in the early tenth century in gathering Islamic silver, but after about 970 that source of wealth was closed to them, and Ingvar's belated expedition was widely proclaimed to have been a disaster (p. 32). There were still opportunities in the lands south of the Baltic among the Slavs, who were then becoming richer thanks to the German silver that began to reach that region in large quantities by the end of the century. Some Scandinavians turned to the areas raided by earlier Vikings. Frisia still offered tempting targets: Stavoren was raided in 991, Tiel in 1006 and Utrecht in 1007. According to *Víkingavísur*, Olaf Haraldsson campaigned in Frisia before attacking England, and then fought battles in western France and Spain (p. 33). It was in England that these Vikings found the richest rewards.

The first raids were on a small scale: Southampton was attacked in 980 by seven ships, and the raid of 982 on Portland was made by three, but the fleets were soon much bigger, as the vulnerability of England to such attacks was demonstrated and the English proved able and willing to pay large sums of silver as the price of peace, however temporary. Ninety-three ships raided the south-east in 991 and forced the English to pay £10,000; three years later a similar fleet, led by the same men, failed to take London but extorted an even larger sum, £16,000, by general violence in the surrounding area. One of the leaders of these attacks was the Danish king, Sven Forkbeard, who returned several times; in 1003 he attacked the south coast, and in 1004, East Anglia. He probably also encouraged the raids of 1006–07 and 1009–12, although they were led by others.

The English were forced to recruit Vikings to reinforce their defences, even though they could not be relied on. Sven's brother-in-law, Pallig, was one leader who was generously treated by Æthelred but changed sides in 1001 to join a raiding fleet. In 1012 forty-five ships commanded by Thorkell the Tall agreed to serve Æthelred, and were based in the Thames to protect London. This was a remarkable development, for Thorkell had been the leader of the army that dispersed in 1012 having been paid the unprecedented sum of £48,000.

There were therefore different ways in which a Scandinavian warrior could share England's wealth – by plunder, as tribute, or as payment for service. After Knut had conquered England in 1016 he was able to maintain a regular fleet with the revenue from English taxation. He used this fleet first to ensure his own succession as king in Denmark, and then to further his ambitions in Sweden and in Norway. Like his grandfather, Harald Gormsson, he claimed to have conquered Norway, and coins were minted for him in Sigtuna, but his so-called 'North Sea Empire' was a fragile structure and collapsed on his death in 1035. It was briefly revived in 1040 when Harthaknut, by then king of the Danes, was chosen by the English as their king. They soon regretted that decision for he increased the fleet from the sixteen ships that Knut had normally maintained to sixty-two, and the English had to pay for them.

When Harthaknut died in 1042 the English chose Æthelred's son, Edward, to succeed him. He had spent his years of exile in Normandy and naturally favoured Normans rather than Danes, but the links with Scandinavia were not easily broken. Edward retained a small Scandinavian fleet until 1051 and when, in January 1066, he died childless, his successor Harold Godwinson was challenged by both Harald Hardrada, king of Norway, and William, Duke of Normandy. They both invaded England. The Norwegians were beaten, and their king killed at Stamford Bridge, east of York, on 25 September. Three weeks later William won the Battle of Hastings. The most persistent opposition he had to face was in the Danelaw, where the resistance was reinforced from time to time by the arrival of a Danish fleet in the Humber. William, like Æthelred, had to pay them to leave, but he did more. Castles were built and manned by loyal garrisons, reinforcements were recruited across the Channel when necessary, and some rebellious areas were ruthlessly devastated. A Danish threat to invade in 1085 was taken very seriously by William, who brought,

> A larger force of mounted men and infantry from France and Brittany than had ever come to this country, so that people wondered how this country could maintain all that army. And the king had the army dispersed all over the country . . . and had the land near the sea laid waste, so that if his enemies landed, they should have nothing to seize on so quickly. (*ASC*, 1085)

His enemies did not land, and England was never again threatened by a large-scale Scandinavian attack. It was only in the northern and western Isles, long settled by Norwegians, that Norwegian kings could hope to extend their authority, but Magnus' attempt to do so ended in disaster in 1102.

The Viking leaders of the eleventh century, if not of the tenth, had perhaps a better claim than their predecessors of the early Viking Age to be considered kings rather than pirates, in St Augustine's terms, for they were Christians. They had an even better claim as the commanders of large fleets. The temptation to treat Knut as an emperor is strong, but that title has little more basis than that acknowledged by St Augustine. He had a large fleet and used it to molest the world. But even the most successful of these kings of the north could not effectively control the whole of their kingdoms. There were still opportunities for men with little ships, or few. Some were adventurers, outlaws who could at least be licensed like the pirates of Öresund (p. 39), if they could not be suppressed. Others, however, were men like Erling Skjalgsson, Ingvar or Sibbi the Wise, son of Foldar, who are likely to have been as proud of their ancestry as any man. Royal power had developed greatly in some parts of Scandinavia during the Viking Age but we must not be misled by the propagandists of the twelfth and thirteenth centuries into supposing that power in eleventh-century Scandinavia was exclusively in the hands of the men later generations recognized as the kings of the Danes, Norwegians or Swedes. In the eleventh century, as in the ninth, there were many others, like Östman who converted Jämtland, who had claims to be considered kings by their subjects, if not by their increasingly powerful overlords.

Bibliographical note

This note has two main purposes: to supplement the references given in the text and to serve as a guide for further reading.

General

The best introduction to the whole subject is Musset (1971). The most substantial recent narrative survey, Jones (1968), puts particular emphasis on the literary evidence. Foote and Wilson (1970) is useful as an introduction in English to many topics that are otherwise only discussed in Scandinavian languages. There are several short, general surveys that concentrate on the archaeological evidence, for example Arbman (1961) and Wilson (1980). Graham-Campbell (1980b) has contributions by specialists on ships, runes and religion. Almgren (1966), also by several authors, is lavishly illustrated. Articles in *KHL* are the best guide to most topics and generally have good bibliographies.

Sources

The Frankish and Ottonian sources are fully treated in Wattenbach–Holtzmann (1938–9), Wattenbach–Levison (1953–73) and Molinier (1902); the English in *EHD*; and the Irish in Hughes (1972). Obolensky (1970) is a short introduction to the Byzantine evidence. Most of the Islamic texts are mentioned, and the relevant passages translated into Norwegian by Birkeland (1954).

Turville-Petre (1953) is a good general introduction to the Icelandic texts. *Íslendingabók* and *Landnámabók* are both edited by Benedikts-son (1968). There are translations of *Íslendingabók* by Hermannsson (1930) and Jones (1964, pp. 101–13). One version of *Landnámabók* has been translated by Pálsson and Edwards (1972) and passages from several versions by Jones (1964, pp. 114–42). *Landnámabók* was discussed by Benediktsson (1969) before Rafnsson (1974) challenged many of the assumptions made about it. For more recent comments see Benediktsson (1976; 1978). Magnusson and Pálsson have translated several Icelandic sagas including; *Njála* (1960), *Laxdœla* (1969), *Grœnlendiga* and *Eiriks* (1965). Other translations include *Egils Saga* by Fell (1975), *Heimskringla* by Hollander (1964) and *Sturlunga Saga* by McGrew and Thomas (1970; 1974). The first volume of a translation of *Grágás* by Dennis, Foote and Perkins has been published (1980). Skaldic poetry is discussed and some is translated by Turville-Petre (1976). Frank (1978) is an illuminating discussion of some of the main themes of this poetry.

These, and many other sources, are discussed in *KHL*. Particular attention is drawn here to editions or translations of texts that figure prominently in this book. The *Frankish Royal Annals* are translated by Scholz (1970) and one of their continuations, the *Annals of St Bertin*, edited by Grat, Vielliard and Clémencet (1964) has been discussed recently by Nelson (1981); her unpublished translation is used here. The *Vita Anskarii* and Adam of Bremen's *Gesta Hammaburgensis Ecclesiae Pontificum* are both edited and translated into German in Trillmich and Buchner (1961). Adam of Bremen is translated into English by Tschan (1959). The *Vita Anskarii* is translated by Robinson (1921), but the version used here is from the forthcoming edition by Ian Moxon and myself. The first nine books of Saxo Grammaticus' *Gesta Danorum* have been translated and discussed by Davidson and Fisher (1979; 1980) and the last seven books by Christiansen (1980b; 1981). *Gutasagan* is translated into modern Swedish by Holmbäck and Wessén (1943) but a very different view of that work is put forward by Sjöholm (1977). One version of the *Russian Primary Chronicle* has been translated by Cross and Sherbowitz-Wetzor (1953). The discussion of the treaties in that text by Sorlin (1961) is particularly helpful. Constantine Porphyrogenitus' *De Administrando Imperio* is edited and translated by Moravcsik and Jenkins (1949) and a full commentary is edited by Jenkins (1962). The full text of Ibn Fadlan is translated into French by Canard (1958).

The best introduction to the runic inscriptions of the Viking Age is by Musset and Mossé (1965). Ruprecht (1958) is a detailed study of the inscriptions that mention Scandinavians who went overseas. These are also discussed, more briefly but more critically, by Liestøl (1970). Liestøl's discussion of the Forsa Ring (1979) underlines the difficulty of dating and interpreting some inscriptions. Thompson's discussion

(1975) of the stones carved by one rune master, Asmund, is the most important and critical modern study of any part of the Swedish material.

Malmer (1968) is a comprehensive general survey of the Scandinavian numismatic evidence. Malmer (1966) is the fundamental work on Scandinavian coinages before the year 1000. Skaare (1976) deals very thoroughly with the Viking Age coins in Norway, while Bendixen (1980) briefly indicates ways in which the classic work of Hauberg (1900) on early Danish coinage is being revised. Swedish coin hoards are being systematically published in *CNS*, but only three volumes have so far appeared, and the work will not be completed for many years. In the meantime Hatz (1974) on the hoards containing German coins is of great value. The Islamic coins found in Russia are dealt with by Ianin (1956) whose lists have been brought up to date for the ninth century by Noonan (1981). Islamic coins in Finland are discussed by Granberg (1966). Noonan (1977–8) has also listed and discussed the dirham hoards in the Baltic states. His paper on the early dirham imports into Russia (1980a) is of the greatest importance for the interpretation of the Scandinavian activity in Russia. Recent work on the coinage of Viking Scandinavia is well represented in the papers edited by Blackburn and Metcalf (1981) which give full references to the current literature. Dolley (1965) is a short but authoritative account of the Viking coinages in the British Isles.

Olsen (1928) is a classic study of early Scandinavian society based on the evidence of place names. A more recent contribution on this topic is by Hald (1969), who is also responsible for the standard work on Danish place names (1965). The interpretation of these names is fully discussed by Dalberg and Kousgård Sørensen (1972; 1979) and some of their conclusions are summarized in English by Kousgård Sørensen (1979). Ståhl (1970) and Pamp (1974) are elementary introductions to the vast literature on Swedish place names. Excellent examples of attempts to use place-name evidence to elucidate economic and social developments are provided by Hellberg (1967; 1979; 1980) on Kumla, the Kalmar district and Åland, and by Olsson (1979) on Gotland. District names are discussed by Kousgård Sørensen (1978) and by Andersson (1965; 1974; 1981), and the Swedish literature on this topic is listed by Westberg (1978).

Place names are one of the main sources for the study of Scandinavian settlement overseas. The literature on the English evidence is reviewed by Fellows Jensen (1975). Since then there have been contributions to the discussion by Gelling (1978), Lund (1981) and by Fellows Jensen herself (1978; 1980; 1981). The Scottish names have been discussed by Nicolaisen (1976; 1981) and by Fellows Jensen (1982; forthcoming a). Davey (1978) on the Isle of Man contains contributions that, taken together, show how misleading place-name evidence can be. Scandinavian names in Normandy have been discussed by Musset (1959; 1978) and by Adigard des Gautries (1954). Fellows Jensen (1979) is a helpful, short comparison of the Scandinavian names in Normandy and the Danelaw.

The literature on archaeological investigations is vast and references to publications on specific topics and sites are given elsewhere. Attention should however be drawn here to two exhibition catalogues, Graham–Campbell (1980a) and Roesdahl *et al.* (1981). Some of the greatest advances have been made in the study of ships and seamanship. The evolution of Viking Age ships is now relatively well understood (Crumlin–Pedersen, 1981). Much has been learned by sailing replicas (Binns, 1980) or later types of boat that were of similar design (Nordlandsbåden, 1980).

Scandinavia

Apart from studies of mythology and religion, for example Turville–Petre (1964), there have been very few attempts to deal with Scandinavia as a whole. Phillpotts (1913) on kinship and, more generally, Foote and Wilson (1970) are notable exceptions. Most studies concentrate on particular countries. The most recent general history of Denmark in the Viking period is by Skovgaard Petersen (1977), the archaeological and historical evidence for early Danish society is surveyed by Jensen (1979) and by Lund and Hørby (1980), while Roesdahl (1980) concentrates on the archaeology of Viking Denmark. The best work on early Swedish history is still Hildebrand (1879–1954). He had a remarkable command of the evidence available when he wrote. Rosén (1962a) is the fullest modern treatment of medieval Swedish history. The archaeology of Sweden is surveyed by Stenberger (1979), a work that shows how unevenly distributed the Swedish archaeological effort has been, the main areas that have been investigated being Svealand, Gotland, Öland and Skåne. Norway is well served by Andersen's excellent survey (1977) of both the source material and the historiography of early Norway. Norwegian archaeology is discussed by Hagen

Bibliographical note

(1967) and by Magnus and Myhre (1976). Kivikoski (1973) is the best treatment of the Finnish material.

Jóhannesson (1974) is the most detailed survey of early Icelandic history but Meulengracht Sørensen (1977) can be recommended as a most stimulating discussion of the same topic. The archaeological evidence for early Iceland is discussed by Eldjárn (1956). Krogh (1967) is an excellent introduction to the Scandinavian settlement of Greenland. Dahl (1970) and Thorsteinsson (1981) are the best introductions, in English, to the Faroese evidence.

Western Europe

Viking activity in ninth-century Frankia is very fully discussed by Vogel (1906) and in even greater detail, but for a shorter period, in a series of articles by Lot that have been reprinted in his collected works (1970). Musset has elucidated the early history of Normandy (1970; 1975). Smyth's attempts (1975; 1977; 1979) to deal with Scandinavian activity throughout the British Isles has provoked much criticism but also some support, notably from Wormald (1982). Stenton (1971) remains an important work of reference for Scandinavian activity in England. The best introductions to the role of Scandinavians in Ireland and Scotland are by Ó Corráin (1972) and Duncan (1975).

Russia

A great deal has been written about Scandinavian activity in the east, and there are several helpful contributions in English. Schmidt (1970) can now be supplemented by the survey by Dejevsky (1977). An article by Avdusin (1969) provoked a lively discussion with particularly illuminating contributions by Bulkin (1973) and by Lebedev and Nazarenko (1973).

Scandinavian Settlements

Viking period settlements have been thoroughly surveyed in some parts of Scandinavia; in Mälardalen by Ambrosiani (1964), and Hyenstrand (1974; 1981), in Skåne by Strömberg (1961), and in Fyn by Grøngaard Jeppesen (1981). The evidence for northern Norway is surveyed by Sjøvold (1974). Carlsson (1979) draws attention to some interesting features of settlement in Viking Gotland. A number of

153

settlements have been thoroughly investigated, especially in Denmark; see Becker (1979). Most attention has, however, been paid to market places and early towns. The classic work on Hedeby is Jankuhn (1963), but his conclusions are being greatly modified by the more recent excavations, whose results are being reported in the *Berichte über die Ausgrabungen in Haithabu,* edited by Kurt Schietzel, sixteen of which have so far appeared. Stolpe's excavations in Birka have not yet been fully published. The grave finds were published by Arbman (1940; 1943), the burial customs discussed by Gräslund (1980), the pottery by Selling (1955) and the textiles by Geijer (1938), but on these now see Hägg (1974) and Geijer (1979). The recent small excavation of part of the harbour at Birka is reported by Ambrosiani *et al.* (1973). The definitive publication of the Kaupang excavations has begun with Blindheim *et al.* (1981), but the earlier interim reports, for example Blindheim (1969, 1975), will remain an important source of information about this site for some time.

Bibliography

Abbreviations are listed on p. viii.

Abrahamowicz, Z. (1970) 'The expressions "Fish-tooth" and "Lion-fish" in Turkish and Persian', *Folia Orientalia* 12, pp. 25–32.

Adigard des Gautries, J. (1954) *Les noms de personnes scandinaves en Normandie de 911 à 1066*, Lund.

Almgren, B. (ed.) (1966) *The Viking*, London.

Ambrosiani, B. (1964) *Fornlämningar och bebyggelse. Studier i Attundalands och Södertörns förhistoria*, Stockholm.

Ambrosiani, B. *et al.* (1973) *Birka. Svarta jordens hamnområde. Arkeologisk undersökning 1970–71* (Riksantikvarieämbetet rapport C 1), Stockholm.

Ambrosiani, K. (1981) *Viking Age Combs, Comb making and Comb makers in the Light of Finds from Birka and Ribe*, Stockholm.

Andersen, H. H., Madsen, H. J. and Voss, O. (1976) *Danevirke*, 2 vols, København.

Andersen, P. S. (1977) *Samlingen av Norge og Kristningen av Landet 800–1130*, Oslo.

Andersson, T. (1965) *Svenska Häradsnamn*, Lund.

Andersson, T. (1974) 'Hæraþ und Hundare. Zwei Bezeichnungen nordischer Bezirke in alter Zeit', *Actes du XIe Congrès International des Sciences Onomastiques*, Sofia, pp. 41–9.

Andersson, T. (1981) 'Siedlungsgemeinschaften im mittelalterlichen Uppland beleuchtet durch die Bezirknamen', *Collected Papers Presented at the Permanent European Conference for the Study of the Rural Landscape held at Roskilde, Denmark, 3–9 June 1979*, Hansen, V. (ed.) Copenhagen, pp. 85–92.

Andersson, T. and Sandred, K. I. (eds) (1978) *The Vikings. Proceedings of the Symposium of the Faculty of Arts of Uppsala University 6–9 June 1977*, Uppsala.

Annals of Fulda (1891), Kurze, F. (ed.) Hanover.

Annals of Ulster, Hennessy, W. H. (ed.) (1887–93), Dublin.

Arbman, H. (1940; 1943), *Birka I: Die Gräber*, 2 vols, Uppsala.

Arbman, H. (1961) *The Vikings*, London.

Arne, T. J. (1947) 'Bishop Osmund', *Fornvännen* 42, pp. 54–6.

Arwidsson, G. (1942) *Vendelstile. Email und Glas im 7.-8. Jahrhundert*, Uppsala.

Arwidsson, G. (1977) *Valsgärde 7*, Uppsala.

Arwidsson, G. (1978) 'Viking Society in Central Sweden. Traditions, Organization and Economy', in Andersson and Sandred (1978) pp. 154–60.

Avdusin, D. A. (1969) 'Smolensk and the Varangians according to the Archaeological Data', *NAR* 2, pp. 52–62.

Bailey, R. N. (1980) *Viking Age Sculpture in Northern England*, London.

Bakka, E. (1965) 'Ytre Moa. Eit gardsanlegg frå vikingtida i Årdal i Sogn', *Viking* 29, pp. 121–45.

Bakka, E. (1971) 'Scandinavian trade relations with the Continent and the British Isles in pre-Viking times', *Early Medieval Studies* (Antikvariskt Arkiv 40), Stockholm, pp. 37–51.

Bannerman, J. (1974) *Studies in the History of Dalriada*, Edinburgh.

Barrow, G. W. S. (1973) *The Kingdom of the Scots*, London.

Bately, J. (1980) *The Old English Orosius*, London.

Beck, C. W. (1970) 'Amber in Archaeology', *Archaeology* 23, pp. 7–11.

Becker, C. J. (1979) 'Viking-age settlements in western and central Jutland. Recent excavations. Introductory remarks', *AA* 50, pp. 89–94.

Beckwith, J. (1972) *Ivory Carvings in Early Medieval England*, London.

Bencard, M. (ed.) (1981) *The Ribe Excavations 1970–76*, 1, Esbjerg.

Bencard, M. *et al.* (1978) 'Wikingerzeitliches Handwerk in Ribe. Eine Übersicht', *AA* 49, pp. 113–38.

Bendixen, K. (1974) 'The first Merovingian coin-treasure from Denmark', *Medieval Scandinavia* 7, pp. 85–101.

Bendixen, K. (1978) 'Møntcirkulation i Danmark fra Vikingetid til Valdemarssønnerne', *ANOH*, pp. 155–90.

Bendixen, K. (1981) 'Sceattas and other coin finds', in Bencard (1981), pp. 63–101.

Benediktsson, J. (ed.) (1968) *Íslendingabók Landnámabók*, Reykjavík.

Benediktsson, J. (1969) 'Landnámabók', SBVS 17, pt 4, pp. 275–92.

Benediktsson, J. (1976) Review of Rafnsson (1974), in SBVS 19, pts 2–3, pp. 311–18.

Benediktsson, J. (1978) 'Some problems in the history of the settlement of Iceland', in Andersson and Sandred (1978), pp. 161–5.

Binchy, D. A. (1962) 'The passing of the old order', in The Impact of the Scandinavian Invasions on the Celtic-Speaking Peoples, c.800 –1000 A.D., B. Ó Cuív, B. (ed.) Dublin, pp. 119–32.

Binchy, D. A. (1943) 'The Linguistic and historical value of the Irish law tracts', Proceedings of the British Academy 29, pp. 195–227.

Binns, A. (1980) Viking Voyagers. Then and Now, London.

Biornstad, M. (1966) 'Spångas förhistoria', in Spånga Sockens Historia, Stockholm, pp. 1–81.

Birkeland, H. (1954) Nordens historie i middelalderen etter arabiske kilder. (Skrifter utg. av det Norske Videnskaps-Akademi i Oslo. II Hist.-filos. kl. 2), Oslo.

Birkeli, F. (1961) 'Hadde Håkon Adalsteinsfostre likevel en biskop Sigfrid hos seg?', Historisk Tidsskrift (Oslo) 40, pp. 113–36.

Birkeli, F. (1973) Norske Steinkors i tidlig Middelalder (Skrifter utg. av det Norske Videnskaps-Akademi i Oslo. II Hist.-filos. kl., ny serie, 10), Oslo.

Bjørkvik, H. (1965) 'Leiglending', KHL 10, cols 460–2.

Bjørkvik, H. (1969) 'Rektegn', KHL 14, cols 35–7.

Bjørkvik, H. et al. (1965) 'Leidang', KHL 10, cols 432–59.

Blackburn, M. A. S. and Metcalf, D. M. (eds) (1981), Viking-Age Coinage in the Northern Lands (BAR Int. Ser. 122), Oxford.

Blindheim, C. (1969) 'Kaupangundersökelsene avsluttet', Viking 33, pp. 5–39.

Blindheim, C. (1975) 'Kaupang by Viksfjord, I and II', in Herteig, A. E., Lidén, H. E. and Blindheim, C. Archaeological Contributions to the Early History of Urban Communities in Norway, Oslo.

Blindheim, C., Heyerdahl-Larsen, B. and Tollnes, R. (1981) Kaupang-Funnene I, Oslo.

Blok, D. P. (1978) 'Die Wikingen in Friesland', Naamkunde 10, pp. 25–47.

Blok, D. P. (1979) Die Franken in Nederland, 3rd edn, Bussum.

Blomqvist, R. (1951) Lunds Historia. I Medeltiden, Lund.

Bøe, A. (1965) 'Lendmann', KHL 10, cols 498–505.

Bøe, A. and Lárusson, M. M. (1965) 'Leysingi', KHL 10, cols 521–26.

Bolin, S. (1931) 'Danmark och Tyskland under Harald Gormsson.

Grundlinjer i dansk historia under 900-talet', *Scandia* 4, pp. 184 –209.

Brøgger, A. W. (1916) *Borrefundet og Vestfoldkongernes Graver* (Skrifter udg. af Videnskabsselskabet i Christiania. II Hist.-filos. kl. 1916 no. 1).

Brooks, N. (1971) 'The development of military obligations in eighth- and ninth-century England', in *England before the Conquest, Studies in Primary Sources Presented to Dorothy Whitelock*, Clemoes, P. and Hughes, K. (eds) Cambridge, pp. 69–84.

Brooks, N. (1979) 'England in the ninth century: the crucible of defeat', *Transactions of the Royal Historical Society*, fifth series, 29, pp. 1–20.

Bulkin, V. A. (1973) 'On the classification and interpretation of archaeological material from the Gnezdovo cemetery', *NAR* 6, pp. 10–13.

Bulkin, V. A. (1975) 'Bol'shie kurgany Gnezduskogo mogil'nika', *Skandinavskij sbornik* 20, pp. 134–46.

Byrne, F. J. (1971) 'Tribes and tribalism in early Ireland', *Ériu* 22, pp. 128–66.

Campbell, A. (ed.) (1949) *Encomium Emmae Reginae*, London.

Canard, M. (1958) 'La relation du voyage d'Ibn Fadlan chez les Bulgares de la Volga', *Annales de l'institut d'etudes orientales. Alger* 16, pp. 41–145.

Carlsson, D. (1979) *Kulturlandskapets utveckling på Gotland. En studie av jordbruks – och bebyggelseförändringar under järnåldern*, Visby.

Carlsson, G. (1961) 'Historieskrivning. Sverige och Finland', *KHL* 6, cols 587–91.

Chesnutt, M. (1981) 'Afterword' to Ross (1940).

Christensen, A. E. (1969) *Vikingetidens Danmark paa oldhistorisk baggrund*, København.

Christensen, A. E. (1974) 'Birka-Hedeby myntene som kilde til skipets historie på 800-tallet', in *Norsk Sjøfartsmuseum 1914–1964*, Oslo, pp. 7–12.

Christiansen, E. (1980) *The Northern Crusades. The Baltic and the Catholic Frontier 1100–1525*, London.

Christiansen, E. (1980a; 1981) *Saxo Grammaticus Books x–xvi* (BAR, Int. ser. 84, 118), Oxford.

Christiansen, T. E. (1968) 'De gyldne Altre 1. Tamdrup-pladerne', *ÁNOH*, pp. 153–205.

Bibliography

Clarke, H. (ed.) (1979) *Iron and Man in Prehistoric Sweden*, Stockholm.

Craigie, W. A. (1897) 'The Gaels in Iceland', *Proceedings of the Society of Antiquaries of Scotland* 31, pp. 247–64.

Crawford, I. A. (1981) 'War or peace. Viking colonization in the Northern and Western Isles of Scotland', *Viking Congress VIII*, pp. 259–69.

Cross, S. H. and Sherbowitz-Wetzor, O. P. (1953) *The Russian Primary Chronicle. Laurentian Text*, Cambridge, Mass.

Crumlin-Pedersen, O. (1978a) 'The Ships of the Vikings', in Andersson and Sandred (1978), pp. 32–41.

Crumlin-Pedersen, O. (1978b) *Søvejen til Roskilde*, Roskilde.

Crumlin-Pedersen, O. (1981), 'Skibe på Havbunden: Vragfund i danske farvande fra perioden 600–1400', *Handels og Søfartsmuseets Årbog*, Kronborg, pp. 28–65.

Dahl, S. (1970) 'The Norse Settlement of the Faroe Islands', *Medieval Archaeology* 14, pp. 60–73.

Dalberg (formerly Christensen), V. and Kousgård Sørensen, J. (1972; 1979) *Stednavneforskning*, 2 vols, Kobenhavn.

Davey, P. (ed.) (1978) *Man and Environment in the Isle of Man*, (BAR British ser. 54(ii)), Oxford.

Davidan, O. I. (1970) 'Contacts between Staraja Ladoga and Scandinavia', in Schmidt (1970), pp. 79–94.

Davidson, H. E. and Fisher, P. (1979; 1980) *Saxo Grammaticus. The History of the Danes, Books i–ix*, 2 vols, Cambridge.

Dejevsky, N. J. (1977) 'The Varangians in Soviet archaeology today', *Mediaeval Scandinavia* 10, pp. 7–34.

Demidoff, L. (1973) 'The Poppo Legend', *Mediaeval Scandinavia* 6, pp. 39–67.

Dennis, A., Foote, P. and Perkins, R. (1980) *Laws of Early Iceland I*, Winnipeg.

De Vries, J. (1928) 'Die Entwicklung der Sage von den Lodbrokssöhnen in den historischen Quellen', *Arkiv för Nordisk Filologi* 44, pp. 117–63.

Dhondt, J. (1962) 'Les problèmes de Quentovic', *Studi in Onore di Amintore Fanfani* i, Milan, pp. 183–248.

Dickins, B. (1939) 'The cult of St Olave in the British Isles', *SBVS* 12, pt 2, pp. 53–80.

Dolley, M. (1965) *Viking Coins of the Danelaw and of Dublin*, London.

Dolley, R. H. M. (1966) *The Hiberno-Norse coins in the British Museum*, London.

Douglas, D. (1947) 'The Rise of Normandy', *Proceedings of the British Academy* 33, pp. 101–31.

Douglas, M. (1978) *Sigtuna* (Medeltidsstaden 6) Stockholm.

Dumville, D. N. (1977) 'Kingship, genealogies and regnal lists', in *Early Medieval Kingship*, Sawyer, P. H. and Wood, I. N. (eds) Leeds, pp. 72–104.

Duncan, A. A. M. (1975) *Scotland. The Making of the Kingdom*, Edinburgh.

Dunlop, D. M. (1954) *The History of the Jewish Khazars*, Princeton.

Eck, A. (1933) *Le Moyen age russe*, Paris.

Eckstein, D. and Schietzel, K. (1977) 'Zur dendrochronologischen Gliederung und Datierung der Baubefunde von Haithabu', *Berichte über die Ausgrabungen in Haithabu*, 11, pp. 141–64.

Eggers, H.-J. (1951) *Der Römische Import im freien Germanien*, Hamburg.

Ehrhardt, H. (1977) *Der Stabreim in altnordischen Rechtstexten*, Heidelberg.

Eldjárn, K. (1956) *Kuml og haugfé ur heiðnum sið á Íslandi*, Akureyri.

Eldjárn, K. (1961) 'Bær í Gjáskógum í Thjórsárdal', *Árbok hins íslenzka fornleifafélags*, pp. 7–46.

Ettinghausen, R. (1950) *Studies in Muslim Iconography I. The Unicorn* (Freer Gallery of Art, Occasional Paper 1, no. 3), Washington D.C.

Farrell, R. T. (ed.) (1982) *Viking Civilization; contributions . . . from the Cornell Viking Series 1980*, London.

Fell, C. E. (1973) 'A note on Pálsbók', *Mediaeval Scandinavia* 6, pp. 102–8.

Fell, C. E. (1975) *Egils Saga*, London.

Fell, C. E. (1981) 'Víkingavísur', *Speculum Norroenum*, pp. 106–22.

Fellows Jensen, G. (1972) *Scandinavian Settlement Names in Yorkshire*, Copenhagen.

Fellows Jensen, G. (1975) 'The Vikings in England: a review', *Anglo-Saxon England*, 4, 181–206.

Fellows Jensen, G. (1978) *Scandinavian Settlement Names in the East Midlands*, Copenhagen.

Fellows Jensen, G. (1979) 'Viking settlement in Normandy. The place-name evidence as seen from the Danelaw', *Souvenir Normand*, pp. 15–24.

Fellows Jensen, G. (1980) 'Conquests and the place names of England, with special reference to the Viking settlements', *Norna-Rapporter* 17, pp. 192–209.

Fellows Jensen, G. (1981) 'Scandinavians settlement in the Danelaw in the light of the place names of Denmark', *Viking Congress VIII*, pp. 133–45.

Fellows Jensen, G. (1982) 'Viking Settlement in the northern and western isles – the place-name evidence as seen from Denmark and the Danelaw', *Northern and Western Isles in the Viking World. Survival Continuity and Change*, Fenton, A. and Pálsson, H. (eds), Edinburgh.

Fellows Jensen, G. (forthcoming a) 'Scandinavian settlement in Cumbria and Dumfriesshire: the place-name evidence', *The Scandinavians in Cumbria*, Whyte, I. and Baldwin, J. (eds).

Fellows Jensen, G. (forthcoming b) 'Scandinavian settlement in the Isle of Man and north-west England; the place-name evidence', *Proceedings of the Ninth Viking Congress, 1981*.

Foote, P. (1975) 'Træl', *KHL* 19, cols 13–19.

Foote, P. (1978) 'Wrecks and Rhymes', in Andersson and Sandred, pp. 57–66.

Foote, P. and Wilson, D. M. (1970) *The Viking Achievement*, London.

Foster, C. W. and Longley, T. (eds.) (1924) *The Lincolnshire Domesday and the Lindsey Survey*, Lincoln Record Society.

Fox, R. (1967) *Kinship and Marriage*, Harmondsworth.

Frank, R. (1978) *Old Norse Court Poetry. The Dróttkvætt Stanza*, Ithaca.

Frank, R. (1981) 'Snorri and the mead of poetry', *Speculum Norroenum*, pp. 155–70.

Frye, R. N. (ed.) (1975) *The Cambridge History of Iran*, vol. 4, Cambridge.

Gallén, J. (1958) 'Kring det s.k. Florensdokumentet från omkring år 1120', *Historisk Tidskrift för Finland* 43, pp. 1–26.

Ganshof, F. L. (1962) 'A propos du tonlieu sous les mérovingiens' *Studi in onore di Amintore Fanfani*, 1, Milan, pp. 291–315.

Geijer, A. (1938) *Birka III. Die Textilfunde aus den Gräbern*, Uppsala.

Geijer, A. (1979) 'The Textile Finds from Birka. *Birka III, Die Textilfunde aus den Gräbern*, revised by the author', *AA* 50, pp. 209–22.

Gelling, M. (1978) *Signposts to the Past*, London.

Gibson, M. and Nelson, J. (eds) (1981) *Charles the Bald: Court and*

Kingdom. Papers based on a Colloquium held in London in April 1979 (BAR, International Series 101), Oxford.

Gillingham, J. (1981) 'Ademar of Chabannes and the history of Aquitaine in the reign of Charles the Bald', in Gibson and Nelson, pp. 3–14.

Goedheer, A. J. (1938) *Irish and Norse Traditions about the Battle of Clontarf*, Haarlem.

Gordon, B. (1963) 'Some Norse place-names in Trotternish, Isle of Skye', *Scottish Gaelic Studies* 10, pp. 82–112.

Gräslund, A.-S. (1980) *Birka IV. The Burial Customs. A Study of the Graves on Björkö*, Stockholm.

Gräslund, B. (1973) 'Äring, näring, pest och salt', *Tor* 15, pp. 174–93.

Graham-Campbell, J. (1980a) *Viking Artefacts. A Select Catalogue*, London.

Graham-Campbell, J. (1980b) *The Viking World*, London.

Granberg, B. (1966) *Förteckning över Kufiska Myntfynd i Finland* (Studia Orientalia 34), Helsinki.

Granlund, J. (1958) 'Disting', *KHL* 3, cols 112–15.

Granlund, J. (1972) 'Storfamilj', *KHL* 17, cols 230–6.

Grat, F., Vielliard, J. and Clémencet, S. (eds) (1964) *Annales Bertiniani*, Paris.

Grierson, P. (1981) 'The *Gratia Dei Rex* coinage of Charles the Bald', in Gibson and Nelson, pp. 39–51.

Grøngaard Jeppesen, T. (1981) *Middelalderlandsbyens Opståen* (Fynske Studier 11), Odense.

Grøtvedt, P. N. (1965) 'Sårbøter og Drapsbøter i brev fra Norsk Senmiddelalder', *Historisk Tidsskrift* (Oslo) 44, pp. 105–40.

Hårdh, B. (1976a) *Wikingerzeitliche Depotfunde aus Südschweden. Katalog und Tafeln*, Lund.

Hårdh, B. (1976b) *Wikingerzeitliche Depotfunde aus Südschweden. Probleme und Analysen*, Lund.

Hårdh, B. (1978) 'Trade and money in Scandinavia in the Viking Age', *MLUHM*, new ser. 2, pp. 157–71.

Hägg, I. (1974) *Kvinnodräkten i Birka. Livplaggens Rekonstruktion på Grundval av det Arkeologiska Materialet* (Aun 2), Uppsala.

Hafström, G. (1949) *Ledung och Marklandsindelning*, Uppsala.

Hafström, G. (1957) 'Bordsrätt', *KHL* 2, cols 509–12.

Hagberg, U. E. (1967) *The Archaeology of Skedemosse. II The Votive Deposits in the Skedemosse Fen and their Relation to the Iron-Age Settlement on Öland, Sweden*, Stockholm.

Bibliography

Hagen, A. (1967) *Norges Oldtid*, Oslo.

Hald, K. (1933) 'Om rekkr og höldr i danske stednavne', *Danske Folkemaal* 7, pp. 73–80.

Hald, K. (1965) *Vore Stednavne*, 2nd edn, København.

Hald, K. (1969) *Stednavne og Kulturhistorie*, 2nd edn, København.

Hall, R. (1981) 'Markets of the Danelaw', in Roesdahl *et al.*, pp. 95–9.

Hallberg, P. (1978) 'The ship – reality and image in Old Norse poetry', in Andersson and Sandred, pp. 42–56.

Hasselberg, G. *et al.* (1957) 'Böter', *KHL* 2, cols 519–37.

Hatz, G. (1974) *Handel und Werkehr zwischen dem Deutschen Reich und Schweden in der späten Wikingerzeit. Die deutschen Münzen des 10. und 11. Jahrhunderts in Schweden*, Stockholm.

Hauberg, P. (1900) *Myntforhold og Udmyntninger i Danmark indtil 1146*, Kjøbenhavn.

Hedager, L. (1979) 'Processes towards State formation in Early Iron Age Denmark' in *New Directions in Scandinavian Archaeology*, Kristiansen, K. and Paludan–Müller, C. (eds) Lyngby, pp. 217–23.

Helgö I–VI, Holmqvist W. *et al.* (1961–81) *Excavations at Helgö*, 6 vols, Stockholm.

Hellberg, L. (1967) *Kumlabygden III. Ortnamn och Äldre Bebyggelse*, Kumla.

Hellberg, L. (1978) 'Schwedische Ortnamnen und altwestnordische Dichtersprache', in Andersson and Sandred, pp. 67–77.

Hellberg, L. (1979) 'Forn-Kalmar. Ortnamnen och stadens förhistoria', *Kalmar Stads Historia* I, Hammarström, I. (ed.) Kalmar, pp. 119–66.

Hellberg, L. (1980) *Ortnamnen och den Svenska Bosättningen på Åland* (Ortnamn och samhälle 2), Uppsala.

Hemmer, R. (1969) 'Yngre straff – och processrättsliga stadganda i Dalalagen', *Tidskrift utgiven av Juridiska föreningen i Finland* 150, pp. 29–60.

Hermannsson, H. (1930) *The Book of the Icelanders (Íslendingabók) by Ari Thorgilsson*, Ithaca.

Hildebrand, H. (1879–1954) *Sveriges Medeltid. Kulturhistorisk Skildring*, 3 vols and index, Stockholm.

Hodges, R. (1981) 'Trade and market origins in the ninth century: an archaeological perspective of Anglo-Carolingian relations', in Gibson and Nelson, pp. 213–33.

Hollander, L. M. (1964) *Heimskringla. History of the Kings of Norway by Snorri Sturluson*, Austin, Texas.

Holmbäck, Å. and Wessén, E. (1943) *Svenska Landskapslagar, 4. Skånelagen och Gutalagen*, Stockholm.

Holmqvist, W. (1979) *Swedish Vikings on Helgö and Birka*, Stockholm.

Holtsmark, A. (1961) 'Historieskrivning: Norge', *KHL 6*, cols 595–7.

Hrbek, I. (1960) 'Bulghar', *EI* 1, pp. 1304–8.

Hughes, K. (1972) *Early Christian Ireland. Introduction to the Sources*, London.

Hulthén, B. (1978) 'Keramiktillverkning i kv. Tankbåten i Ystad', *Ystadiana* (Ystads Fornminnesförening 23), pp. 103–13.

Hunter Blair, P. (1939) 'Olaf the White and the Three Fragments of Irish Annals', *Viking* 3, pp. 1–35.

Hvass, S. (1979) 'Jernalderlandsbyerne ved Vorbasse', *Fra Ribe Amt*, pp. 357–91.

Hvass, S. (1979) 'Vorbasse. The Viking-age settlement at Vorbasse, Central Jutland', *AA* 50, pp. 137–72.

Hyenstrand, A. (1974) *Centralbygd–Randbygd. Strukturella, Ekonomiska och Administrative Huvudlinjer i Mellansvensk Yngre Järnålder*, Stockholm.

Hyenstrand, A. (1981) *Excavations at Helgö VI. The Mälaren Area*, Stockholm.

Ianin, V. L. (1956) *Denezhno-vesovye Sistemy Russkogo Srednevekov'ia: Domongol'skii Period*, Moscow.

Ilisch, P. (1981) 'German Viking-age coinage and the North', in Blackburn and Metcalf, pp. 129–48.

Ingstad, A. S. (1970) 'The Norse settlement at l'Anse aux Meadows, Newfoundland. A preliminary report from the excavation 1961–68', *AA* 41, pp. 109–54.

Jacobsen, L. and Moltke, E. (1942) *Danmarks Runeindskrifter*, København.

Jankuhn, H. (1963) *Haithabu. Ein Handelsplatz der Wikingerzeit*, 4th edn, Neumünster.

Jansson, S. B. F. (1962) *The Runes of Sweden*, London.

Jenkins, R. J. H. (ed.) (1962) *Constantine Porphyrogenitus, De Administrando Imperio, II, Commentary*, London.

Jensen, J. (1979) *Oldtidens Samfund. Tiden indtil år 800* (Dansk social historie 1) Copenhagen.

Jensen, S. (1976) 'Byhøjene i Thy og aspekter af samfundsudvikling i ældre jernalder', *Museerne i Viborg Amt* 6, pp. 64–77.

Jóhannesson, J. (1974) *A History of the Old Icelandic Commonwealth*, Winnipeg.

Johnsen, A. O. (1948) *Fra Ættesamfunn Til Statssamfunn*, Oslo.

Jones, G. (1964) *The Norse Atlantic Saga*, Oxford.

Jones, G. (1968) *A History of the Vikings*, Oxford.

Keynes, S. (1978) 'The Declining reputation of King Æthelred the Unready', *Ethelred the Unready*, Hill D. (ed.) (BAR, British ser. 59), Oxford, pp. 227–53.

Kivikoski, E. (1937) 'Studien zu Birkas Handel im östlichen Ostseegebiet', *AA* 8, pp. 229–50.

Kivikoski, E. (1973) *Die Eisenzeit Finnlands*, new ed., Helsingfors.

Kluge, B. (1978) 'Bemerkungen zur Struktur der Funde europäischer Münzen des 10. und 11. Jahrhunderts im Ostseegebiet', *Zeitschrift für Archäologie* 12, pp. 181–90.

Kluge, B. (1981) 'Das angelsächsische Element in den slawischen Münzfunden des 10. bis 12. Jahrhunderts. Aspekte einer Analyse', in Blackburn and Metcalf, pp. 257–327.

Korkukhina, G. F. (1971) 'Kurgan v urochishche Plakun bliz Ladogi', *Kratkie Soobshcheniya Instituta Arheologii Akademii Nauk* 125, pp. 59–64.

Kousgård Sørensen, J. (1978) 'Toponymic evidence for administrative divisions in Denmark in the Viking Age', in Andersson and Sandred, pp. 133–41.

Kousgård Sørensen, J. (1979) 'Place-names and settlement history', *Names, Words and Graves: Early Medieval Settlement*, Sawyer P. H. (ed.), Leeds, pp. 1–33.

Krogh, K. J. (1965) 'Thjodhildes kirke på Brattahlid', *Nationalmuseets Arbejdsmark* 1963–65, pp. 5–18.

Krogh, K. J. (1967) *Viking Greenland*, Copenhagen.

Krogh, K. J. and Voss, O. (1961) 'Fra hedenskab til kristendom i Hørning', *Nationalmuseets Arbejdsmark*, pp. 5–34.

Lair, J. (ed.) (1865) *Dudonis Sancti Quintini De Moribus et Actis Primorum Normanniae Ducum*, Paris.

Larsen, J. H. (1980) 'Vikingtids handelsplass i Valle, Setesdal', *Universitetets Oldsaksamling Skrifter*, ny rekke 3, pp. 143–8.

Lárusson, O. (1960) 'Grágás', *KHL* 5, cols 410–12.

Lebedev, G. S. and Nazarenko, V. A. (1973) 'The Connections between Russians and Scandinavians in the 9th–11th centuries', *NAR* 6, pp. 4–9.

Lewicki, T. (1962) 'Ecrivains arabes du siècle ix au xvie traitant de l'ambre jaune de la Baltique et de son importation en pays arabes', *Folia Orientalia* 4, pp. 1–39.

Lichačev, D. S. (1970) 'The legend of the calling-in of the Varangians, and political purposes in Russian chronicle-writing from the second half of the 11th to the beginning of the 12th century', in Schmidt, pp. 170–85.

Lidén, H.-E., Holmqvist, W. and Olsen, O. (1969) 'From pagan sanctuary to Christian Church. The excavation of Mære church in Trøndelag', *NAR* 2, pp. 3–32.

Liestøl, A. (1958) 'Runene fra Gamle Ladoga', *Kuml*, pp. 133–5.

Liestøl, A. (1970) 'Runic Inscriptions', in Schmidt, pp. 121–31.

Liestøl, A. (1971) 'The literate Vikings', *Proceedings of the Sixth Viking Congress* Foote P. and Strömbäck, D. (eds) Uppsala, pp. 69–78.

Liestøl, A. (1973) 'Runenstabe aus Haithabu–Hedeby', *Berichte über die Ausgrabungen in Haithabu* 6, pp. 96–119.

Liestøl, A. (1979) 'Runeringen i Forsa. Kva er han, og når vart han smidd?', *Saga och Sed*, pp. 12–27.

Linder Welin, U. S. (1938) 'En Uppländsk silverskatt från 800-talet', *Nordisk Numismatisk Årsskrift*, pp. 109–24.

Linder Welin, U. S. (1956) 'Arabiska mynt', *KHL* 1, cols. 182–91.

Linder Welin, U. S. (1974) 'The first arrival of Oriental coins in Scandinavia and the inception of the Viking Age in Sweden', *Fornvännen* 69, pp. 22–9.

Lindqvist, S. (1922) 'Jarlabankes-slätkens minnesmärken', *Berättelse över det Nordiska Arkeologmötet i Stockholm 1922*, pp. 123–41.

Lindqvist, S. (1941) *Gotlands Bildsteine*, 2 vols, Stockholm 1941–42.

Lot, F. (1915) 'La Loire, l'Aquitaine et la Seine de 862 à 866. Robert le Fort', *Bibliothèque de l'Ecole des Chartes* 76, pp. 473–510.

Lot, F. (1970), *Recueil des Travaux Historiques de Ferdinand Lot*, vol. 2, Geneva.

Lucas, A. T. (1966) 'Irish-Norse relations: time for a reappraisal?', *Journal of the Cork Historical and Archaeological Society* 71, pp. 62–75.

Lucas, A. T. (1967) 'The plundering and burning of churches in Ireland, 7th to 16th Century', Rynne, E. (ed.) *North Munster Studies. Essays in Commemoration of Monsignor Michael Moloney*, Limerick, pp. 172–229.

Lund, N. (1976) '*Thorp*-names' Sawyer, P. H. (ed.) *Medieval Settlement: Continuity and Change*, London, pp. 223–5.

Bibliography

Lund, N. (1981) 'The settlers: where do we get them from – and do we need them?', *Viking Congress VIII*, pp. 147–71.

Lund, N. and Hørby, K. (1980) *Samfundet i Vikingetid og Middelalder* 800–1500 (Dansk social historie 2), Copenhagen.

Lundström, P. (1981) *De kommo vida . . . Vikingars Hamn vid Paviken på Gotland*, Stockholm.

McGrew, J. and Thomas, R. G. (1970; 1974) *Sturlunga Saga*, 2 vols, New York.

McKerral, A. (1951) 'The lesser land and administrative divisions in Celtic Scotland', *Proceedings of the Society of Antiquaries of Scotland* 85, pp. 52–64.

Magnusson, M. (1980) *Vikings!*, London.

Magnusson, M. and Pálsson, H. (1960) *Njal's Saga*, Harmondsworth.

Magnusson, M. and Pálsson, H. (1965) *The Vinland Sagas. The Norse Discovery of America*, Harmondsworth.

Magnusson, M. and Pálsson, H. (1969) *Laxdaela Saga*, Harmondsworth.

Malmer, B. (1966) *Nordiska Mynt före år 1000*, Lund.

Malmer, B. (1968) *Mynt och Människor*, Stockholm.

Malmer, B. (1981a) 'Importen av tyska och engelska mynt till Sverige under vikingatiden', *Nordisk Numismatisk Unions Medlemsblad* 1981, pp. 24–7.

Malmer, B. (1981b) 'Om Danmarks näst äldsta myntort och depåfyndet från Igelösa kyrkogård', *Nordisk Numismatisk Unions Medlemsblad* 1981, pp. 62–7.

Martens, I. (1972) 'Mösstrond i Telemark – en jernproduserende fjellbygd for svartedauen', *Viking* 36, pp. 83–114.

Martens, I. (1981) 'Some reflections on the production and distribution of iron in Norway in the Viking Age', Wilson, D. M. and Caygill, M. L. (eds) *Economic Aspects of the Viking Age*, (British Museum occasional paper no. 30), London, pp. 39–46.

Marwick, H. (1949) 'Naval defence in Norse Scotland', *Scottish Historical Review* 28, pp. 1–11.

Megaw, B. (1978) 'Norseman and native in the kingdom of the Isles: a re-assessment of the Manx evidence', in Davey, pp. 265–314.

Metcalf, D. M. (1981) 'Some twentieth-century runes: statistical analysis of the Viking-age coin hoards and the interpretation of wastage rates', in Blackburn and Metcalf, pp. 329–82.

Meulengracht Sørensen, P. (1977) *Saga og Samfund. En Indføring i Oldislandsk Litteratur*, København.

Mierow, C. C. (1915) *The Gothic History of Jordanes*, 2nd edn, Princeton.

Miles, G. C. (1960) 'A ninth-century hoard of dirhams found at Suza', *Mémoires de la mission archéologique en Iran* 37, pp. 68–145.

Minorsky, V. (1937) *Hudūd al-' Ālam 'The Regions of the World'; A Persian Geography* 372 A.H. – 982 A.D., London.

Minorsky, V. (1942) *Marvazi, Sharaf al-Zaman Tahir on China, the Turks and India*, London.

Miqel, A. (1971) 'Ibn Hawkal', *EI* 3, pp. 786–8.

Modéer, K. Å. (1976) 'Ættleiing', *KHL* 20, cols 608–13.

Molinier, A. (1902) *Les sources de l'histoire de France*, 1–2, Paris.

Moltke, E. (1976) *Runerne i Danmark og deres Oprindelse*, København.

Moravcsik, G. and Jenkins, R. J. H. (eds) (1949) *Constantine Porphyrogenitus, De Administrando Imperio*, 1, Budapest.

Morris, R. (1982) *The Church in British Archaeology* (Council for British Archaeology, Research Report), London.

Müller–Wille, M. (1970) *Bestattung im Boot. Studien zu einer nordeuropäischen Grabsitte, Offa* 25–6.

Müller–Wille, M. (1978) 'Das Schiffsgrab von der Île de Groix (Bretagne) – Ein Exkurs zum Bootkammergrab von Haithabu', *Berichte über die Ausgrabungen in Haithabu* 12, pp. 48–84.

Musset, L. (1959) 'Pour l'étude des relations entre les colonies scandinaves d'Angleterre et de Normandie', in *Mélanges de Linguistique et de Philologie Fernand Mossé in Memoriam*, Paris, pp. 330–9.

Musset, L. (1970) 'Naissance de la Normandie', in *Histoire de la Normandie*, de Bouard, M. (ed.) Toulouse, pp. 75–130.

Musset, L. (1971) *Les Invasions: le second assaut contre l'Europe chrétienne (viie–xie siècles)*, 2nd edn, Paris.

Musset, L. (1974) 'La renaissance urbaine des xe et xie siècles dans l'ouest de la France: problèmes et hypothèses de travail', in *Etudes de civilisations médiévale (ixe–xiie siècles). Mélanges E. – R. Labande*, Poitiers, pp. 563–75.

Musset, L. (1975) 'Pour l'étude comparative de deux fondations politiques des Vikings: Le royaume d'York at le duché de Rouen', *Northern History* 10, pp. 40–54.

Musset, L. (1978) 'Participation de Vikings venus des pays celtes à la colonisation scandinave de la Normandie', *Cahiers du centres de recherches sur les pays du nord et du nord-ouest* (Caen) 1, pp. 107–17

Bibliography

Musset, L. and Mossé, F. (1965) *Introduction à la runologie*, Paris.

Myhre, B. (1974) 'The iron age farm in southwest Norway', *NAR* 6, pp. 14–29.

Myhre, B. (1977) 'Nausttuft fra eldre jernalder på Stend i Fana', *Viking* 40, pp. 29–78.

Myrvoll Lossius, S. (1979) *Skien i Middelalderen, en Antikvarisk Registrering*, Oslo.

Nelson, J. L. (1981) 'The Annals of St Bertin', in Gibson and Nelson pp. 15–36.

Nerman, B. (1958) *Grobin–Seeburg. Ausgrabungen und Funde*, Stockholm.

Neveus, C. (1975), 'Træl', *KHL* 19, cols 21–5.

Nicolaisen, W. F. H. (1976) *Scottish Place-Names*, London.

Nicolaisen, W. F. H. (1982) 'The Viking settlement of Scotland: the evidence of place-names', in Farrell.

Noonan, T. S. (1974) 'The nature of medieval Russian–Estonian relations, 850–1015', *Baltic History*, Columbus, Ohio, pp. 13–20.

Noonan, T. S. (1977–8) 'Pre-970 dirham hoards from Estonia and Latvia', *Journal of Baltic Studies* 8, pp. 238–59, 312–23; 9, pp. 7–19, 99–115.

Noonan, T. S. (1978) 'Suzdalia's eastern trade in the century before the Mongol conquest', *Cahiers du monde russe et soviétique* 19, pp. 371–84.

Noonan, T. S. (1980a) 'When and how dirhams first reached Russia: a numismatic critique of the Pirenne theory', *Cahiers du monde russe et soviétique* 21, pp. 401–69.

Noonan, T. S. (1980b) 'Monetary circulation in early medieval Rus: a study of Volga Bulgar dirham finds', *Russian History/Histoire Russe* 7, part 3, pp. 294–311.

Noonan, T. S. (1980c) 'The circulation of Byzantine coins in Kievan Rus', *Byzantine Studies/Etudes Byzantines* 7, pp. 143–81.

Noonan, T. S. (1981) 'Ninth-century dirham hoards from European Russia, a preliminary analysis', in Blackburn and Metcalf, pp. 47–118.

Norborg, L.-A. (1965) 'Landbo', *KHL* 10, cols. 201–3.

Nordlandsbåden (1980) *Nordlandsbåden analyseret og prøvesejlet af Vikingeskibshallens Bådelaug* (National Museum of Denmark, Working papers, 12), Copenhagen.

Nylén, E. (1978) *Bildstenar*, Visby.

Ó Corráin, D. (1972) *Ireland before the Normans*, Dublin.

Ó Corráin, D. (1978) 'Nationality and kingship in pre-Norman Ireland', Moody, T. W. (ed.), *Nationality and the Pursuit of National Independence*, Belfast, pp. 1–35.

Ó Máille, T. (1910) *The Language of the Annals of Ulster*, Manchester.

Obolensky D. (1962) Commentary on *De Administrando Imperio*, ch. 9, in Jenkins, pp. 16–61.

Obolensky, D. (1970) 'The Byzantine sources on the Scandinavians in eastern Europe', in Schmidt, pp. 149–64.

Oftedal, M. (1954) 'The Village names of Lewis in the Outer Hebrides', *Norsk Tidsskrift for Sprogvidenskap* 17, pp. 363–408.

Oftedal, M. (1955) 'Norse place-names in the Hebrides', Falck, K. (ed.), *Annen Viking Kongress*, Bergen, pp. 107–22.

Oftedal, M. (1962) 'On the frequency of Norse loanwords in Scottish Gaelic', *Scottish Gaelic Studies* 9, pp. 116–27.

Ohlsson, T. (1976) 'The Löddeköpinge investigation I. The settlement at Vikhögsvägen', *MLUHM*, new ser. 1, pp. 59–161.

Ohlsson, T. (1980) 'The Löddeköpinge investigation II. The northern part of the village area', *MLUHM*, new ser. 3, pp. 68–111.

Olsen, M. (1928) *Farms and Fanes of Ancient Norway*, Oslo.

Olsen, O. and Crumlin-Pedersen, O. (1978) *Five Viking Ships from Roskilde Fjord*, Roskilde.

Olsson, I. (1976) 'Tuna-namnen i Sverige', *Fornvännen* 71, pp. 71–81.

Olsson, I. (1979) *Gotländsk Natur och Historia Speglade i Ortnamnen*, Visby.

Owen, D. M. (1971) *Church and Society in Medieval Lincolnshire*, Lincoln.

Ozols, J. (1976) 'Der Bernsteinhandel und die skandinavischen Kolonien in Kurland', *Bonner Hefte zur Vorgeschichte* 11, pp. 153–9.

Page, R. I. (1979) 'Dumézil Revisited', *SBVS* 20, parts 1–2, pp. 49–69.

Page, R. I. (1980) 'Some thoughts on Manx runes', *SBVS* 20, part 3, pp. 179–99.

Pálsson, H. (1952) 'Keltnesk mannanöfn í íslenzkum örnefnum', *Skírnir* 126, pp. 195–203.

Pálsson, H. (1953) 'Um Íra-örnefni', *Skírnir* 127, pp. 105–11.

Pálsson, H. and Edwards, P. (1972) *The Book of Settlements*, Winnipeg.

Pamp, B. (1974) *Ortnamnen i Sverige*, Lund.

Pedersen, B. H. (1960) 'Bebyggelsesnavne på – by sammensat med personnavn', *Ti Afhandlinger* (Navnestudier udg. af Stednavneud-valget 2), København, pp. 10–46.

Petersen, J. (1933) *Gamle Gårdsanlegg i Rogaland fra Forhistorisk Tid og Middelalder*, Oslo.

Petersen, J. (1936) *Gamle Gårdsanlegg i Rogaland. Fortsettelse*, Oslo.

Petersson, H. (1976) 'Vängåva', *KHL* 20, cols 303–7.

Phillpotts, B. (1913) *Kindred and Clan in the Middle Ages and After: A Study in the Sociology of the Teutonic Races*, Cambridge.

Pilz, E. (1981) 'Schwedisches Mittelalter und die Byzantinische Frage', *Konsthistorisk Tidskrift* 50, pp. 17–32.

Pliny, *Natural History*, libri 36–7, Eichholz, D. E. (trans.) (Loeb Classical Library, 1962).

Pollock, F. and Maitland, F. W. (1895) *The History of English Law before the Time of Edward I*, Cambridge.

Pritsak, O. (1970) 'An Arabic text on the trade route of the corporation of the ar-Rus in the second half of the ninth century', *Folia Orientalia* 12, pp. 241–59.

Radner, J. N. (1978) *Fragmentary Annals of Ireland*, Dublin.

Rafnsson, S. (1974) *Studier i Landnámabók. Kritiska Bidrag till den Isländsk Fristatstidens Historia*, Lund.

Ramskou, T. (1950) 'Viking-age cremation graves in Denmark', *AA* 21, pp. 137–82.

Ramskou, T. (1965) 'Vikingerne ofrede mennesker', *Nationalmuseets Arbejdsmark* 1963–5, pp. 79–86.

Randsborg, K. (1980) *The Viking Age in Denmark; The Formation of a State*, London.

Rasmusson, N. L. *et al.* (1957) 'Bysantinska mynt', *KHL* 2, cols 428–31.

Rasmusson, P. *et al.* (1962) 'Jordejendom', *KHL* 7, cols 654–77.

Robertson, A. J. (1956) *Anglo-Saxon Charters*, 2nd ed., Cambridge.

Robinson, C. H. (1921) *Anskar, the Apostle of the North*, London.

Roesdahl, E. (1977) *Fyrkat. En jysk Vikingeborg. II Oldsagerne og Gravpladsen*, København.

Roesdahl, E. (1980) *Danmarks Vikingetid*, København. (An English translation is to be published in London, 1982.)

Roesdahl, E. (1981) 'Aggersborg in the Viking Age', in *Viking Congress VIII* pp. 107–22.

Roesdahl, E. *et al.* (1981) *The Vikings in England*, London.

Rolfsen, P. (1981) 'Den siste hedning på Agder', *Viking* 44, pp. 112–28.

Kings and Vikings

Rosén, J. (1962a) *Svensk Historia: I Tiden före 1718*, Stockholm.

Rosén, J. (1962b) 'Husaby', *KHL* 7, cols 94–6.

Ross, A. S. C. (1940) 'The Terfinnas and Beormas of Ohthere (Leeds School of English Language Texts and Monographs, no. 7). Reprinted by the Viking Society for Northern Research, London, see Chesnutt, 1981.

Ruprecht, A. (1958) *Die ausgehende Wikingerzeit im Lichte der Runeninschriften* (Palaestra 224), Göttingen.

Sawyer, P. H. (1971) *The Age of the Vikings*, 2nd edn, London.

Sawyer, P. H. (1976) 'Harald Fairhair and the British Isles', in Boyer, R. (ed.) *Les Vikings et leur civilisation. Problèmes actuels*, Paris, pp. 105–9.

Sawyer, P. H. (1978a) *From Roman Britain to Norman England*, London.

Sawyer, P. H. (1978b) Some sources for the history of Viking Northumbria', Hall, R. A. (ed.) *Viking Age York and the North*, (Council for British Archaeology, Research Report 27), London, pp. 3–7.

Sawyer, P. H. (1981) 'Conquest and colonization: Scandinavians in the Danelaw and in Normandy', *Viking Congress VIII*, pp. 123–31.

Sawyer, P. H. (1982) 'The Vikings and Ireland', in Whitelock, D., McKitterick, R. and Dumville, D. N. (eds) *Ireland in Medieval Europe*, Cambridge, pp. 345–6.

Schietzel, K. and Crumlin Pedersen, O. (1980), 'Havnen i Hedeby', *Skalk* 1980, no. 3, pp. 4–10.

Schledermann, H. *et al.* (1975) 'Tyende', *KHL* 19, cols 98–117.

Schmid, T. (1934) *Sveriges Kristnande: fran verklighet till dikt*, Stockholm.

Schmidt, K. R. (ed.) (1970) *Varangian Problems* (Scando-Slavica. Supplementum I), Copenhagen.

Schönbäck, B. (1974) 'L'Anse-aux-Meadows, June to September 1974', *Parks Canada Research Bulletin* 20, Ottawa.

Schönbäck, B. (1976) 'Progress report on archaeological fieldwork at L'Anse-aux-Meadows, June to October 1975', *Parks Canada Research Bulletin* 33, Ottawa.

Schönbäck, B. (1980) 'Båtgravskicket', in Sandwall A. (ed.) *Vendeltid*, (Statens Historiska Museum), Stockholm, pp. 108–22.

Scholz, B. W. (1970) *Carolingian Chronicles*, Ann Arbor.

Schreiner, K. E. (1927) 'Menneskeknoklene fra Osebergskibet og andre Norske Jernalderfund', in Brøgger A. W. and Schetelig, H. (eds) *Osebergfundet*, vol. 5, Oslo, pp. 81–279.

Bibliography

Selling, D. (1955) *Wikingerzeitliche und frühmittelalterliche Keramik in Schweden*, Stockholm.

Serning, I. (1956) *Lapska Offerplatsfynd från Järnålder och Medeltid i de Svenska Lappmarkerna*, Stockholm.

Shepard, J. (1974) 'Some problems of Russo-Byzantine relations c.860–c.1050', *The Slavonic and East European Review* 52, pp. 10–33.

Shepard, J. (1979) 'The Russian steppe-frontier and the Black Sea', *Archeion Pontou* 35, pp. 218–37.

Sjöholm, E. (1977) *Gesetze als Quellen mittelalterlicher Geschichte des Nordens*, Stockholm.

Sjövold, T. (1974), *The Iron Age Settlement of Arctic Norway*, II, Tromsö.

Sjøvold, T. (1979), *The Viking Ships in Oslo*, Oslo.

Skaare, K. (1964), 'Skipsavbildninger på Birka-Hedeby mynter', *Norsk Sjøfartsmuseum 1914–1964*, Oslo.

Skaare, K. (1976), *Coins and Coinage in Viking-Age Norway*, Oslo.

Skovgaard-Petersen, I. *et al.* (1977), *Danmarks historie, I, Tiden indtil 1340*, Copenhagen.

Skyum-Nielsen, N. (1974) 'Slaveriet i Norden set mod international baggrund', in *Beretning. Foredrag of Forhandlinger ved det Nordiske Historikermøde i København 1971*, København, pp. 301–23. (An English translation is published in *Mediaeval Scandinavia* 11 (1981).)

Smyth, A. P. (1976) 'The Black Foreigners of York and the White Foreigners of Dublin', *SBVS* 19, parts 2–3, pp. 101–17.

Smyth, A. P. (1977), *Scandinavian Kings in the British Isles 850–880*, Oxford.

Smyth, A. P. (1975; 1979) *Scandinavian York and Dublin*, 2 vols, Dublin.

Sogner, S. B. (1961) 'Herse', *KHL* 6, cols 512–3.

Sorlin, I. (1961) 'Les traités de Byzance avec la Russie au xe siècle', *Cahiers du monde russe et soviétique*, 2, pp. 313–60, 447–75.

Sorlin, I. (1965) 'Le témoignage de Constantin VII Porphyrogénète sur l'état ethnique et politique de la Russie au début du xe siècle', *Cahiers du monde russe et soviétique* 6, pp. 147–88.

Speculum Norroenum Norse Studies in Memory of Gabriel Turville-Petre (1981), Dronke, U., Helgadottir, G. P., Weber, G. W. and Bekker-Nielsen, H. (eds) Odense.

Ståhl, H. (1970) *Ortnamn och Ortnamnsforskning*, Stockholm.

Kings and Vikings

Stalsberg, A. (1979) 'Skandinaviske vikingetidsfunn fra det gamelrussiske riket', *Fornvännen* 74, pp. 151–60.

Steffensen, J. (1968) 'Population: Island', *KHL* 13, cols 390–2.

Stenberger, M. (ed.) (1943) *Forntida Gårdar i Island*, København.

Stenberger, M. (1955) 'The reasons for the abandonment of Vallhagar', in Stenberger, M. and Klindt-Jensen, O. (eds) *Vallhagar. A Migration Period Settlement in Gotland, Sweden*, 2 vols, Copenhagen, pp. 1161–85.

Stenberger, M. (1956a) 'Tuna in Badelunda. A grave in central Sweden with Roman vessels', *AA* 27, pp. 1–21.

Stenberger, M. (1956b) *Västeråstraktens Förhistoria*, Västerås.

Stenberger, M. (1979) *Det Forntida Sverige*, 3rd edn, Stockholm.

Stenton, F. M. (1971) *Anglo-Saxon England*, 3rd edn, Oxford.

Stewart, I. (1981) 'How did Anglo-Saxon coins reach Finland?', in Blackburn and Metcalf, pp. 491–94.

Stewart, J. (1965) 'Shetland farm names', in Small, A. (ed.) *The Fourth Viking Congress*, Edinburgh, pp. 247–66.

Stoumann, I. (1979) 'Sædding. A Viking-age village near Esbjerg', *AA* 50, pp. 95–118.

Strand, B. (1980) *Kvinnor och Män i Gesta Danorum*, Göteborg.

Strömberg, M. (1961) *Untersuchungen zur jüngeren Eisenzeit in Schonen. Völkerwanderungszeit–Wikingerzeit*, 2 vols, Lund.

Strömberg, M. (1963) 'Handelsstråk och vikingabygd i sydöstra Skåne. Om Hagestadsundersökningen', *Ale* 1963:3, pp. 1–25.

Strömberg, M. (1978) 'En kustby i Ystad – före stadens tillkomst', *Ystadiana* 1978 (Ystads fornminnesförening 23), pp. 7–101.

Svensson, J. V. (1917) 'De nordiska folknamnen hos Jordanes', *Namn och Bygd* 5, pp. 109–57.

Tallgren, A. M. (1931) 'Biarmia', *Eurasia Septentrionalis Antiqua* 6, pp. 100–20.

Tallgren, A. M. (1934) 'Die "altpermische" Pelzwarenperiode an der Pečora', *Finska Fornminnesföreninge Tidskrift* 40, pp. 152–81.

Thompson, C. W. (1975) *Studies in Upplandic Runography*, Austin, Texas.

Thórarinsson, S. (1967) *The Eruptions of Hekla in Historical Times. A Tephrochronological Study* (The Eruption of Hekla 1947–48, I), Reykjavík.

Thórarinsson, S. (1976) 'Gjóskulög og gamlar rústir', *Árbok Hins Íslenzka Fornleifafélags* 1976, pp. 5–38.

Thorsteinsson, A. (1981) 'On the development of Faroese settlements', *Viking Congress VIII*, pp. 189–202.

Thorvildsen, E. (1972) 'Dankirke', *Nationalmuseets Arbejdsmark*, pp. 47–60.

Todd, J. H. (1867) *Cogadh Gaedhel re Gallaibh* (Rolls Ser. 48), London.

Tornberg, M. (1972) 'Storfamiljinstitutionen i Finland', *Nord-Nytt* 1972, pp. 4–17.

Trillmich, W. and Buchner, R. (1961) *Quellen des 9. und 11. Jahrhunderts zur Geschichte der Hamburgischen Kirche und des Reiches*, Berlin.

Trimpe Burger, J. A. (1973) 'Oost-Souburg, Province of Zeeland: a preliminary report on the excavation of the site of an ancient fortress (1969–1971)', *Berichten van de Rijksdienst het Oudheidkundig Bodemonderzoek* 23, pp. 355–65.

Tschan, F. J. (1959) *History of the Archbishops of Hamburg–Bremen by Adam of Bremen*, New York.

Turville-Petre, E. O. G. (1953) *Origins of Icelandic Literature*, Oxford.

Turville-Petre, E. O. G. (1965) *Myth and Religion of the North*, London.

Turville-Petre, E. O. G. (1976) *Scaldic Poetry*, Oxford.

Utterström, G. (1975) 'Die mittelalterliche Rechtssprache Schwedens. Einige quellenkritische und sprachliche Beobachtungen', in Dahlstedt, K.-H. (ed.) *The Nordic Languages and Modern Linguistics* 2, pp. 734–48.

Utterström, G. (1978) 'Ålderdomlighet utan ålder? En replik om Dalalagen', *Namn och Bygd* 93, pp. 199–204.

Van Es, W. A. (1969) 'Excavations at Dorestad; a pre-preliminary report: 1967–1968', *Berichten van de Rijksdienst voor het Oudheidkundig Bodemonderzoek* 19, pp. 183–207.

Van Es, W. A. *et al.* (1978) 'Dorestad', *Spiegel Historiael* 13, no. 4 (April).

Van Es, W. A. and Verwers, W. J. H. (1980) *Excavations at Dorestad 1 – The Harbour: Hoogstraat 1* (Nederlandse Oudheden 9), Amersfoort.

Van Regteren Altena, H. H. and Heidinga, H. A. (1977), 'The North Sea region in the early medieval period (400–950)', in van Beek, B. L., Brandt, R. W. and Groenman-van Waateringe, W. (eds) *Ex Horreo*, Amsterdam, pp. 47–67.

Van Werveke, H. (1965) 'De oudste Burchten aan de Vlaamse en de Zeeuwse Kust', *Mededelingen van de Koninklijke Vlaamse Academie voor Wetenschappen, Letteren en Schone Kunsten van Belgie, Klasse der Letteren*, 37, no. 1, pp. 3–22.

Veale, E. M. (1966) *The English Fur Trade in the Later Middle Ages*, Oxford.

Vercauteren, F. (1936) 'Comment s'est-on défendu, au ix⁰ siècle dans l'empire franc, contre les invasions normandes?' *Annales du xxx⁰ congrès de la fédération archéologique de Belgique*, Bruxelles, pp. 117–32.

Viking Congress VIII, *Proceedings of the Eighth Viking Congress. Århus 24–31 August 1977*, Bekker-Nielsen, H., Foote, P. and Olsen, O. (eds), Odense, 1981.

Vilkuna, K. (1956) 'Bjarmer och Bjarmaland', *KHL* 1, cols 647–51.

Vilkuna, K. (1969) *Kainuu-Kvänland, ett Finsk-Norsk-Svenskt Problem*, Uppsala.

Vogel, W. (1906) *Die Normannen und das fränkische Reich bis zur Gründung der Normandie (799–911)*, Heidelberg.

Wåhlin Andersen, V. (1964) 'Skuldelev skibene i perspektiv', *Skalk*, no. 4, pp. 10–15.

Wallace Hadrill, J. M. (1975) *The Vikings in Frankia*, reprinted in Wallace Hadrill, J. M. *Early Medieval History* 1975, pp. 217–36.

Wallén, P.-E. (1962) 'Hämnd', *KHL* 7, cols 239–46.

Wallén, P.-E. *et al.* (1966) 'Mansbot', *KHL* 11, cols 327–38.

Wattenbach, W. and Holtzmann, R. (1938–9) *Deutschlands Geschichtsquellen im Mittelalter. Die Zeit der Sachsen und Salier*, rev. edn, F.-J. Schmale, h. 1–2, Darmstadt.

Wattenbach, W. and Levison, W. (1953–76) *Deutschlands Geschichtsquellen im Mittelalter. Vorzeit und Karolinger*, rev. edn, H. Löwe, h. 2–5, Weimar.

Wessén, E. (1930) 'Schwedische Ortsnamen und altnordische Mythologie', *Acta Philologica Scandinavica* 4, pp. 97–115.

Wessén, E. (1960) *Historiska Runinskrifter*, Stockholm.

Westberg, B. (1978) *Litteratur om Svenska Distriktsbeteckningar och Distriktsnamn. En bibliografi* (Ortnamn och samhälle 4), Uppsala.

Wideen, H. (1955) *Västsvenska Vikingatidsstudier*, Göteborg.

Wild, J. P. (1976) 'Loan-words and Roman expansion in north-west Europe', *World Archaeology* 8, pp. 57–64.

Wilson, D. M. (1974) *The Viking-Age in the Isle of Man. The Archaeological Evidence*, Odense.

Bibliography

Wilson, D. M. (1980) *The Vikings and their Origins*, new edn, London.

Wilson, D. M. and Klindt-Jensen, O. (1966) *Viking Art*, London.

Winberg, C. (1975) *Folkökning och Proletarisering*, Göteborg.

Wormald, C. P. (1982) 'Viking studies: whence and whither?', in Farrell.

Yrwing, H. (1969) 'Rysslandshandel', *KHL* 14, cols 528–34.

Index

Abbreviations: abp – archbishop; bp – bishop; D. – Danish; Got. – Gotland; k. – king; run. ins. – runic inscription; V. – Viking(s)

Plate I Model of a tenth-century cargo-boat. This model, made for the Viking Ships Museum in Roskilde by Leo Larsen, is based on Skuldelev 1, one of the boats that were deliberately sunk to block a channel in Roskilde Fjord in the eleventh century (Olsen and Crumlin-Pedersen 1978). That boat was probably built in western Norway and measures over 16 m. long and 4.5 m. broad. The hold has space for over 30 cubic metres of cargo. *Photo: Vikingeskibshallen, Roskilde*

Plate II Rune-stone near Randbøl, Jutland. This stone vividly illustrates the vulnerability of these monuments. In 1874 it had fallen so that the inscription was no longer visible and a stone-mason cut it up to make mile-stones. When he realized that it had an inscription he did his best to restore it with cement. The inscription, which fortunately survived, is partly poetic and records that the monument was erected by Tue, described as a *bryde*, in memory of his wife, who may have been buried in the mound on which the stone stands. This is the only inscription that certainly refers to a *bryde* (see p. 55; Moltke 1976, pp. 240, 248; Lund and Hørby 1980, pp. 21, 25–6). *Photo: Steen Hvass*

Plate III Inscriptions carved by Asmund Karasun (see figure 3, p. 31).

a. Järvsta, Valbo parish, Gästrikland (Gä 11). This inscription is signed by Asmund Karasun. It was erected by three brothers in memory of their father Thiuðmund. Its Christian character is shown not only by the cross but also by the invocation 'God and God's mother help his soul'. The interpretation of the last words is disputed (see p. 30). They include the name Æimund, who may have been a son of Thiuðmund who had died before him (Thompson 1975, pp. 84–7). For other views see the discussion under Gä 11. *Photo: ATA* (Antikvarisk-Topografiska Arkivet)

b. Yttergärde, Orkesta parish, Uppland (U 344). This inscription is unsigned but is clearly shown to be the work of Asmund Karasun by its general style, by the form of some of the letters and by some spelling peculiarities (Thompson 1975, pp. 120–21). The inscription reads: 'Ulf took three gelds in England. That was the first which Tosti paid. Then Thorkel paid. Then Knut paid' (see p. 32). It was originally one of a pair of stones, both carved by Asmund, that formed a single monument to Ulf. The other stone, now lost (U 343), read: 'Karsi and [. . .]rn had this stone raised in memory of Ulf, their father. God and God's mother help his [soul]'. It is therefore a Christian stone despite the absence of a cross. Ulf lived at Bårresta near Yttergärde and is named in at least two other inscriptions (U 161, 336). *Photo: ATA*

Plate IV Rune-stones commemorating members of Ingvar's expedition (see figure 3 and pp. 32, 35).

a. Gripsholm, Kärnbo parish, Södermanland (Sö 179). In this largely poetic inscription Tola commemorates his son Harald, Ingvar's brother. It ends;

> They fared like men
> far after gold
> and in the east
> gave the eagle food.
> They died southward
> in Serkland

(Jansson 1962, p. 41)

The expression 'give the eagle food' was a well-known kenning for 'kill enemies'. The meaning of Serkland, which occurs on other stones, is uncertain; suggested interpretations include 'the land of the Saracens' and 'the land of silk' (Ruprecht 1958, p. 55). Other Ingvar stones, e.g. at Varpsund (U 654), show that the expedition failed in the east, probably somewhere in Russia. *Photo: ATA*

b. Svinnegarn Church, Uppland (U 778). This stone was erected in memory of Banke by his parents. He is said to have owned a ship and to have steered eastward with Ingvar. The cross and the invocation 'May God and God's mother help Banke's soul' suggest that he, or his parents, were Christian. The inscription is signed by Askil. The Ingvar stones are stylistically very different from those carved by Asmund (see plate III; Wessén 1960, p. 31). *Photo: ATA*

Plate V Matrices from Hedeby Harbour. The excavation of the harbour of Hedeby in 1979 recovered many remarkable things, including a leather bag containing these 42 bronze matrices. There are 14 different designs, each in three sizes. They could be used to make moulds into which silver, gold or other metal could be poured to provide the basis for more elaborately worked ornaments (see p. 37; Schietzel and Crumlin-Pedersen 1980). *Photo: Schleswig-Holsteinisches Landesmuseum für Vor- und Frühgeschichte, Abteilung für Wikingerforschung*

Plate VI (on facing page) Mounds at Borre (see figure 5, p. 49. *Photo: Universitetets Oldsaksamling, Oslo).*

Plate VII Boat-grave at Tuna in Badelunda (see p. 49). This boat was about 6 m long. It contained the remains of an elderly woman dressed in silk and linen with brooches, arm-rings and a remarkable necklace of coloured glass beads with silver pendants made from dirhams. The burial can be dated to the late ninth century. *Photo: Else Nordahl and Bengt Schönbäck*

Plate IX Møsstrond. A general view showing part of the area covered by figure 10. The wooded hills contain many charcoal pits and iron-extraction sites (see pp. 61–3). *Photo: Irmelin Martens*

Plate VIII (on facing page) Eleventh-century house at Vorbasse, Jutland. The traces of walls and supporting posts of this large house can clearly be seen in this photograph. It was 24 m long and 7 m wide in the centre. It had entrances in the gable-end walls and was divided into three rooms, the central one having a hearth. It formed part of the last phase of Vorbasse, before the village was permanently fixed on its medieval, and modern, site (see p. 59; Hvass 1979, pp. 159–61, 165, House XLI). *Photo: Steen Hvass*

Plate X Birka in winter. This aerial photograph of the northern part of the
island of Björkö, looking north-east over the site of Birka, shows the wide
expanse of the frozen surface of Lake Mälaren. Birka lay on the shore between
the fort, on the higher ground nearest the camera, and Hemlanden, the densely
wooded area in which most of the Birka graves lie. In these conditions
communications are relatively easy and the ice provided additional space on
which winter markets could be held (Ambrosiani 1981, pp. 50–2).   *Photo:
Björn Ambrosiani. Reproduced with the permission of Försvarsstaben.*

Plate XI   Limfjord. This aerial view shows Limfjord east of Gjøl, the village in the foreground. Ålborg can be seen on the south bank, where the fjord narrows, and Lindholm Høje stands on the opposite side. The eastern entrance to the Fjord is about 40 kilometres away.   *Photo: Svend Tougaard*

Plate XII   Ships depicted on Gotlandic Picture stones (see p. 76).

a. Riddare, Hejnum parish. Photo: ATA

Plate XIII   Ships depicted on early-ninth-century Hedeby coins (see p. 76). *Enlargement 3×. Photo: ATA*

b. Hunninge I, Klinte parish.
Photo: ATA

a. Burgh on Schouwen.

Plate XIV   Circular forts near the Scheldt Estuary (see figure 13, p. 82).

b. Oost Souburg on Walcheren.

These aerial photographs show how the ninth-century fortifications have determined the shape of the later settlements.   *Photos: Rijksdienst Oudheidkundig Bodemonderzoek*

a. from Rondarve, Eksta parish, Gotland (*CNS* 1.3.13). This hoard, found in 1897, included five silver rods in the form of spirals and 305 dirhams struck between 842 and 955. 117 of the coins are fragments similar to the four shown here. Most dirham fragments found in Gotland are regular and neatly cut. Many, like these, are cut in half but smaller pieces, for example quarters, are also found.

b. Tingstad, Östergötland. This hoard, found in 1968, contained various silver objects, one Scandinavian coin, 54 complete dirhams and 498 fragments of dirhams. These coins were struck, as far as can be determined, between 742 and 963. Dirham fragments found in mainland Sweden tend to be crudely broken and irregular, like these.   *Photos: Jüri Tamsalu*

Plate XVI   Erling Skjalgsson's Cross (see pp. 140). This cross formerly stood
by the main road leading out of Stavanger but is now in Stavanger Arkeologisk
Museum. It stands 3.8 metres high and has a badly defaced inscription on the
other face.   *Photo: Stavanger Arkeologisk Museum*